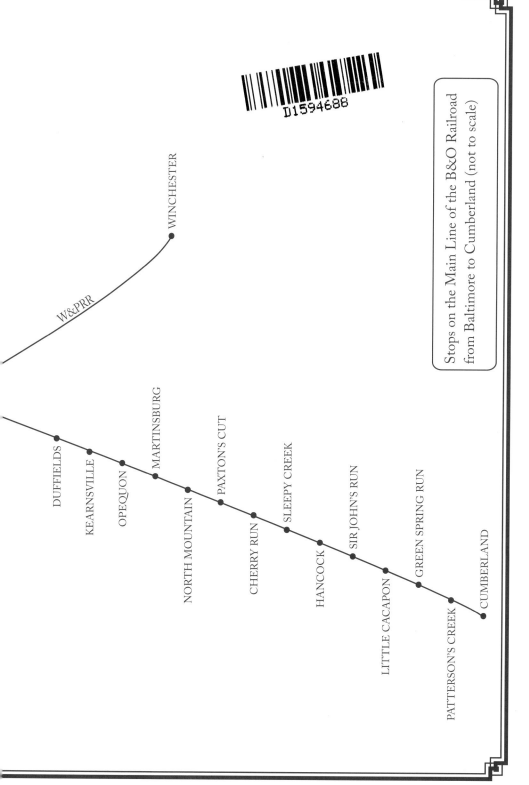

Stops on the Main Line of the B&O Railroad from Baltimore to Cumberland (not to scale)

WINCHESTER

W&PRR

DUFFIELDS
KEARNSVILLE
OPEQUON
MARTINSBURG
NORTH MOUNTAIN
PAXTON'S CUT
CHERRY RUN
SLEEPY CREEK
HANCOCK
SIR JOHN'S RUN
LITTLE CACAPON
GREEN SPRING RUN
PATTERSON'S CREEK
CUMBERLAND

THE WAR CAME BY TRAIN

THE BALTIMORE & OHIO RAILROAD DURING THE CIVIL WAR

Daniel Carroll Toomey

Baltimore & Ohio Railroad Museum
Baltimore, Maryland

Other titles by the author:

The Civil War in Maryland

Baltimore During the Civil War

Marylanders in Blue

Hero at Front Royal: The Life of General John R. Kenly

Marylanders at Gettysburg

A History of Relay, Maryland and the Thomas Viaduct

The Johnson-Gilmor Raid July 9-13, 1864

The Maryland Line Confederate Soldiers' Home

Designed by Merrifield Graphics and Publishing Service, Baltimore, MD

Printed in the United States of America by H. G. Roebuck & Son, Inc., Baltimore, MD

Library of Congress Cataloging-in-Publication Data
Toomey, Daniel Carroll, 1948–
The War Came by Train: The Baltimore & Ohio Railroad During the Civil War /
Daniel Carroll Toomey
p. cm.
Includes biographical references and index.
ISBN 978-1-886248-01-4

1. United States – History – Civil War, 1861-1865 – Transportation. 2. Railroads – United States – History – 19th century. 3. Confederate States of America. Army – Transportation. 4. United States. Army – Transportation – History – 19th century. United States – History – Civil War Veterans, 1866-1938 – Transportation. I Title.
L/C 2012954184

To Joseph H. Toomey, Sr.
Locomotive Engine, B&O Railroad 1861–1865

and

All the volunteers who have ever served at the
Baltimore & Ohio Railroad Museum

Photographic Sources

The following abbreviations are use to identify repetitive sources. Individuals are noted within the accompanying captions.

Baltimore & Ohio Railroad Museum (B&ORRM)

Harpers Weekly (H. W.)

Library of Congress (L. C.)

Frank Leslie's Illustrated Newspaper (L. I. N.)

Millers Photographic History of the Civil War (Miller's)

National Archives (N. A.)

Paul L. Roy (P. L. R.)

Daniel Carroll Toomey Collection (D. C. T.)

United States Army Military History Institute (USAMHI)

West Virginia Division Culture & History (WVDC&H)

CONTENTS

FOREWORD

In another life, time and place in the mid-1970's when I decided to enter the venerable full-time vocation of Civil War antiques dealer, I was introduced to Daniel Carroll Toomey. We instantaneously became friends. As a collector, historian, author, lecturer and scholar of all things Maryland during the American Civil War he excels at every turn. During the ensuing years of friendship and collegiality, I watched Dan diligently research and publish a number of important works; notably his bestselling work, *The Civil War in Maryland* (1983), and those to follow.

Fast forward to 1997 when I was engaged as a consultant to the City of Baltimore seeking to establish the Baltimore Civil War Museum in the historic Philadelphia, Wilmington & Baltimore Railroad's President Street Station (1851). As a result of that job I was offered and accepted an opportunity to become the Chief Curator of the Baltimore & Ohio Railroad Museum in downtown Baltimore, Maryland. In January 2000, I was selected to be the Museum's Executive Director.

After some thirty-five years of friendship it is my sincere pleasure and honor to introduce you to *The War Came by Train*. The inspiration for this work came directly from an embryonic idea to create a Civil War sesquicentennial exhibit at the Museum to commemorate the role of the railroad, specifically, the B&O during the American Civil War. About a year ahead of the kick off for the 2011-2015 commemoration, the concept of this exhibit came into focus. The Museum holds the world's largest collection of Civil War period locomotives, freight and passenger cars as well as a number of horse drawn vehicles from the period. This, along with the rich Civil War archival materials in the Museum's library and archives, made this a natural fit. Of course one of my first calls was to Dan Toomey.

I invited Dan to our first staff meeting organized to lay out the plans for the proposed exhibit. Dan clearly had a brilliant vision for a vibrant four-year program and exhibition that utilized all of the Museum's resources, his knowledge of Maryland Civil War history and his many colleagues in the Civil War collecting field. At the end of that very first meeting it was clear to all in the room that Dan should lead the intellectual effort and given the title Guest Curator. His reputation would lend scholarly credence to our effort. Indeed, Dan himself coined the exhibition's title, The War Came by Train. Add up more than thirty years of friendship, a shared passion for the Civil War, and the Museum's amazing collections and you have a dream come true.

Within weeks of that meeting, Dan approached me with his concept for this book. Obviously a great deal of primary source research would have to be completed for the exhibition along with image searches and scanning already published articles and the many references to the B&O Railroad in general and monographic Civil War books. Why not preserve this experience for generations of readers and historians to come?

The only other work published on this subject, *The Baltimore and Ohio in the Civil War*, was written by an Associate Professor of History at West Virginia University, Festus P. Summers, in 1939! Still a viable reference, it is centered largely on the corporate history of the B&O during the conflict, its profits and losses and the big stories of the war. Dan's work is a far more personal and tactical account of lesser known campaigns, personalities, railroad workers and amazing anecdotal stories pulled from the depths of the Museum's archives, private collections and other rarely tapped institutional collections all woven in the context of the larger war. Full of raging battles, espionage, politics and drama, this is a book on railroads during the Civil War like none other.

After I had read Dan's manuscript for the second time we were chatting in my office when he asked me a very pointed question, "If you could choose one seminal fact you learned that you didn't know before reading the book, what would it be?" My pause was brief and my answer thus, "I never knew that so many important campaigns of the Civil War were tactically planned and executed specifically to destroy the B&O."

Many books have been written about the B&O Railroad from its inception in 1827 to its final merger into CSX in 1987. Many of these works have highlighted its pioneering technologies, political and financial fits and starts, the Great Railroad Strike of 1877 and, of course, its magnificent locomotives and equipment. *The War Came by Train* reveals, in rich detail, what may be the crowning achievement of any railroad in American history and so perfectly fills a gap formerly occupied by a work now nearly seventy-five years old.

Courtney B. Wilson
Executive Director
Baltimore & Ohio Railroad Museum
Baltimore, Maryland

INTRODUCTION

The American Civil War has often been referred to as the last romantic and the first modern war. The number of technological advancements either begun or accelerated during the war years is truly amazing. Some inventions like the submarine and Gatling gun would not reach their deadly potential until World War I. On the other hand, two technologies that were well established before the war began were the railroad and the telegraph. Together they made it possible to support and manage the largest armies ever assembled on the North American Continent until the beginning of the Twentieth Century.

The term "first in history" is often a debatable point. This author has tried to qualify his claims whenever using the reference. For instance, the first documented use of a railroad in time of war occurred during the Crimean War when a single track was laid between the port city of Balaklava and Sevastopol to facilitate the delivery of food and ammunition. The first railroads to operate in the United States were short lines with a single purpose – usually the movement of natural resources from their point of extraction to a canal or river landing. The Baltimore & Ohio was not the first railroad in the United States, but it was the first railroad company in the world to successfully carry passengers, freight and mail over a long-distance. Finally, the first wartime troop movement engaged in by the B&O was not to Harpers Ferry in 1859 but during the Mexican War when four companies of the Baltimore and Washington Battalion were transferred to Washington from whence they sailed to Texas. However, the movement of 88 marines and two cannons from Washington to Harpers Ferry to subdue John Brown was the first tactical deployment of troops by rail in the United States.

In 1939, Festus P. Summers wrote *The Baltimore and Ohio in the Civil War*. For the most part, Summers presented an administrative history of the B&O during the war years under its highly efficient president, John Work Garrett. Garrett's difficulties with competing lines, government policies during the first year of the war and the company's profit and loss statements are well documented, but only the largest of military operations affecting the B&O are discussed. From then until now, it has remained the only book length study of the B&O Railroad during the Civil War. In the past decade, several authors have put forth excellent works that focus on events large and small relating to the B&O Railroad. Hunter Lesser's *Rebels at the Gate* tells the story of West

Virginia's statehood; Roger Pickenpaugh's *Rescue by Rail* details one of the largest troop movements by rail during the war; and Steve French accounts for many of the Confederate cavalry attacks on B&O trains in *Rebel Chronicles*, to name a few.

The War Came by Train is not meant to replace Summers' book but to stand next to it by telling the Civil War history of the B&O Railroad from an operational perspective. The people who worked for, travelled on, attacked or defended the railroad, as well as the trains and the technologies used to keep them moving, are all part of the story. The scope of the book, beginning with John Brown's Raid on Harpers Ferry in 1859 and ending with Garrett's immediate post war aims, allows the reader to see how each event affected the operation of the railroad and in turn the Union war effort. The administrative accomplishments of President Garrett and his right hand man, Master of Transportation William Prescott Smith, show brightly through each crisis but await their own well-deserved biographies.

In writing this book I have had the opportunity to travel through the Lower Shenandoah Valley of Virginia and the state of West Virginia in order to learn about the events that occurred outside my native state of Maryland relative to the history of the Baltimore & Ohio Railroad during the Civil War. It has been a journey well worth the effort.

To bring this book to print required a small army of friends both old and new. The first person I would like to acknowledge is Paul Bridges. Paul is a long time volunteer at the B&O Railroad Museum. He not only reviewed the manuscript but also supplied a great deal of information from the museum's archives on John Work Garrett. A new trio of friends, Hunter Lesser, Richard Wolf and Steve French introduced me to the war in West Virginia. Hunter schooled me on the process of West Virginia statehood and Richard on the life of General B. F. Kelley. Steve gave me a guided tour of the area around Martinsburg where many of the events described in the book took place. Dr. Tom Clemens, an old acquaintance and recently retired history professor was my second reader. Tom is one of the leading experts on the Antietam Campaign and the war in Western Maryland. His numerous recommendations took the text to a completely new level of refinement. Mr. Herbert Harwood was Tom's counterpart. As an expert on the history of the B&O Railroad, he made a number of key recommendations that kept me on the right track so to speak. Another newfound friend that had a significant impact on this project is Art Candenquist. Art readily shared his considerable research on Captain Thomas Sharp and "the great train raid." Likewise, Doyle Vincent allowed me to view his extensive material on blockhouses. I would also like to thank

David P. Bridges of Richmond, Virginia, for his suggestions and encouragement along the way as well as Becky Ebert and her staff at the Handley Library in Winchester, Virginia, and Ben Ritter of that same city. Michelle Hammer, Museum Specialist with the National Park Service was most helpful in securing photographs associated with the events that occurred at Harpers Ferry.

My sincere appreciation goes out to Mr. Francis X. Smyth, Chairman of the Board of the B&O Railroad Museum, for his generous and enthusiastic support for this book and all things associated with The War Came by Train project.

I would also like to acknowledge the technical assistance given to me by the Chief Curator at the Baltimore & Ohio Railroad Museum Dave Shackelford and his staff, Jane Harper, Curator, and Ryan McPherson, Archivist. They worked tirelessly to supply the maps and photographs for the book. And to Jean Safrit for her diligent proof reading of the manuscript one last time. Finally, my deepest appreciation goes to a friend of over thirty years, Courtney Wilson. As Executive Director of the B&O Museum, Courtney has given me the opportunity to both design The War Came by Train exhibit and write this book. It has truly been a journey well worth the effort.

Daniel Carroll Toomey
Guest Curator
The Baltimore & Ohio Railroad Museum

B&O train crossing the North Branch Bridge east of Cumberland, Maryland. This photograph was taken in 1858 and shows one of the many Bollman Truss bridges on the main line of the B&O. (B&ORRM)

CHAPTER ONE

THE MOST FAMOUS
RAILROAD IN
AMERICA

R ailroading in America on the eve of the Civil War was an industry with unknown potential. Its success in challenging time and distance was not unlike the space race a century later. Completing the transcontinental railroad in 1869 was the nineteenth century equivalent to landing on the moon. It required a vast array of technological advancements in bridge building, tunneling, and locomotive design. The oldest railroad in the United States was the Baltimore and Ohio Railroad. By 1860, it consisted of three operating units – a main line running from Baltimore to Wheeling, 380 miles; the Washington Branch, 30 miles; and the Northwestern Virginia Railroad running from Grafton to Parkersburg, 104 miles. Supporting their operation were 236 locomotives, 3,579 passenger and freight cars, and over 6,000 employees, plus an extensive system of telegraph lines, repair shops, and train stations. To put this into perspective, there were a dozen railroads operating in the state of Virginia in 1861. Combined, these twelve railroads had almost 1,500 fewer rail cars in service than the B&O.[1]

In the B&O Railroad's annual report for 1860 President John Work Garrett proudly stated, "The Company has continued to make its purchases for cash, and it is entirely free from floating debt." Elsewhere it was reported that, "Our road has now attained a condition to challenge comparison with any line in the country." Finally, it was noted that in an era of fatal train wrecks, no passenger had lost his or her life for a period of eight years and that no accident had occurred during the past fiscal year.[2]

Founded in 1827, the Baltimore & Ohio had not attained this level of success without a struggle. Its chartered purpose was to connect Baltimore City with the Ohio River in order to develop trade with the Ohio Valley re-

Charles Carroll of Carrollton at the laying of the First Stone of the Baltimore and Ohio Railroad July 4, 1828. (B&ORRM)

gion. During a spectacular groundbreaking ceremony on July 4, 1828, Charles Carroll of Carrollton was the guest of honor and laid the first stone. Charles Carroll was both the last living signer of the Declaration of Independence and an investor in the railroad. In May of 1830, the first 13 miles of commercial railroad in the United States was completed. The first trains were pulled by horses and the first tracks were laid on granite stringers.

The B&O did not reach its namesake river until Christmas Eve 1852. To get there it had to perform one engineering feat after another in order to penetrate the Allegheny Mountains. Tunnels were bored and bridges designed that had never been built before. Its employees literally had to invent wheels, rails, switches, locomotives, railcars and the terminology of railroading. Once the B&O had passed through the Allegheny Mountains, it rapidly developed a completely new line of business, the coal trade. In the company's annual report for the fiscal year ending September 30, 1860, it recorded the movement of 46,268 carloads of coal. This was 55% of all freight cars moved during that period. To accommodate the ever-increasing tonnage, the B&O built specially designed "pot hopper" cars that could be filled from the top and emptied from the bottom. By 1861, coal trains were moving day and night on the main line of the B&O and represented a major source of revenue for the company. Its future success, both in the coming war and the peace that followed, would be attributed to its current president, John Work Garrett. So successful was Garrett's stewardship that future experts would refer to the history of the B&O as having three time-periods, before Garrett, Garrett and after Garrett.[3]

No event in the antebellum period polarized the attitudes between North and South and at the same time displayed the talents of future Civil War leaders more than John Brown's Raid on Harpers Ferry, Virginia (now West Virginia), in 1859. It was the final lap in a decade-long race toward open conflict between the states. John Brown became a national figure as a result of the Kansas-Nebraska Act. When these two territories began to organize themselves prior to statehood, the issue of slavery reared its ugly head. The Kansas-Nebraska Act of 1854 attempted to resolve the problem by calling for Popular Sovereignty. Each territory or proposed state would have the opportunity to vote itself into the Union as free or slave. It was a foregone conclusion that Nebraska would enter as a free state, but Kansas' fate was yet to be determined. Both sides flooded the territory with armed men and the ensuing conflict gave rise to the term "Bleeding Kansas." As an ardent abolitionist, John Brown entered the fray and murdered five pro-slavery settlers in what became known as the "Potawatomi Massacre." Returning to the East, Brown was hailed as a hero by the abolitionists in the North. Their financial support allowed him to put his next project into motion. Brown planned to capture the United States Arsenal at Harpers Ferry and use the weapons stored there to form an army of freed slaves that would sweep through the Southern states and exterminate the institution of slavery and all of those who supported it.[4]

Brown, his sons Owen and Oliver, and a long time associate named Jeremiah Anderson arrived in Hagerstown on July 3, 1859, via the Cumberland Valley Railroad from Chambersburg. Using the alias Isaac Smith and the cover story that he was looking to purchase farmland near Harpers Ferry, he rented the Kennedy farm located on the Boonsboro Road about five miles north of the town. For the next few months men, supplies, and weapons were smuggled into the Kennedy farmhouse. On the night of October 16, Brown ordered his "Army of Liberation" into action. He led 18 men towards Harpers Ferry. Captain Owen Brown and two men remained behind to guard their supplies.

Their first objective was the 837-foot long covered bridge that carried the Baltimore and Ohio Railroad and pedestrian traffic across the Potomac River. At 10:30 that evening, two of Brown's men entered the bridge and captured the

Coal cars lined up in front of the Roundhouse at Martinsburg. (B&ORRM)

night watchman, William Williams. The little army then proceeded across the river to occupy the United States arsenal. Around midnight, Williams' replacement, Patrick Higgins, entered the bridge oblivious to the danger that awaited him. Brown had left two men to guard the bridge and they attempted to seize Higgins who fought off his attackers and escaped into the night with a bullet wound to the scalp.[5]

John Brown. (D. C. T.)

At the opposite end of the bridge, the B&O tracks curved sharply to the right and ran along the south bank of the Potomac River past the government musket factory and arsenal on their way to Cumberland, Maryland, and Wheeling, Virginia (now West Virginia). Near the southern entrance to the bridge was the Wager Hotel, which doubled as the town's train station. At 1:30 on the morning of October 17, the eastbound train was stopped in front of the station. Brown and a number of his men blocked the entrance to the bridge. Conductor A. J. Phelps and his crew dismounted and approached the strangers along with Heyward Shepherd, a baggage porter at the station. Shots rang out in the darkness with unintended consequences. Heyward Shepherd, a free black man employed by the Baltimore and Ohio Railroad, was shot through the body and died a few hours later.

At 3:00 a.m., Brown sent word to Phelps that he could proceed, but that his would be the last train to do so. Fearing an attack or sabotage on the bridge, Phelps waited until first light and then ordered his engineer, William McKay, to cross slowly over the Potomac River before racing full throttle to Monocacy Junction where he sent a telegram to William Prescott Smith, the Master of Transportation for the Baltimore and Ohio Railroad. "Express train bound east under my charge was stopped this morning at Harpers Ferry by armed Abolitionist. Myself and baggagemaster (sic) have been fired at and Heyward, the colored porter, is wounded...The doctors say he cannot survive."

Considering the fact that no military operation had taken place in the state of Maryland since the War of 1812, Smith may have found the communication incredulous. Two hours later he sent a reply which Conductor Phelps found waiting at the Ellicott's Mills station. "Your dispatch is evidently exag-

Pre-war view of Harpers Ferry showing covered railroad bridge and Maryland Heights. (B&ORRM)

gerated and written under excitement. Let me know at once before we respond to extremities." Phelps was in no mood for criticism and fired back, "I have not made it half as bad as it is....I will call at your office immediately on my arrival and tell you all."[6]

Things moved quickly after this. Smith informed John W. Garrett, the president of the B&O, who in turn had telegrams sent to the President of the United States James Buchanan, the governors of Maryland and Virginia, and General George Hume Steuart of the Maryland Militia, informing them that an insurrection was in progress at Harpers Ferry! To Secretary of War John B. Floyd he inquired, "Can you authorize the government officers and military from Washington to go on our train at 3:20 this afternoon to the scene?" Having used the telegraph to spread the alarm, the B&O would be the first railroad in the United States to move United States forces to the scene of an armed conflict.

The Regular Army of the United States at this time consisted of just over 16,000 officers and enlisted men – nearly all of which were somewhere other than the nation's capital. President Buchanan was forced to turn to his Secretary of the Navy, Isaac Toucey, for manpower. He ordered Colonel John Harris, Commandant of the United States Marine Corps, to organize a force for immediate deployment to Harpers Ferry. First Lieutenant Israel Greene left the Washington Depot on the 3:20 p.m. train with 87 men and two 12-lb. howitzers. His orders were to report to the senior U.S. Army officer at or near Harpers Ferry. Their first stop was Relay Station where the Washington Branch joined the main line of the B&O about seven miles south of Baltimore City. The Marines and their two cannon were off loaded to await the arrival of a westbound express that would take them as close to Harpers Ferry as possible.

While the Marines waited in Relay, the Secretary of War was still in search of an army officer to take charge of the situation. Lieutenant

William Prescott Smith, Master of Transportation for the B&O Railroad. (L. C.)

Colonel Robert E. Lee had recently returned from an assignment and was spending a few days leave at Arlington, his mansion across the river in Virginia. Floyd issued an order to send a special messenger to summon Lee to report to the War Department Immediately. By coincidence, Lieutenant John Ewell Brown (J.E.B.) Stuart of the First U.S. Cavalry was outside the Secretary's office seeking an interview on personal business. Sensing something important was afoot, he volunteered to deliver the message.[7]

While all of this was transpiring, events at Harpers Ferry were not standing still. Several Virginia militia units and many armed civilians were swarming into Harpers Ferry. By mid-afternoon, the arsenal buildings had been recaptured. Five of Brown's men and three citizens of the town had been killed. One of these was Fontaine Beckham, the B&O's station agent and mayor of the town. Brown, with the five surviving members of his band and a number of hostages, had take refuge in the fire engine house located outside the entrance to the arsenal complex. The structure later became known as John Brown's Fort. With telegraph lines cut, the authorities could receive no creditable re-

Relay House was also known as Washington Junction. Both the U.S. Marines and Colonel Robert E. Lee waited here for trains to take them to Harpers Ferry. (D. C. T.)

ports. Rumors spread that up to a thousand armed insurgents controlled the town.

Maryland, being both a slave state and a major investor in the B&O Railroad, had a dual interest in the crisis. The first contingent of Maryland troops to arrive on the scene were three militia companies from Frederick City, commanded by Colonel Edward Shriver. They had left Frederick at 3:45 p.m. on a special train provided by the B&O Railroad. Arriving at the now-famous covered bridge after dark, Shriver led them across the Potomac River and offered their services to the ranking Virginia Militia officer, Colonel R. W. Baylor. Among the men serving under Shriver were William P. Maulsby, future colonel of the First Potomac Home Brigade U.S. and Bradley T. Johnson, the future colonel of the First Maryland Infantry C.S. and brigadier general in the Confederate Army.

At the same time the Frederick troop movement was under way, five additional militia companies from Baltimore City were boarding a second train provided by the B&O Railroad. They were commanded by General Charles C. Egerton, Jr. of the Second Light Brigade. With them, President Garrett sent Master of Transportation William Prescott Smith to insure that none of the troop trains bound for Harpers Ferry were unnecessarily delayed. En route, this train stopped at Relay to pick up the Marines from Washington. Continuing on, it deposited both units at Sandy Hook on the Maryland side of the Potomac River with instructions to await the arrival of Lieutenant Colonel Lee.[8]

When Stuart arrived at Arlington, he simultaneously delivered the order for Lee to report to the War Department and offered his services as Aide-de-Camp. The two men left immediately, Lee not even taking the time to change into his uniform. No sooner had they arrived at the War Department than the Secretary escorted them to the White House for a meeting with the President. Buchanan and Floyd took turns briefing the two Army officers with what little information they had concerning the insurrection. Then Lee was given his marching orders – go to Harpers Ferry and end it.

From the White House, Lee and Stuart headed for the Washington Depot and boarded the next train out. By the time they reached the station at Relay, the Marines were gone. Lee wired instructions to Lieutenant Green not to enter Harpers Ferry until he arrived. Greene received the telegram when he passed through Monocacy Junction. A third special train was dispatched by Garrett to take Lee and Stuart to Harpers Ferry. It consisted solely of B&O Locomotive #22 and its tender. As the special pulled up to the platform at Relay sometime after 2:00 a.m. on October 18, Engineer G. F. Gilbert invited the two officers to climb aboard and the locomotive sped off into the darkness. Their first ride on a train to a war zone would be a memorable one. The old design of Engine 22 did not include an enclosed cab. Thus, the two passengers had no protection from the wind and damp night air. At Sandy Hook, Lee received a situation report from Lieutenant Greene, the first reliable information that he could use to formulate his plans. Lee ordered Greene to take his Marines across the river and surround the engine house. Fearing for the safety of the hostages, no attack would be made until after sun up and only the bayonet would be used. At 7:00 a.m., Stuart delivered a final demand for Brown to surrender which he refused. Then the Marines stormed the fire engine house killing two of Brown's men and capturing three plus their leader who was also wounded in the attack. The Marines lost one killed, Private Luke Quinn, and one wounded, Private Matthew Ruppert.[9]

As soon as the situation allowed, Lee sent a telegram to the Secretary of War with the welcome news that the revolt had been crushed. Master of Transportation Smith also sent a message to his boss, John Garrett, detailing the valiant charge of the Marines and the capture of Brown. He then sent telegrams to newspapers as far west as Cincinnati announcing the restoration of peace in Harpers Ferry – no doubt with an eye to getting passengers back on the train and the trains back on schedule.[10]

The next day the Marines escorted their prisoners through a howling lynch mob to the depot of the Winchester & Potomac Railroad where they were transferred to the custody of Virginia officials. As a security measure, Lieutenant Greene and a detachment of his men accompanied the party on the short train ride to Charles Town where John Brown would be tried and eventually executed. Later the same day Green received a telegram with orders to return to headquarters in Washington.

Lee and Stuart joined the Marines as they boarded the 1:15 train on the morning of October 19 for the return run to Relay Station. The B&O's dress rehearsal for the Civil War was over. Through its telegraph lines, it had given the governors of the affected states and the President the first notice of a national emergency and the means to respond to it. Its Telegraph Department was not a public utility, but an internal communication system. As the latest form of communication technology, the telegraph would be invaluable to the management of field armies in the coming war. The federal government established its own system in April of 1861.[11]

The more obvious accomplishment was that of troop movements by rail. Never before had troops and artillery been moved to the point of conflict with such speed and efficiency. Travel time was reduced from days to hours. The key to this success was the management skill of Garrett and Smith and their subordinates who used a combination of scheduled service with specially arranged trains to deliver the troops in the shortest amount of time. Additionally, the events at Harpers Ferry introduced the potential of the railroad in time of war to three future Confederate generals and numerous lesser officers that would serve in both armies.

On a national level, John Brown's Raid on Harpers Ferry drove a mighty wedge between North and South. Southerners saw the combination of the abolitionist movement with the newly formed Republican Party as a direct threat to their way of life. In the North, the slavery issue was pushed front and center. Many who had been indifferent to the plight of Southern slaves now took up the cause of emancipation. Both regions saw an increase in the formation of independent military companies and a renewed interest in the state militias. The presidential election of 1860 would be the last pause before Civil War. For many, their first glimpse of that war would be a B&O train carrying troops somewhere between Baltimore and Wheeling – the terminal points of America's most famous railroad.

U.S. Marines attacking the engine house at Harpers Ferry on the morning of October 18, 1859. (Harpers Ferry National Historic Park)

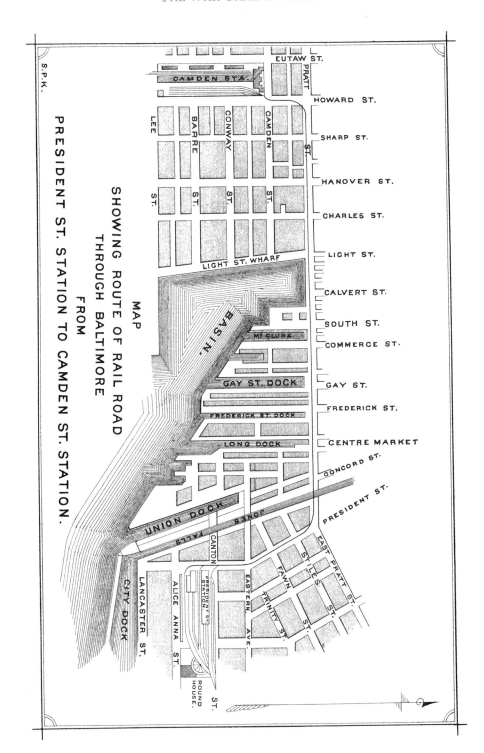

MAP
SHOWING ROUTE OF RAIL ROAD
THROUGH BALTIMORE
FROM
PRESIDENT ST. STATION TO CAMDEN ST. STATION.

S.P.K.

Chapter Two

1861
THE FIRST
FRONT

During the election of 1860, four candidates vied for the highest office in the land. Regional interests conspired to make it two separate contests. The old line Southern Democrats supported former Vice-President John C. Breckenridge with a view toward protecting slavery. Border State Conservatives and refugees from the old Whig and dying Know Nothing parties ran John Bell in an attempt to avert war by calling for a strict adherence to the Constitution. Northern Democrats nominated Stephen A. Douglas to run against the lesser known Republican candidate Abraham Lincoln. Both Breckenridge and Bell knew they had little chance of success in the North and confined their campaigning to the Southern states. Their only hope was that a split in the North would give one or the other a victory. Likewise, Lincoln and Douglas conceded the Southern states and campaigned against each other in the North and West with the realization that the superior number of electoral votes would decide the election. With the Democratic Party split three ways, Lincoln received more than twice as many electoral votes than his nearest rival Breckenridge did. At this time the Baltimore and Ohio Railroad was located wholly within two Southern states, Maryland and Virginia, and both voted decidedly against Abraham Lincoln.[12]

As soon as the results of the election were known, states in the Deep South began to call secession conventions. South Carolina led the way when it passed an ordinance of secession on December 20, 1860. Mississippi, Florida, Alabama, Georgia, Louisiana and Texas followed in what became known as the Secession Winter. The border and upper southern states hesitated, their citizens not fully committed to a separation from the Union. Maryland was tied to Virginia and could go nowhere without its sister state to the south. The last four states to join the Confederacy did not do so until after the fall of Fort Sumter, beginning with Virginia on April 17. With the entire length of the Baltimore & Ohio Railroad located below the Mason-Dixon Line, its future was anything but certain.[13]

Abraham Lincoln was not the first President to travel to his inauguration by train, but he was the first President to use the railroad to his political advantage. Both Lincoln and the Republican Party were relatively new to national politics. In order to introduce himself to the people who had elected him and garner their support in the looming struggle to preserve the Union, he arranged a circuitous route through eight states that would include seventy different whistle stops and major speeches. Leaving Springfield, Illinois, on February 11, he began a twelve-day journey that would cover over 1,900 miles and utilize eighteen different railroads. The final stop was to be Baltimore City on February 23.[14]

As Lincoln traveled through the northeast, the border states simmered with talk of secession. Samuel M. Felton, president of the Philadelphia, Wilmington & Baltimore Railroad, hired Allan Pinkerton, head of the Pinkerton's National Detective Agency, to investigate rumored plans to attack his railroad if engaged in troop movements against the Confederacy. Pinkerton sent a number of his detectives into Baltimore City to work the bars and street corners for any hint of a conspiracy against the railroad. What they found, according to Pinkerton, was a plot to assassinate the president-elect as he changed trains in Baltimore! Although confirmed by a second source from New York City, one must consider the possibility that Pinkerton was only attempting to ingratiate himself with the new administration with an eye towards future contracts. Until now, only circumstantial evidence has been provided to prove his allegations.

Plot or no plot, Felton and the PW&B Railroad quickly became the solution to the problem. Lincoln was scheduled to raise a 34-star flag at Independence Hall when he arrived in Philadelphia to welcome the new state of Kansas into the Union. Then he would go to Harrisburg to address the state legislature and spend the night. The next day Lincoln, his wife Mary Todd and their sons would travel by the Northern Central to Baltimore City where they would change trains and complete their epic journey on the Washington Branch of the B&O Railroad.[15]

Lincoln kept his schedule as far as Harrisburg. Then, after he addressed the legislature, a special two-car train was provided by the Pennsylvania Railroad to carry him back to Philadelphia. Extreme measures were taken to keep the move a secret. The telegraph was cut between the two cities and everyone functioned on a need-to-know basis. Because double tracking was not universal at the time, it was necessary for trains to run on schedule. The image of a conductor with his gold watch was not just a popular railroading theme, it was essential to avoid head-on collisions. Felton devised a clever cover story to keep the trains waiting. He had his general superintendent, Mr. H. P. Kenney, instruct the conductor to hold the train for a vital package that must go through to Washington on the night train. Once Pinkerton, Lincoln, and his bodyguard Ward H. Lamon were safely aboard in the rear sleeping car, the package was handed to the conductor, and the train departed the station thirty minutes late. In reality, the package only contained obsolete reports.

The train arrived at the President Street Station in Baltimore about 3:00 a.m. on February 23. The cars were detached and pulled by horse power, one at a time, to Camden Station where the B&O's Locomotive No. 25 (later named the William Mason after its famous designer) waited to make the Washington run. As soon as the President's party arrived at the Washington Depot, Pinkerton telegraphed the anxious Samuel Felton a cryptic message, "Plums delivered nuts safely," confirming Lincoln's safe arrival. At 12:30 p.m. the same day, the president-elect's special train arrived at the Northern Central's Calvert Street Station. On board were Mrs. Lincoln, her three sons, and John Hay, Lincoln's private secretary. At trackside, 10,000 people waited to see the man that most of them had not elected President. Their disappointment caused some agitation but no violence. Mrs. Lincoln was entertained at the home of Mr. John S. Gittings, the president of the Northern Central Railway, until it was time to take the afternoon train from Camden Station to Washington. No one can blame the President for erring on the side of caution but his nocturnal passage

Baltimore & Ohio Locomotive No. 25, the "William Mason," pulled the train that took Lincoln to his inauguration in 1861. Now in the collection of the B&O Railroad Museum, it is the only operating Civil War locomotive in the United States. (B&ORRM)

through Baltimore City eliminated the possibility of wooing any Southern-leaning Marylanders back into the Union and brought forth a deluge of criticism from the Southern press. A political cartoonist depicted him as hiding in a boxcar and wearing a dress to conceal his identity. This would not be the end of Lincoln's difficulties with Maryland. In fact, it was only the beginning.[16]

Baltimore

On March 4, Lincoln took the oath of office. In his inaugural address, Lincoln made one final plea to the Southern states for a unified nation.

"In your hands, my dissatisfied fellow-countrymen, and not mine, is the momentous issue of civil war. The government will not assail you. You can have no conflict without being yourselves the aggressor. *You* have no oath registered in heaven to destroy the government, while *I* shall have the most solemn one to 'preserve, protect and defend it.'"

His eloquent words fell on deaf ears. At 4:30 in the morning of April 12, a signal gun was fired from Fort Johnson in Charleston Harbor and all the batteries under the command of Confederate General P. G. T. Beauregard commenced a bombardment on Fort Sumter. The last symbol of federal authority in the state surrendered the next day. The Civil War had begun.[17]

Events now occurred almost faster than they could be recorded. On April 15, Lincoln called for 75,000 volunteers to suppress the rebellion. Two days later Virginia voted to secede from the Union. Now all eyes were on Maryland, the only southern state north of Washington, DC. If Maryland joined the secession movement, Lincoln and the nation's capital would be located behind enemy lines! A humiliating escape by sea to New York or Philadelphia would be the only alternative for the government's leaders. The key to maintaining the capital was Baltimore City and the B&O Railroad. All the railroads from the north funneled into Baltimore and out on the main line of the B&O. Troops and supplies coming from the Ohio Valley traveled east from Wheeling, Virginia. Both movements would converge on the tiny town of Relay where the Washington Branch joined the main line of the B&O seven miles southwest of Baltimore. The single-tracked, thirty-mile-long Washington Branch was truly the lifeline of the Union in the spring of 1861.

On April 18, five companies of Pennsylvania volunteers left Harrisburg, Pennsylvania, on a Northern Central train that took them to Baltimore along the identical route Mary Lincoln had traveled two months earlier. On the same train were forty men of Company H, Fourth U.S. Artillery commanded by Lt. John C. Pemberton. The Regulars were under orders to reinforce the garrison

Political cartoon by Albert J. Volck depicts Lincoln passing through Baltimore City on the night of February 22-23, 1861 in a Philadelphia, Wilmington & Baltimore boxcar. (D. C. T.)

at Fort McHenry. Lt. Pemberton resigned his commission on April 24 and entered the Confederate Army. Rising to the rank of lieutenant general, he surrendered Vicksburg, Mississippi, on July 4, 1863.

The Regulars passed through the city with little difficulty. A different fate awaited the volunteers. Only one company, the Logan Guards, was armed and its members carried obsolete flintlock muskets without any ammunition. As they proceeded from the Northern Central Railway's Bolton Station to the B&O's Mount Clare Station, they were set upon by a crowd of pro southern supporters. A contingent of Baltimore City policemen attempted to restrain

First Defenders' ribbon for the veterans of the five companies of Pennsylvania Volunteers that passed through Baltimore on April 18, 1861. (D. C. T.)

the rioters but a number of the soldiers were struck by stones and other objects that caused severe injuries but no deaths. Nick Biddle, a free black man in the service of Captain James Wren who commanded The Washington Artillerists of Pottsville, was struck in the face with a paving stone and "bled profusely." He is considered by some to have been the first casualty of the war. When the Pennsylvania volunteers arrived at Mount Clare, they were quickly loaded onto a waiting train of boxcars and arrived in Washington City, as it was then known, at 7:00 p.m. The first troops to arrive in the capital after Lincoln's call for volunteers, they assumed the title "First Defenders" and celebrated this accomplishment after the war with an annual pilgrimage to Baltimore City.[18]

April 19, 1861, was in many ways as historic as the firing on Fort Sumter a week earlier. On April 17, the militia companies that composed the Sixth Massachusetts Infantry Regiment were summoned to Boston in response to Lincoln's call for volunteers. Hailing from Boston and the surrounding towns of Acton, Lowell and Lawrence to name a few, these Minute Men of 61 were direct descendents of the Revolutionary War patriots who fought the British at Lexington and Concord. Commanded by Colonel Edward F. Jones, the Sixth Massachusetts was 800 men strong and included a 16-piece band. It was the first fully armed and

Sixth Massachusetts Regiment leaving the Jersey City railroad depot for Philadelphia. (L. I. N.)

equipped regiment to answer the call. Its transportation by train to Washington City was unprecedented in military history moving 450 miles over seven different railroads to arrive in only 48 hours. Their route took them through Baltimore, sparking another significant event.

The regiment spent the night in Philadelphia and was awakened at an early hour when news arrived of the events in Baltimore the day before. Colonel Jones conferred with Samuel M. Felton, president of the PW&B. To avoid any sabotage of the line, Felton provided a pilot engine to run in advance of the troop train. Jones ordered the train loaded in a specific sequence of companies so that if forced to disembark suddenly he could immediately form a line of battle. The headquarters personnel were in the first car and the regimental band in the rear. Before departing, parts of two Pennsylvania regiments under the command of Colonel William F. Small, known as the Philadelphia Brigade, joined the movement south. These men were from the Twenty-Sixth and Twenty-Seventh regiments and were in civilian dress without any kind of weapons or equipment. The train now totaled 35 cars and was over twice the length of a normal passenger train.

At this time no bridge existed across the Susquehanna River between Perryville and Havre de Grace, Maryland. The railroad relied on the 238-foot iron ferryboat *Maryland* to cross the river. The boat had fixed tracks on its upper deck that could accommodate 20 railcars. Passengers traveled on the lower deck. It was here that Jones began to learn the complexities of railroad operations south of the Mason-Dixon Line. The cars were not rolled off in the same order they had been loaded. The headquarters car was still in front and the band in the rear but all the others were haphazardly attached to the waiting locomotive.

The train arrived at President Street Station on the east side of Baltimore's harbor early on the morning of April 19. Jones expected it to pass through Baltimore and on to Washington without interruption. What he did not know was that a city ordinance enacted in 1831 prohibited the movement of any rail cars through Baltimore by steam power. Although the track gauges were the same, any transfers between terminals had to be by draft animals, one car at a time. Several factors may have led to the implementation of the law. First, the steam and noise of the locomotives often scared horses and other draft animals. Second, the embers from the flue occasionally set wooden structures on fire. Finally, the teamsters wanted to maintain their monopoly of the city's transit business and so lobbied for the law.[19]

One at a time, the cars were uncoupled and drayed down President Street to Pratt Street where they traveled along the waterfront, what is now the western edge of Baltimore's famous Inner Harbor, to Howard Street. From Howard Street it was a mere two blocks to Camden Station. The total distance was only about two miles, but for half the regiment it would seem like an eternity. The first seven cars containing the regimental staff and six infantry companies moved along Pratt Street in this fashion. With each passing car, the citizens grew more hostile. When the eighth car left President Street Station with Company K aboard, it was derailed by an anchor thrown in its way as it turned on to Pratt Street. Major Benjamin F. Watson jumped to the ground and forced a passing teamster to aid in re-railing the car. The street was now packed on both sides with a mixture of rebel sympathizers, unionists, gang members and innocent spectators. It was impossible for the soldiers to know who was who. Major Watson climbed back on board and, with pistol in hand, urged the driver to continue in the direction of Camden Station. The forward motion of the car resulted in a deluge of rocks, bottles, pieces of scrap iron, and random gunfire being sent in its direction. Despite many injuries, the soldiers did not open fire on their attackers until one of them had his thumb shot off. The shattered coach was forced to stop near Howard Street when it was discovered that the tracks had been ripped out of the ground. From there Company K marched the rest of the way to Camden Station taking their wounded with them.

Four companies totaling 220 men, the band, and the unarmed Pennsylvania volunteers remained at President Street Station. After the departure of Company K, they were informed that no more cars would attempt a passage

Camden Station viewed from the east side. It was both the corporate headquarters of the B&O Railroad and the destination of the Sixth Massachusetts Regiment on April 19, 1861. (B&ORRM)

through the city. Leaving the band behind, the senior officer, Captain A. S. Follansbee, formed up companies C, I, L and D and began to march along the railroad tracks in order to rejoin the regiment. As they turned onto Pratt Street, they discovered the floor of the bridge over the Jones Falls had been removed. Jumping from stringer to stringer, they passed over it amid the now familiar array of missiles. Once across the bridge the amount of gunfire coming from the mob increased, and Follansbee gave the order to return fire. Sometimes the

The first battle of the Civil War was fought on Pratt Street April 19, 1861. (D. C. T.)

soldiers took aim at an armed citizen. At other times, the men in the rear rank would simply put their muskets on their shoulders and fire a blind volley.

That all the residents of Baltimore were against the soldiers was simply not the case. When Mayor George W. Brown was informed that a riot was taking place he rushed to the scene and marched beside Captain Follansbee for a while in an unsuccessful attempt to calm the attackers. Along the entire route, wounded soldiers were taken into businesses and private homes where they were protected from further harm and given medical attention. Finally, near Howard Street, Marshal George P. Kane of the Baltimore City Police Department arrived with a detachment of 50 policemen who, with drawn revolvers, backed the rioters down. The "lost battalion" then had to fight its way into Camden Station where it boarded a train waiting to take the regiment to Washington. The regiment's losses were four killed and 36 wounded. Colonel Jones reluctantly ordered the train to depart knowing he was leaving about 130 men behind and unaccounted for. Many of these were given shelter in the various police stations and eventually reunited with their regiment.

Having lost their prey on Pratt Street, the mob then besieged the unarmed band members and Pennsylvania volunteers still waiting at President Street Station. The band members were chased from their car and beaten as were many of the Pennsylvania soldiers. Eventually the tracks were cleared and Colonel Small's brigade was sent back to Philadelphia along with the bandsmen by train. A strong detachment of Baltimore City policemen escorted them to the city limits. The Pennsylvania volunteers' losses were one man killed and five wounded. George Leisenring was stabbed in the chest and died three days later in Philadelphia. He was the first Pennsylvania citizen to give his life for the Union. Many others had run from the train and it took them several days to make their way back to Philadelphia.[20]

The arrival of the Sixth Massachusetts Regiment in Washington did not mean an end to the difficulties in Baltimore. On the night of April 19, the mayor, governor, and city council met to determine a course of action for the city. It was an undeniable fact that if more troops came, more blood would be spilled. To prevent this from happening, orders went out from Governor Hicks and Mayor Brown to burn the railroad bridges north of the city and cut the telegraph lines. Three bridges on the Northern Central and two on the PW&B were destroyed. Lincoln's worst nightmare had come true. The Nation's Capital was cut off from direct resupply from the loyal states. Baltimore, in the words of Mayor Brown, "entered into a period of armed neutrality." Militia units from all over the state swarmed into the city and Isaac Ridgeway Trimble, a future major general in the Confederate Army, was given command of a 10,000 man non-uniformed volunteer corps. Trimble was no stranger to railroad operations. A West Point graduate, he participated in the original surveys for the B&O Railroad and at one time was the superintendent of the PW&B. He also invented a system for splicing adjacent rails. Know as the Trimble Splice, it was manufactured by the firm of Trimble & Houston in Wilmington, Delaware. Lincoln, realizing his precarious position, sent the following telegram on April 20.

> Governor Hicks:
> I desire to consult with you and the mayor of Baltimore related to preserving the peace of Maryland. Please come immediately by special train, which you can take at Baltimore; or if necessary, one can be sent from here. Answer forthwith.
>
> LINCOLN

These negotiations were complicated by the arrival of an additional 2,500 Union Volunteers along the banks of the Gunpowder River at Cockeysville, Maryland. Swarms of armed Marylanders gathered to oppose their advance. Realizing that Maryland was on the brink of secession, Lincoln was forced to back down and ordered the troops returned to Harrisburg. It would fall to a political general from Massachusetts to save the day.[21]

Traveling by rail 24 hours behind the Sixth Massachusetts Regiment was the Eighth Regiment and Brigadier General Benjamin Franklin Butler. But-

Burning of the Philadelphia, Wilmington & Baltimore Railroad bridge over the Gunpowder River after the Pratt Street Riot. (L. I. N.)

ler was a pre-war Democrat turned Radical Republican. After the war, he served in Congress, was elected governor of his state in 1882, and ran as a presidential candidate for the Greenback Party in 1884. As military governor of Louisiana in 1862, he garnered the sobriquets "Beast Butler" for his heavy-handed control of the civilian population and "Spoons" for the amount of silverware that he took home with him. He failed miserably as commander of the Army of the James and Grant ordered him home to await orders in November of 1864. A second failure while in command of the expedition against Wilmington, North Carolina, ended his military career.

Brigadier General Benjamin F. Butler occupied Annapolis, Relay and Baltimore in April and May of 1861. (D. C. T.)

When Butler arrived at Philadelphia, he met with General Robert Patterson, then commanding the Department of Pennsylvania. He ordered Butler to bypass Baltimore and go to Washington via Annapolis. This Butler did by seizing the railroad ferryboat *Maryland* at Perryville and sailing down the Susquehanna River to the Chesapeake Bay. It was well that he did because on the same day, April 20, Marshal Kane of the Baltimore City Police Department ordered Major James J. Archer of Harford County to seize or destroy the *Maryland* in order to keep it from being used to transport Northern soldiers through the state. Soon after this, Archer resigned his commission in the U.S. Army and entered Confederate service. He commanded the Tennessee Brigade at the battle of Gettysburg where he earned the dubious honor of being the first general officer of the Army of Northern Virginia captured during the war.

Butler moved by train to within a mile of Perryville where he stopped and deployed one company, the Salem Zouaves, to advance as skirmishers on either side of the track. The rest of the regiment followed in silent route step until they arrived at their objective. Boat, captain and crew were quickly captured without a shot being fired. The vessel only contained enough coal to cross the river. In order to expedite their departure four rail cars loaded with coal were pushed on board and unloaded as they sailed down the Susquehanna River. The ferryboat arrived at the Naval Academy dock before dawn the next day.

General Butler received a warm welcome from Captain George S. Blake, commandant of the Academy. He had greatly feared an attack by Southern sympathizers who might capture or destroy the training ship USS *Constitution*. [22]

A second ship arrived on the morning of April 22 carrying the Seventh New York National Guard commanded by Colonel Marshall Lefferts. The Seventh Regiment had marched in a farewell parade down Broadway and then been ferried over to Jersey City where it boarded a New Jersey Railroad & Transportation Co. train that would interchange with the Camden & Amboy line before arriving in Philadelphia. There, informed by Mr. Felton of the prevailing conditions on the PW&B, Colonel Lefferts took it upon himself to charter the steamer *Boston* and sail to Washington if possible or, if the Potomac River was blocked, to Annapolis. Unarmed and without an escort, he judged ascending the Potomac River too great a risk and put into Annapolis on the morning of April 21, where he found the *Maryland* aground off the Naval Academy dock.

The men in the two regiments worked well together despite a clash of personalities by their respective commanders. Butler claimed overall command by virtue of his star. Not yet federalized, no New York colonel was going to take orders from another state's militia general. The ships were unloaded and the Naval Academy grounds secured. Annapolis was the state capital and a colonial seaport. Between November of 1783 and August of 1784, it had served as the capital of the nascent United States of America, and it was in the Maryland State House that General George Washington relinquished his command of the Continental Army. Annapolis was also located in Southern Maryland where tobacco plantations and slavery were the norm. The Annapolis and Elk Ridge Railroad operated a single line track that ran from the city to Annapolis Junction. There it connected with the Washington Branch of the B&O 20 miles west of Annapolis. Pro-Confederate militia companies opposed the advance by Union troops along this route by removing rails and burning bridges. [23]

Butler sent a force to occupy the Annapolis and Elk Ridge train station near the beginning of West Street in Annapolis and ordered two of his companies to march out along the tracks for a distance of two miles and hold their position until reinforced. Breaking open a train shed, some of Butler's men found a disassembled locomotive. When asked if anyone knew how to fix it, Private Charles Homans of Company E, stepped forward and announced that he could. He worked at the Portland locomotive works where the *J. H. Nicholson* had been built. Missing parts were located, and in a short time, Private Homans had the engine back in working order. At the same time, a detail of twenty men with railroad experience set about replacing the missing rails at that end of the line.

The advance on Annapolis Junction began early on the morning of April 24. The track gang had been fired on and the strength of the opposing force was unknown. To supply fire support for the advancing column Butler created the first war train in military history. The sides of two cattle cars were cut down to make flat cars. On the first flat car, a 6-pound howitzer was mounted and loaded with grape shot and protected by 16 riflemen. On the second car, the gun's ammunition was stacked and guarded by an additional six men. Next came the locomotive driven by Private Homans followed by two passenger cars, each carrying a company from the Seventh New York.[24]

Passing through the advanced guard of the Eighth Massachusetts, the New Yorkers found their progress halted about three miles farther on. The two flat cars were uncoupled and drag ropes were attached. Sufficient repairs were made to allow the flat cars to be pulled manually over the damaged section of the track and the advance continued. The rest of the train waited for the rails to be properly replaced.

Colonel Lefferts left the Annapolis Depot at about 8:00 a.m. with the balance of his regiment. They brought along two additional flat cars. One carried medical supplies and was fitted up as a crude ambulance car. The other one carried a second howitzer and its ammunition. Skirmishers were deployed for half a mile on either side of the tracks to prevent an ambush. They were also ordered to look for rails and crossties that had been thrown about by the track wreckers. Just beyond the water station at Millersville, the railroad bridge that crossed over a wagon road had been burned. The structure was 20 feet high and 16 feet long. It took several hours to rebuild it. During the delay, the Eighth Regiment arrived and many of its men joined in the reconstruction project. The project was completed near sundown and the Seventh New York, with their flat cars in tow, again took the lead. The locomotive was used to shuttle men and supplies between them and Annapolis.

Despite the day long exertions, Lefferts pushed his men through the darkness. Railroad sidings were cannibalized to replace missing rails, spikes and ties. As the hours passed the men's fatigue mounted. Soldiers marched with eyes closed and fell to the ground like dead men at every halt. At dawn, the regiment reached the outskirts of Annapolis Junction. Lefferts halted the column and advanced into the Junction with a force of about 150 men. He found it deserted and immediately ordered his men to make camp and procure provisions from the local community.

The Washington Branch had not been damaged. Expecting the arrival of the regiment, but having no way to communicate with it, the officials in Washington began sending a train out each day to meet it at the Junction. Not knowing this, a detail was sent out on a handcar to find a train or some-

The Seventh New York advancing along the Annapolis & Elk Ridge Railroad followed by Butler's "War Train." (D. C. T.)

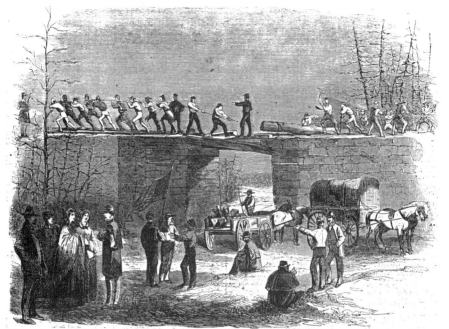

Men of the Eighth Massachusetts Regiment rebuilding the railroad bridge south of Annapolis, Maryland. (H. W.)

how communicate their arrival to the government. On the morning of April 25, the connection was made and the Seventh New York was on its way to Washington City. Their arrival not only brought badly needed reinforcements to the poorly defended capital, it also meant Lincoln now had a route around Baltimore that other regiments could follow.[25]

Butler was considered the hero of the day. On April 25, General Winfield Scott sent a letter to him requesting that he take charge of the City of Annapolis and disburse a regiment of infantry along the critical points of the railroad between Annapolis and Washington to ensure its safety. He concluded with instructions to "Send to this place all spare troops from Annapolis as fast as you may find means of transportation, and report often." This was followed up two days later with General Orders No. 12 that created the Department of Annapolis and made General B. F. Butler its commander. His area of authority was uniquely defined as "…the country for twenty miles on either side of the railroad from Annapolis to the city of Washington as far as Bladensburg, Maryland." By now, at least four more regiments had arrived at the Naval Academy dock and the flow of troops and supplies began in earnest.

Acting on orders from General Scott, Butler occupied Relay on May 5 with two regiments and six guns of the Boston Battery. Here the Washing-

The Seventh New York Regiment arriving at the B&O terminal in Washington City. (H. W.)

ton Branch connected with the mainline of the B&O Railroad over a massive stone arch bridge known as the Thomas Viaduct. His mission was two-fold; first, to stop the flow of supplies and recruits from Baltimore to the rapidly forming Confederate Army at Harpers Ferry and second, to act as a blocking force should the enemy advance from Harpers Ferry toward that point. Butler immediately placed two guns in battery on Elk Ridge Heights to cover the bridge and distributed troops up and down both lines to protect switches and other vulnerable points.[26]

While Butler's force was at Relay two events related to the renowned locomotive builder and inventor Ross Winans took place. The first occurred on May 11. Butler was absent and Colonel Jones of the Sixth Massachusetts, acting on information that a secret weapon had left Baltimore and was en route to Harpers Ferry, immediately halted a westbound train and loaded two companies of infantry and two pieces of artillery on it with orders to intercept the weapon. The weapon was actually invented by a man named Charles Dickinson. A steam-powered machine gun, it was supposedly capable of firing 100 to 500 rounds per minute. Having failed to sell his invention to the City of Baltimore, Dickinson was attempting to take it west along the National Road and eventually South to sell it to the Confederate government. The gun had been assembled in Winans machine shop and erroneously given the name Winans Steam Gun. By the time the train arrived, a group of citizens had already seized the weapon. The soldiers loaded it on a rail car and returned with it to Relay. The inventor managed to escape with some critical components that rendered the weapon inoperable. Thus, its true capability was never known.

Early in his career, Ross Winans had worked for the B&O Railroad designing wheels, rail cars and even locomotives before starting his own firm that evolved into one of the largest railroad machine shops in America. The B&O was his largest customer, purchasing 140 locomotives between 1848 and 1864. Despite his northern birth and industrial based fortune, Winans was an ardent secessionist. He manufactured over 4,000 pikes in his machine shop to arm the citizens of Baltimore against Northern soldiers and as a member of the Maryland State Legislature, railed against Lincoln's policies. Butler arrested him on May 14 as he was returning home from the special session of the

The Boston Battery on Elk Ridge Heights guarding the Thomas Viaduct after General Butler occupied Relay on May 5, 1861. (D. C. T.)

legislature held in Frederick City. After a short confinement at Fort McHenry, he was released upon signing a parole not to take any hostile action against the federal government.[27]

By now, Baltimore City had enjoyed two weeks of "Armed Neutrality" and the State Legislature had convened at Frederick City on April 26. Following the Pratt Street Riot, Governor Hicks had been forced to call a special session of the Legislature to address Maryland's course of action in the unfolding civil war. No one could tell if this special session would result in Maryland leaving the Union, and Lincoln was helpless to influence its outcome. Butler, believing that Baltimore was within his area of operation, took matters into his own hands. On May 13, he requested a special train from the B&O. It was to be a very large train with a locomotive at each end. His cover story was that he was going to Frederick City. When the train arrived at Relay, Butler placed a thousand men and several pieces of artillery on board and headed up the main line toward Frederick. At a blind spot on the tracks, he had the train broken in half. The first part continued on its way. Butler and the rear section of the train ran back down the main line passing Relay. It arrived at Camden Station near nightfall amidst a thunderstorm. He quickly detrained his men and marched them to the top of Federal Hill, a commanding eminence that overlooked the

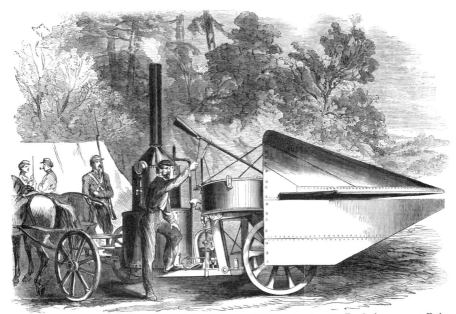

The Winans steam-gun was captured in Ellicott's Mills and taken to Butler's camp at Relay. (H. W.)

waterfront and much of the city, where he dug in for the night. Butler also sent a dispatch to Fort McHenry informing its commander that, "I have taken possession of Baltimore. My troops are on Federal Hill, which I can hold with my artillery. If I am attacked tonight, please open fire on Monument Square with your mortars." The next day the citizens of Baltimore awoke to find the U.S. flag flying on Federal Hill and guarded by the same men they had attacked on the 19th of April, the Sixth Massachusetts Regiment. [28]

Ross Winans. Originally, an employee of the B&O Railroad, he designed locomotives and railcars before opening his own locomotive works in Baltimore City. Despite his Northern birth, he was an ardent secessionist. (B&ORRM)

This bold action essentially ended all overt opposition to the federal government in Maryland. Those young men who hoped to join the Confederate Army on Maryland soil were forced to abandon their homes and travel to Richmond or Harpers Ferry to enlist. When General Winfield Scott learned of the unauthorized operation, he had Butler removed from command – ironically for performing his most vital service for the Union. A final review of Butler's accomplishments is in order. Beginning on April 20, he seized the ferryboat *Maryland* before it could be captured or destroyed by Major Archer. Then, moving in a giant clockwise circle, he secured the U.S. Naval Academy, occupied the state capital, and worked with the Seventh New York to reopen the Annapolis & Elk Ridge Railroad that linked Maryland's capital to the B&O's Washington Branch. In addition, he secured the entire length of the Washington Branch and the vital Thomas Viaduct and ended the stalemate in Baltimore City. In short, he transferred the opening battle lines of the Civil War from the Susquehanna River to the Potomac.

Harpers Ferry

Located at the confluence of the Shenandoah and Potomac rivers, Harpers Ferry, West Virginia, is a place of both natural beauty and historic significance. The town was named after Robert Harper, who operated a mill and ferry during the middle of the eighteenth century. Due to the influence of President George Washington, a federal arsenal was located there towards the end of the same century. It was the Harpers Ferry rifle that Lewis and Clark carried on their great exploration of the West. One of several different types of weapons manufactured at the arsenal, the U.S. Model 1803 was the first rifle produced for the United States Army. Industrialization of the town was further enhanced by the arrival of the B&O Railroad in 1834. The railroad constructed a retaining wall on the Virginia side of the Potomac. Its purpose was to allow the tracks to be laid between the river and the arsenal. From Harpers Ferry, the line continued up the Virginia side, reaching Martinsburg on May 21, 1842. After bridging the river to the Maryland side again, just above Green Spring Run, the B&O introduced service to Cumberland, Maryland, on November 3 of that same year.[29]

Virginia's long delayed vote for secession passed on April 17, 1861. The next day as Union volunteers boarded a train in Harrisburg, Pennsylvania, bound for their confrontation on the streets of Baltimore, three small troop trains containing Virginia militia companies traveled along the Orange & Alexandria Railroad to Manassas Junction where they were transferred to the Manassas Gap line and continued on to Strasburg in the Shenandoah Valley. Riding in the first train was Captain John D. Imboden of the Staunton Artillery. Realizing that Lincoln's call for troops to suppress the rebellion would push Virginia out of the Union, Ex-Governor Henry Wise summoned Imboden and a number of militia officers on the night of April 16, to a conference at the Exchange Hotel in Richmond. Once the details were worked out, he ordered Captain Imboden to present Governor John Letcher with their plan to capture the U.S. Arsenal at Harpers Ferry with a rapid deployment of troops by rail. Brigadier General William H. Harman was in overall command of this novel expedition.

The Harpers Ferry Arsenal contained what the fledgling Confederacy would need to wage war – a stockpile of weapons and the machinery and components to make more of them. First Lieutenant Roger Jones of the U.S. Mounted Rifles commanded the post with a guard detail of less than 50 men. Learning of the advance by Virginia troops, he ordered his small force of soldiers and factory workers to spread combustible materials throughout the complex and notified his superiors in Washington City that if he was not reinforced immediately he would be compelled to abandon Harpers Ferry. On the night of April 18, he received "positive and reliable information" that 2,500 to 3,000 state troops were advancing from Winchester and that a smaller force from Halltown was only 20 minutes away. Vastly outnumbered, Lieutenant Jones gave the order to set fire to the armory buildings and retreat with his men across the Potomac River into Maryland.[30]

One problem that delayed the advance on Harpers Ferry and would plague both armies in the lower Shenandoah Valley during the war was the lack of rail service between Strasburg and Winchester, Virginia. An 18-mile gap existed between these two points forcing all traffic onto the Valley Turnpike. The Winchester & Potomac Railroad was the second oldest railroad in the state of Virginia. It operated a single line track 32 miles long between Winchester and Harpers Ferry. Requests to extend the rail line to Strasburg had been denied by the State Legislature. Leaving Strasburg before noon on the eighteenth, the last of Harman's column did not reach Winchester until near sundown. As the units arrived, they boarded a Winchester and Potomac train that shuttled them to Charles Town and Halltown, the latter only four miles south of Harpers Ferry.

As dispositions were being made to capture the town, a bright light arose over the target area around 10:00 p.m. Lieutenant Jones had fired the arsenal and made good his escape. The Virginia militia rushed into Harpers Ferry to find the two arsenal buildings that contained about 10,000 finished weapons completely ablaze. Fortunately, for the Southern forces, sympathetic workers had cut the powder trains and saved the vital machine shops and a large supply of gunstocks and other components. Major General Kenton Harper assumed command of the post while militia companies with a wide range of uniforms and weapons continued to report for duty. A strategic advantage of occupying Harpers Ferry for the Southern forces was the fact that they were firmly astride the main line of the B&O and in a position to influence the rail traffic between there and Cumberland, Maryland.[31]

Between April 19 and the end of May, something of a phony war existed between the two sides. It was still possible to mail letters and send telegrams between cities in the North and cities in the South. More remarkable, the B&O was still allowed to operate trains in both directions on its main line albeit with some minor interference from the Virginians at Harpers Ferry. The militia units congregating at the Ferry were poorly led and poorly trained which was the norm for both armies at the time. Other than confiscating some grain from local farmers on the Maryland side of the Potomac, their only real military duty was to stop and search all trains passing through to prevent the movement of Union soldiers. Troops and cannon were positioned on both sides of the Potomac River bridge to ensure compliance. Near the end of April, a train was stopped with Brigadier General William S. Harney on board. One

Thomas J. Jackson. A veteran of the Mexican War and a professor at the Virginia Military Institute, he was assigned by Governor Letcher to command the Virginia Volunteers at Harpers Ferry in 1861. (D. C. T.)

of four general officers in the Regular Army at the beginning of the war, he had been relieved of his command in St. Louis, Missouri, and ordered to report to the War Department in Washington. To Harney goes the distinction of being the first general officer in either army captured during the war.

The relaxed atmosphere at Harpers Ferry came to an abrupt end on April 29 with the arrival of Virginia Military Institute professor Thomas J. Jackson. A West Point graduate and veteran of the Mexican War, Jackson had been teaching at VMI since 1851. Although only a colonel in the state militia, Governor Letcher ordered him to relieve General Harper and assume command of the Virginia forces at Harpers Ferry. He was to organize and train the mass of volunteers he found there into a cohesive military unit and, at the same time, remove all of the machinery and gun parts captured at the U.S. Arsenal to Winchester via the Winchester & Potomac Railroad and the Valley Turnpike to Strasburg where they would be transshipped to Richmond. He would also take more than a passing interest in the Baltimore & Ohio Railroad.

Believing that Maryland was still a candidate for secession, General Robert E. Lee, commander of all Virginia State forces, wrote Jackson on May 9, "In your preparation of the defense of your position it is considered advisable not to intrude upon the soil of Maryland, unless compelled by the necessities of war." With that went the admonishment not to harm the B&O Railroad as it was hoped that it would soon be serving the Confederacy. Jackson's men did not harm the B&O, but they did stop and search passenger and freight trains. On one occasion, a train containing four cattle cars and one carload of horses was stopped and the animals seized for use by Virginians. Jackson's quartermaster, Major John Harmon, selected two of the animals for the general's use. One of these would become his favorite mount, "Little Sorrell."[32]

The Great Train Raid

The following narrative is based on existing sources. There are those who believe that the event never took place. It is the author's opinion that to exclude this story from the book would deprive the reader of a significant piece of Baltimore and Ohio Railroad history. Conversely, to ignore the "legend" factor would be an injustice to history. Therefore, I will first present the controversy and then tell the story. The readers may judge for themselves the significance of the event.

Between 1884 and 1887, the *Century Magazine* published a series of articles that were primarily written by Civil War veterans. In 1887, these articles were republished in a magnificent leather bound four-volume set entitled *Battles and Leaders of the Civil War*. The primary source for the following narrative is an article written by John D. Imboden entitled "Jackson at Harpers Ferry in 1861." No other primary source is known to exist that can confirm his story. Imboden was a colonel at the time and a major participant in the raid. He was later promoted to brigadier general and commanded an independent brigade of cavalry. His successful defense of the Confederate hospital train at the battle of Williamsport would forever link him to the icons of the Gettysburg Campaign. In challenging the validity of his story, one must pose the question, with his reputation safe and "Stonewall Jackson" immortalized, what did he have to gain by fabricating the story? As a counterpoint, one could argue that the astute John Work Garrett and his Master of Transportation William Prescott Smith would never have fallen for such a trick. To this indictment, one could argue that Garrett was a victim of circumstance. The popular opinion at the time was that the war would only last ninety days. Garrett's logic may have been to give Jackson whatever it took to keep the trains running. After all, the war would be over in a couple of weeks and everything would return to normal. A counter to this defense is the fact that this event is not chronicled in the otherwise highly detailed Annual Reports of the B&O Railroad. Due to the military actions along the main line of the B&O during the first year of the war, the annual report for 1861 was not published until 1863. Two years after the fact, Garrett may have decided that the story no longer needed to be told for his sake and that of the railroad's. Finally, if not a collaborating witness, the annual report for 1861 does itemize the number of locomotives and rail cars captured or burned by the Confederates. If "The Great Train Raid" never happened, how does one account for the equivalent of twenty-five full trains being present when Jackson occupied Martinsburg in May of 1861?

Jackson was not a trained railroad man as many future Civil War generals were, but he did appreciate the imbalance of resources between Northern and Southern railroads. At this time, the main line of the B&O was double tracked for a distance of 44 miles from Point of Rocks east of Harpers Ferry westward to Cherry Run. Day and night, freight and passenger trains ran in both directions, as well as coal trains with their distinctive iron pot-hopper cars destined for the Washington Naval Yard where the coal would eventually be loaded into naval vessels assigned to blockade the Southern ports.

Once General Butler occupied Baltimore on May 13, it became obvious that Maryland was not going to leave the Union and the B&O Railroad suddenly became a legitimate military target. A few days later Jackson devised a plan to strike the first great blow against the Baltimore & Ohio Railroad. He notified President Garrett of the B&O Railroad that the incessant rail traffic at night was disturbing the sleep of his soldiers and the B&O would have to confine its operations to daylight hours only. Garrett and his ever-efficient Master of Transportation William Prescott Smith, complied and quickly established daylight-only timetables for both east and west bound traffic. For a few days, things went smoothly, and then Jackson issued a second directive to Garrett. He complained that the constant traffic was disrupting the training of his men and further restricted the passage of trains to the hours of 11:00 a.m. and 1:00 p.m. Garrett was in a desperate situation. The coal and other supplies moving to Washington were vital for the Union war effort, and the long haul freight from Wheeling was a key revenue source for the company. As long as Jackson sat astride the main line, it was useless to protest.

To comply with the new schedule, trains would be backed up nose to tail on the single tracks leading into the two-way section past Harpers Ferry. Then they would enter the doubled tracks simultaneously so that the last west bound train would clear the single track before the first east bound train arrived. This was allowed to continue until May 23 when Jackson snapped the trap. He ordered Captain Imboden to take his men and occupy Point of Rocks on the Maryland side of the Potomac River where the east end of the double tracks was located. He was ordered to let the westbound trains proceed at 11:00 a.m. but to close the east bound track immediately. The now Colonel Kenton Harper of the Fifth Virginia Infantry was sent to Cherry Run at the opposite end of the line to perform the same mission. Then, at exactly noon, Imboden closed the eastbound track, Harper the west. Trapped in between were 56 locomotives and 386 rail cars. Jackson had captured approximately 25 complete trains without firing a shot![33]

The question now was what to do next. Jackson essentially owned the B&O Railroad between Harpers Ferry and Martinsburg, but without a connecting line to Strasburg there was no way to move this valuable property south – no conventional way that is. The W&P was poorly constructed. Its tracks consisted of stringers. These were wooden rails covered with metal straps 3/8 of an inch thick and only two inches wide, and nailed on top to resist wear. The bridges were designed for locomotives of 20 tons or less and were too weak to handle the massive weight of a Winans locomotive or the other first class engines taken from the B&O. Jackson selected four of the smallest engines and had them transferred onto the W&P where they were run south to Winchester along with a number of rail cars. At Winchester, the locomotives were partially disassembled and taken off the tracks. They were then hauled up the Valley Turnpike by teams of horses to Strasburg where they were reassembled on the Manassas Gap Railroad and utilized by Southern railroads during the war.

Before Jackson could transfer any more light engines amongst those captured around Martinsburg an overzealous officer ordered the 147-foot bridge over the Opequon Creek destroyed. This severed the main line of the B&O, approximately five miles east of Martinsburg, trapping all the valuable railroad property captured there. Jackson ordered his men back to Harpers Ferry. Before leaving, they set fire to a number of locomotives and rail cars. Fifty loaded coal cars were run into the gap left by the missing bridge and then set on fire. A newspaper correspondent for the *National Intelligencer* passed through the area during the brief occupation of Martinsburg by Union forces in July and filed the following report:

"All along the railroad were scattered coal cars in long lines, with the coal still burning… They had kindled huge fires around them, burning all the wood work and a great deal of the iron. They were all fine iron cars, holding about twenty tons each.

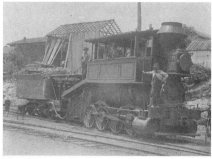

The Winans Camel with its distinctive cab over the boiler and eight drive wheels. Many of the 56 locomotives captured by Jackson between Harpers Ferry and Martinsburg were of this type. (B&ORRM)

A typical Civil War Boxcar. These were also referred to as house cars. (B&ORRM)

Specially designed B&O coal car. When Jackson abandoned Martinsburg, fifty of these cars were run off the tracks and set on fire. The coal inside burned for weeks thereafter. (B&ORR)

Here and there, the road led above them, and, looking down we could see the inside – a mass of red hot coals. Some small bridges had been burnt with the cars on them, and giving way, the cars were left piled one on another in the small streams below, all battered and bent. We counted the locomotives that had been burnt (forty-one or forty-two in all) red and blistered with heat. The destruction is fearful to contemplate."

Jackson's attack against the B&O signaled the end of the "phony war" along the railroad. This was confirmed on a national level by the federal government's announcement that the U.S. Post Office would discontinue mail service between the Union and Confederate states at midnight on May 31. Jackson's independent command was also about to end.[34]

On May 7, the state of Virginia was formally accepted into the newly formed Confederate States of America. Governor Letcher issued a proclamation on June 8, transferring Virginia's state forces to the control of the Confederate government. On May 15, Brigadier General Joseph E. Johnston was given command of all Confederate forces in the lower Shenandoah Valley including Jackson's men. He assumed command at Harpers Ferry on May 24. Jackson was assigned a brigade consisting of five Virginia regiments that became the legendary Stonewall Brigade.

Joseph Johnston was a native Virginian and West Point classmate of Robert E. Lee. When the war began, he was Quartermaster General of the United States Army. Jackson and Johnston differed in their estimations of the Harpers Ferry position. Jackson considered it the key to the Shenandoah Valley and wanted to defend it with the spirit of Thermopylae. Johnston considered it indefensible and lobbied with Richmond for permission to fall back to Winchester once General Patterson's long awaited advance got under way.

When General Johnston took command at Harpers Ferry, he had a force of about 5,200 men to cover the river crossings along the Potomac between Point of Rocks and Williamsport, a distance of nearly 50 miles. He placed a strong force of infantry and artillery at the ferry crossing opposite Williamsport and a similar force at the bridge near Point of Rocks. A smaller force guarded the bridge at Shepherdstown. Both of these bridges and the one at Harpers Ferry were prepared for demolition in case the order for evacuation came through. Reports continued to filter into these posts concerning the Union buildup in Chambersburg, Pennsylvania.[35]

Patterson's Advance

In late May, the Union army finally made an appearance in Western Maryland. The Department of Pennsylvania was established on April 27, 1861, with Major General Robert Patterson commanding. The department included all of

Pennsylvania, Delaware, and the counties comprising Western Maryland, with headquarters in Harrisburg. Patterson was an old warhorse, having served in both the War of 1812 and the war with Mexico. To Patterson fell the task of equipping and training an army of 90-day volunteers before their enlistments expired. When ordered by General Winfield Scott to protect the Northern Central line between Harrisburg and Baltimore, he replied, "…a very large proportion of my men are without muskets, all are without ammunition, service clothing, greatcoats, blankets, knapsacks, haversacks, canteens, Etc."[36]

By the first week of June General Patterson had moved his headquarters to Chambersburg where he would be closer to his forward area of operation and at the same time provide a margin of security for the southern boundary of Pennsylvania. From here, he could use the Cumberland Valley Railroad to move his troops to Hagerstown, Maryland, prior to an advance into Virginia. The limited capacity of the railroad restricted their movement to only six regiments a day.[37]

Forced to utilize its volunteer army before their 90-day enlistments expired, plans were under way for a major Union advance on Richmond via Manassas Junction. Patterson's primary mission was to keep Joe Johnston from joining forces with General P. G. T. Beauregard's army defending that area of Virginia. Reclaiming the main line of the B&O Railroad was somewhat of a secondary mission. On June 8, General Winfield Scott wrote to Patterson, "I think your expedition against Harpers Ferry well projected, and that success in it would be an important step in the war…" but he cautioned "…attempt nothing without a clear prospect of success…" He also informed Patterson that a secondary expedition of about 2,500 men under Colonel Stone would advance from Rockville, Maryland, towards Harpers Ferry as a diversion. In a quest for reinforcements, Patterson wrote directly to the Secretary of State, Simon Cameron, "Remember, I beseech you, that Harpers Ferry is (as I have said from the first) the place where the first great battle will be fought."[38]

Slowly the pressure mounted on the north bank of the Potomac River. Union Colonel Lew Wallace occupied Cumberland on June 10 with his Eleventh Indiana Regiment. Known as the Queen City of the Alleghenies, Cumberland was a key logistics center in the mountain region. Here the B&O met the National Road and the western terminus of the Chesapeake and Ohio Canal. A vital supply base, it remained under Union control for all but one day during the war. Wallace rose to the rank of major general and returned to Maryland in 1864 as a department commander.

On June 13, Johnston received the long awaited approval to fall back on Winchester. The next day he gave Jackson the order to evacuate Harpers Ferry. Before leaving, he was to destroy anything of military value that could not be

Destruction of B&O Railroad bridge over the Potomac River at Harpers Ferry. (B&ORRM)

removed. Jackson did not waste any time. At 5:00 a.m. on June 14, the 800-foot long rail and passenger bridge over the Potomac River was destroyed by placing gunpowder charges along its length and setting fire to the structure. The resulting explosion was both spectacular and effective. All that remained were the stone piers spaced out across the river. Captured B&O cars were loaded with the remaining machinery from the armory and sent up the W&P to Winchester. Then the armory buildings were demolished. The wooden deck on the W&P's bridge was set on fire. Engine #165 and a number of cars were then run through the damaged structure and into the Potomac River.

Johnston's withdraw was a timely maneuver. The next day General Patterson pushed five brigades forward to Williamsport using Hagerstown as their supply base. Learning of the evacuation of Harpers Ferry, he ordered Major General George Cadwalader to send a force across the Potomac River and advance with caution on Martinsburg. Doubting the validity of the report, Patterson added, "If the enemy has abandoned Harpers Ferry, the commanding general wishes it occupied as soon as it can safely be done." At 2:00 p.m. on June 15, Union forces entered Harpers Ferry.[39]

From Harpers Ferry, Johnston led his troops south to Charles Town and then west toward the Valley Turnpike. His plan was to take up a strong defensive position at Bunker Hill ten miles north of Winchester and await the Union advance. In order to prevent Patterson from receiving reinforcements from the west, he ordered Colonel A. P. Hill at Romney to send a force to New Creek Depot (now Keyser, WV) and destroy the bridge there. Known as the 21st Bridge, it was located one and a half miles east of New Creek and carried the B&O Railroad over the North Branch of the Potomac River. The bridge was guarded by 26 men of the Cumberland Continentals, a company from the Fiftieth Regiment of Maryland Militia and two 4-pounder iron cannons under the command of Lieutenants Theodore Luman and James C. Lynn. Both units were camped on the Maryland side of the river, sleeping in tents and boxcars near the bridge.

Hill assigned Colonel John C. Vaughn of the Third Tennessee Infantry the task of destroying the 21st Bridge. His attack force consisted of two companies from his regiment and two from the Thirteenth Virginia. Vaughan's force arrived at dawn on June 19. His scouts reported that there were no pickets on the Virginia side of the bridge. At 5:00 a.m. on June 19, Vaughn launched his attack. After firing a few shots, the Union militiamen abandoned their position and retreated to Cumberland. Vaughn's men swarmed across the river capturing the two pieces of artillery and the camp's flag. Then they set fire to the bridge. In his after action report Vaughn stated that, "...in a few minutes only the piers remained." His men also tore up a half of mile of track on the Maryland side of the river. After setting fire to the boxcars and crossties, the rails were heated over the fires until red-hot and then twisted around nearby trees to render them useless. Although made famous during Sherman's March to the Sea in 1864, the process known as "Sherman's neckties" was first perfected along the main line of the B&O in 1861. When informed of the successful raid, President Jefferson Davis personally congratulated General Johnston and urged him to continue his attacks on the B&O Railroad.[40]

On the same day that Colonel Vaughn attacked New Creek, Johnston received a report from his cavalry commander, Captain J. E. B. Stuart, that the Union forces were preparing to cross the Potomac River at Williamsport. Johnston ordered Jackson to take his brigade north and oppose Patterson's advance on Martinsburg. While there, he was to repeat the cycle of destruction visited on Harpers Ferry. If pressed by the Union advance his orders were to abandon Martinsburg and withdraw up the Shenandoah Valley towards Winchester.

Jackson arrived at Martinsburg on June 20 where he found a roundhouse, machine shops, and an abundance of rails, tools and spare parts desperately needed by the Southern railroads. Also found were locomotives and rail cars that had been captured a month earlier, some of which had been put to the torch. The destruction began anew. Miles of track were removed or rendered useless. The future Stonewall Brigade laid waste to the main line of the B&O east and west of Martinsburg. Seventeen bridges and culverts were destroyed

Remains of a burned out Winans Camel. One of the Many B&O locomotives that the Confederates destroyed at Martinsburg. (B&ORRM)

including the Colonnade Bridge that carried the B&O over East Burk Street in Martinsburg.[41]

Again, Jackson had been ordered to destroy what the Southern railroads needed the most. Even the movement of the lightest engines to Winchester had been precluded by the destruction of the bridges between there and Martinsburg. Those locomotives that had been burned were still highly valuable prizes as there were very few parts on a steam engine that could actually be damaged by fire. The only alternative was to move these stranded locomotives over the Valley Turnpike a distance of 38 miles to Strasburg where they would be put on the Manassas Gap Railroad and sent to Richmond for repairs. The Quarter Master Department in Richmond sent Captain Thomas Sharp to supervise this complicated project. Although born in the North, Sharp had moved with his family to Richmond when his father was appointed superintendent of the Richmond, Fredericksburg & Potomac Railroad in 1840. Trained as a civil engineer, Thomas Sharp became the general superintendent of the Virginia & Tennessee Railroad when only nineteen years of age.

Sharp was aided by another railroad engineer from Richmond, Hugh Longust, a locomotive engineer named John O'Brien, and half a dozen highly skilled machinists. Once a unit was designated for transfer, the tender was separated from the locomotive. Then the engine was raised on jacks and everything possible was removed to lighten the load. This included piston rods, cowcatcher, smoke stack, lamps and whistle. Next, they removed all but the rear drive wheels before swinging the helpless remains onto a specially designed truck with four wooden wheels shod in iron. A huge bolt was dropped through the engine's bumper to secure it to the truck.

Captain Thomas Sharp moved 14 locomotives, 83 railcars and tons of other B&O property from Martinsburg to Strasburg via horse power along the Valley Turnpike. (Art Candenquist)

Hugh Longust worked with the local farmers and blacksmith to acquire the necessary means of moving these oversized loads along the Valley Turnpike. Joseph W. Keeler and his son Charles operated a farm implement business in Stephenson. When the war broke out, they were given a contract to make wagons for the Confederate Army. It was their firm that manufactured the specially designed traces and tongues that were used to attach the draft animals to the wooden trucks.

It must have been an awe-inspiring sight when the first captured locomotive began its trip south on the Valley Turnpike. Forty horses arranged four abreast and ten deep were required to pull the massive load with a teamster cracking his whip over each section of four. It required a chain 100 feet long to secure the ten sections to the front of the locomotive. In front of this was a detachment of cavalry to ward off any raiding bands of Yankees and behind it a string of wagons carrying the disassembled parts. The trip to Winchester could usually be completed in one 24-hour period. From there to Strasburg it took twice as long. When steep hills were encountered up to 200 men with long ropes would add their strength to that of horseflesh. Exhausted men and animals were periodically replaced so that the procession could go on day and night only halting when chains broke or enemy patrols were encountered. It required 20 horses to pull a rail car and 32 to 40 depending on the size of a locomotive.[42]

The lead elements of Patterson's army began crossing the river before dawn on the morning of July 2. Pickets from J. E .B. Stuart's First Virginia Cavalry fired a few shots and fell back slowly. Once he had a sufficient force on the Virginia shore, Patterson ordered an advance on Martinsburg. About four miles from the river, they passed through the village of Falling Waters and continued south along the Valley Turnpike.

In order to both protect his wrecking crews and delay any advance by Patterson on Winchester, Jackson had encamped his brigade halfway between Martinsburg and the Williamsport crossing. When one of Stuart's couriers informed Jackson that the Union advance was near at hand, the latter ordered the tents struck, and set out with Colonel Harper's Fifth Virginia Regiment and one gun from the Rockbridge Artillery to intercept them. The rest of the brigade was to remain in reserve. About two miles from camp the opposing forces collided and the First Battle of Falling Waters was under way (a second battle by the same name took place in 1863 during Lee's retreat from Gettysburg).

Typical of early war engagements, the battle lasted less than an hour and resulted in fewer than a hundred casualties. Outnumbered and out gunned, the Confederates were forced to withdraw. The lack of experience on either side contributed to the small number of casualties sustained despite the presence of both infantry and artillery and a considerable volume of fire. Jackson fell back with his entire command to a ridgeline outside of Martinsburg, expecting Patterson to continue the attack. Patterson stopped his advance at the site of the Confederate camp in order to let his considerably disorganized troops catch up. Realizing that he was facing a much larger force, Jackson retreated through the town of Martinsburg to join Johnston at Winchester.[43]

Patterson's primary mission was to keep Johnston's Army of the Shenandoah from reinforcing Beauregard. He occupied Martinsburg on July 3 and remained there until July 14. On the fourteenth, Patterson moved his command south as far as Bunker Hill where he only remained for one day. Then, instead of threatening Winchester, he relocated his forces to Charles Town and contented himself with reoccupying Harpers Ferry. This gave Johnston the breathing room he needed. Leaving the town in the hands of two militia regiments and Sharp's railroad detachment, he left Winchester on the morning of July 19 with Jackson's command in the lead. By the following morning, they had marched over the Blue Ridge Mountains to Piedmont Station on the Manassas Gap Railroad, where, after some delay, they boarded a train composed of freight and cattle cars for the final leg of their journey. Eight hours later, they arrived at Manassas Junction. The next day the balance of Johnston's command arrived, the first great battle of the Civil War was fought, and the legend of "Stonewall" Jackson was born. To the South, despite its inferior system of railroads, goes the credit for the first large scale tactical deployment of troops by rail during the war.[44]

When Patterson moved south, he failed to leave a covering force at Martinsburg. This allowed Captain Sharp and his mechanics to return and work throughout the summer disassembling and relocating valuable railroad equipment south. The sight of rail cars and locomotives moving along a dirt road became a common occurrence for citizens living along the Valley Turnpike. Several recorded what they saw. Sarah Morgan McKown wrote in her diary on August 22, "We all went to Martinsburg...We met the engines and Cars going up the Pike to Winchester drawn by horses. 32 were hitched to one engine... Our wagon and two horses went to Martinsburg yesterday to help move the Cars today." Julia Chase of Winchester noted in her diary for September 2, "One of the engines (from Martinsburg)...has been brought into town by 32 horses, to be taken to Richmond. It was quite a sight as it passed by ...looking very much like an iron monster."[45]

By March of 1862, 14 locomotives, 83 rail cars and parts of 9 other engines had been taken via the Valley Turnpike to Strasburg along with 9 miles of track, 5 switches and a complete turntable. An additional 386 railcars were burnt before the Confederates left Martinsburg. Not all of the captured locomotives made it to Richmond by the shortest route. B&O No. 199, a Hayes camelback, was stranded at Strasburg because the fighting in Northern Virginia had cut the Manassas Gap line. First designed by the legendary Ross Winans, the camels or camelbacks were so named because the cab was placed on top of the boiler rather than behind it to add weight and thus traction to the drive wheels. When Jackson returned to the Valley in November of 1861, it was still in Strasburg. Realizing the value of this heavy hauler, he ordered the locomotive sent up the Valley to Staunton where it could be put on the Virginia Central and sent east. The Manassas Gap line was still intact as far as Mount Jackson, but this left a gap of 50 miles between railroads. As before, the engine was disassembled and hauled along the Valley Turnpike to Staunton, making the arduous trip in only four days. Just two blocks short of the train station, it broke loose and sank in the mud. A few more days were required to pull it free and do the reassembly before the 199 was off to Richmond. A second avenue for moving captured railroad equipment was now open. As late as 1863, engines and freight cars were still moving south on the Valley Turnpike. [46]

Grafton

The vote that took Virginia out of the Union on April 17 was far from unanimous. The majority of its citizens residing west of the Allegheny Mountains were Unionist. Long ignored by the State Legislature in Richmond, a great gulf had developed between these two regions. Owned by generations of the same families, the slaves and tobacco plantations of Tidewater Virginia were the antithesis of the western counties, where a steady stream of immigrants had followed the B&O Railroad out of the port city of Baltimore to work in the coal mines, on small farms, or the railroad itself. For their economic advancement, they looked to the North and not the South. As in Western Maryland, there were those who embraced the Confederate cause, but they were in the minority.

Unaware of the hostile feelings in the region, General Robert E. Lee sent Major Alonzo Loring to Wheeling on April 29 to recruit troops to protect the western terminus of the B&O Railroad. Just as he had cautioned Jackson at Harpers Ferry in early April not to damage the railroad or offend the state of Maryland in hopes of gaining both for the Confederacy, he cautioned Loring, "It is desirable that business operations of the company (B&O) and peaceful travel not be interrupted, but afforded protection." The next day he sent Major Francis M. Boykin, Jr., to recruit a force for the same purpose at Grafton where the Northwestern Virginia Railroad met the main branch of the B&O 100 miles south of Wheeling. He, too, was cautioned to protect and not damage the railroad.[47]

On May 10, Major Boykin reported great difficulties in recruiting and told Lee that, "This section is verging on a state of rebellion." Loring was able to send a company size unit to Harpers Ferry but could not remain in Wheeling. Frustrated at the lack of progress, Lee sent Colonel George A. Porterfield to Grafton to take charge of the Confederate operations in Western Virginia. Porterfield was a native of Berkeley County, Virginia (now West Virginia). A graduate of the Virginia Military Institute, he had fought in the Mexican War and served on the U.S. Coastal Survey. Lee gave Porterfield instructions for the placement of five regiments of infantry to cover strategic locations near Parkersburg, Wheeling and Grafton.

The B&O's service had not yet been disrupted in this region and Porterfield arrived in Grafton by train from Harpers Ferry on May 14. When he asked a railroad employee where he could find the camp of the Virginia state troops, he was shocked to learn that not a single Southern soldier was in the town. To this was added an admonishment to leave Grafton as soon as possible, as the town's people were up in arms against the Secessionists. In fact, the only troops in Grafton were a single company of home guards commanded by a local lawyer named George Latham. Captain Latham held the town until after the May 23 referendum on secession passed. Then he put his men on a westbound train and set off to Wheeling to fight for the Union. The Grafton

Extremely rare view of the B&O Station and hotel at Grafton, West Virginia, with five locomotives posed in front. On the far right is a Winans Camel No. 91 manufactured in 1852. (Richard Wolf Collection)

Guards would soon become Company B of the Second Virginia Volunteer Infantry U.S. [48]

Porterfield found the militia camp two miles north of Grafton at Fetterman. To his dismay, he found only a few companies, not regiments, of poorly trained and equipped volunteers. He occupied Grafton on May 25 and set up a training camp at Philippi for the men he did manage to recruit.

When Lincoln called for 75,000 volunteers, George B. McClellan was appointed commander of the Department of Ohio with the rank of major general in the Regular Army. His prewar experience, like that of Robert E. Lee's, made him well qualified for the position. McClellan had graduated from West Point in 1846 and immediately went off to the war in Mexico where so many future Civil War generals gained valuable experience. Ranking second in his class, he was assigned to the Corps of Engineers. He went to Europe as an observer during the Crimean War and translated a French manual on the use of the bayonet. His most lasting contribution to the United States Army was designing the "McClellan Saddle" which remained in use until the end of horse cavalry after World War I. In 1857, he resigned his commission to become the chief engineer for the Illinois Central Railroad. When the war began, he was the president of the Ohio and Mississippi Railroad. [49]

At the beginning of hostilities, McClellan faced many problems similar to those Lee did – train and equip raw recruits, guard the state borders of Ohio and Western Pennsylvania and protect the B&O Railroad without offending the people of Western Virginia. In the beginning, just as Lee had misjudged the loyalty of western counties to Virginia, McClellan was uncertain of their loyalty to the Union. He sent a battery of six-pound cannon to Marietta to protect the railroad that ran from there to Cincinnati from a possible attack by secessionists from across the river at Parkersburg. He then marshaled his forces along the Ohio River and awaited the outcome of the statewide voting to confirm Virginia's ordinance of secession on May 23. [50]

Major General George B. McClellan commanded the Department of Ohio and sent Union forces into Western Virginia to protect the B&O Railroad. (D. C. T.)

The seeds of West Virginia's statehood were planted in Clarksburg on April 22 when over a thousand citizens met in opposition to Richmond's secession government. The "Clarksburg Resolutions" called for a convention to be held in Wheeling on May 13. Over 400 delegates from twenty-seven different counties met in an extralegal body to determine their future. Its location was well chosen. Nestled well up in the panhandle between Ohio and Pennsylvania, it was the largest city in Western Virginia and predominantly pro-Union. John Carlile, one of the most outspoken opponents of secession, immediately called for the creation of a new state of Virginia via the division of the old. His revolutionary proposal was countered the next day by a Morgantown lawyer named Waitman T. Willey who declared it "triple treason" – treason against the Constitution, treason against the State of Virginia, and treason against the Confederacy. On the third and final day of the convention, Francis H. Pierpont of Monongalia County rose to offer a compromise. He argued that the U.S. Constitution required the Federal government to protect every state from invasion or domestic violence. They should vote decidedly against the May 23 referendum on secession. In the likelihood that their opposition would fail, he proposed a second Wheeling Convention on June 11 that would consider the formation of a new state. In the interim, Unionists in the region would form military units and solicit aid from the Lincoln administration.

The events of the Nineteenth of April in Baltimore City caused a great deal of excitement in Wheeling. The next day a pro-Union rally was held at the customhouse. By April 23, five companies had been recruited that proved to be the nucleus of the First Regiment Virginia Infantry (U.S.). Within one month, a complete regiment of ten companies was mustered into federal service. Command of the first Union regiment raised in the region was given to Colonel Benjamin F. Kelley. Born in New Hampshire, Kelley moved to Wheeling in 1826 and had been an officer in the local militia. When the war broke out, he was a freight agent for the B&O Railroad.[51]

Porterfield's position was rapidly becoming untenable. The buildup of Union forces on the opposite bank of the Ohio River indicated that an invasion was imminent. In order to delay the anticipated Union advance, Porterfield sent detachments to burn the bridges at Farmington and Mannington on the main line about forty miles northwest of Grafton and one on the Parkersburg line. To add insult to injury they used B&O trains to take them there and bring them back. Virginia Unionists quickly sent word to McClellan at his headquarters in Cincinnati of the Rebel depredations. Now confident that the political situation was on his side and fully understanding the necessity to protect the B&O Railroad, he immediately began to issue orders that ultimately drove the Confederate forces out of Western Virginia and opened the door for West Virginia statehood.

The "Phony War" had not yet ended and the Federal Government was still sending messages from Washington to Wheeling via the telegraph that ran through Grafton. With the aid of two pro-Southern telegraphers at Fetterman, Porterfield was able to read McClellan's mail before he did. Through this early form of wire-tapping, he was made aware of the Union advance on his position. Unable to obtain reinforcements or supplies from Richmond, he abandoned Grafton and moved south to Philippi where he would be in a position to renew his attack on the B&O Railroad once he had gathered sufficient men and supplies there.[52]

Both a railroad man and a soldier, McClellan was perhaps the first Civil War general to maximize the use of the telegraph and the railroad for a tactical advantage on the battlefield. He ordered Colonel Kelley to take his First Regiment and move by train to Grafton and drive out the enemy there. Along the way, he was to repair any damaged bridges and the telegraph lines so that he could remain in contact with headquarters. McClellan ordered the Sixteenth Ohio Infantry to cross the river and support Kelley's advance. The same instructions were wired to Colonel James Steedman who commanded the Fourteenth Ohio Regiment. He was to cross the Ohio River at Parkersburg and advance eastward by rail on the Northwestern Virginia Railroad to Grafton. A second Ohio regiment and two guns from the First Ohio Light Artillery were to follow in support. Mindful of the political situation, he issued a proclamation to the people of Western Virginia.

"Virginians!... The General Government cannot close its ears to the demand you have made for assistance. I have ordered troops to cross the Ohio River. They come as your friends and brothers, – as enemies only to the armed rebels who are preying upon you...Sever the connection that binds you to traitors..."[53]

Kelley's force departed Wheeling on the morning of May 27. The damaged bridges he encountered were made of iron. Only the ties and flooring had been destroyed by the flames and were quickly replaced. Kelley showed great initiative in this, his first military operation. Porterfield only had 550 men to confront a combined Union force of over four regiments. To avoid being caught in a rail borne pincer movement, he abandoned Grafton on the twenty-eighth of May. Kelley arrived at Fairmont the next day. Informed of the retreat, he occupied Grafton on May 30. Colonel Steedman's advance from Parkersburg was attended to with a marked degree of caution, in part because of the terrain features and tunnels along that section of track. The second column did not arrive until June 2.[54]

Porterfield's retreat to Philippi did not ensure the safety of the main line of the B&O Railroad or the Parkersburg branch. With his force encamped only twenty miles south of Grafton, he was in a position to disrupt rail operations anywhere between Clarksburg and Rowlesburg. Realizing this, McClellan assigned a significant portion of his command to protecting the main line of the B&O and the Northwestern Virginia Railroad. An entire regiment was stationed at Rowlesburg to guard the critically important Tray Run Viaduct. Other detachments in company strength were distributed along the B&O northwest of Grafton to guard bridges and other railroad property. The same strategy was applied to the Northwestern Virginia Railroad between there and Parkersburg. As an additional security measure, the military authorities began removing a number of railroad employees known to be aligned with the secession movement. This had an adverse effect on the efficiency of the railroad, and President Garrett was forced to send an official from Baltimore to stabilize the situation. McClellan assigned command of the troops guarding the railroad to General Charles W. Hill. His instructions were both dramatic and precise. "At any cost – that of your last man – you will preserve the Cheat River line, Grafton, and the line thence to Wheeling. On this depends the entire success of the plan of operations."[55]

Colonel Kelley believed the best way to protect the railroad was to push the Rebels far enough away that they could not mount an offensive in the region. He immediately began to plan a two-part attack on Philippi. Before he could take action, Brigadier General Thomas A. Morris of Indiana arrived and, outranking Kelley, took command. Morris readily agreed with the plan and simply delayed its implementation by a single day.

On June 2, Kelley with three regiments totaling 1,600 men boarded a train that would carry them east to Thornton. From there they would march south and strike Porterfield's right flank at dawn the next day. At the same time, General Morris sent a second column of infantry and artillery under the command of Colonel Ebenezer Dumont of the Seventh Indiana Infantry along the Beverly-Fairmont Pike to attack the Rebel camp head on. They were told to arrive at 4:00 a.m. but instructed to hold their position until Kelley opened the attack. Once engaged, Kelley was to assume overall command and pursue the enemy as far as practical.[56]

Porterfield's retreating force had been reinforced by two companies bringing his total strength to about 900 men. However, not all of these were armed. Their camp at Philippi was along the Tygart Valley River where a dual-lane covered bridge had been erected in 1852. On the morning of June 2, Mrs. Whitescarver, the wife of a soldier stationed at Philippi, informed Porterfield that an enemy column was approaching the town. Later that day two young women rode into town with the same information and estimated the enemy's strength at 4,500. Porterfield was again forced to retreat or face a far superior enemy. He gave orders to pack the wagons and prepared his men to move out at midnight. Shortly after sunset, a severe storm struck with a drenching rain that lasted all night. Porterfield postponed the retreat until morning. The inexperienced Southern soldiers on the picket line, drenched and shivering, simply sought shelter where they could find it, leaving the entire camp unguarded.

Dumont's force arrived at 4:00 a.m. on June 3 as scheduled. He placed his two 6-pounder cannons on Talbott's Hill (now the site of Alderson-Broaddus College) and waited for the order to open fire. The plan was for Kelley to open the attack. The signal for the artillery to open fire was to be a pistol shot from one of the officers. The inclement weather and a faulty guide delayed Kelley's arrival. Meanwhile the Confederates slept soundly under the muzzles of the Union guns. In the interim Union soldiers moved about the neighborhood preparing for the attack. Mrs. Thomas Humphreys was awakened by this activity and sent her 12-year-old son, Oliver, on horseback to warn Porterfield. When a couple of quick thinking Union soldiers unhorsed the boy, she pulled a pistol from her bodice and started shooting at them. She missed her mark, but the artillerist took her shots for the prearranged signal and began shelling the Confederate camp. Taken completely by surprise, the Confederate soldiers tumbled out of their tents in various degrees of undress and headed down the road to Beverly in utter confusion. Their route became known as the "Philippi Races."

Shortly after the Union artillery opened fire, Kelley's force arrived. Too late to cut off their retreat, Kelley charged through the Confederate camp eager to capture all that he could. As he did, Porterfield's assistant quartermaster, William Sims, stepped out from behind a wagon and shot Kelley in the right breast. With Kelley out of action, the Union pursuit never materialized. Many thought him mortally wounded.

Kelley's strategy to drive the Confederates away from the B&O Railroad had worked. Porterfield's shattered force passed through Beverly and did not stop until it reached Huttonsville, nearly 70 miles from Grafton. Although most of his men had escaped, much of their arms and equipment had not. General Morris reported the capture of 750 muskets, ammunition, wagons, horses, medical supplies and tents. Porterfield's command would be ineffective for some time to come.

The time and place of the battle of Philippi made it far more important than the number of casualties would imply. In the not-too-distant future, it would barely qualify as a skirmish. Confederate losses were two wounded and five captured including one of the wounded. One soldier on the Union side accidentally shot himself to death and five, including Kelley, were wounded to make the total an even dozen. To Kelley went the honor of being the first Union officer wounded during the war. It was also the first land battle in Western Virginia. Not only was the B&O Railroad put under the protective wing of the Union Army, but also those citizens working towards West Virginia's state-hood were given the opportunity to hold their conventions. Finally, McClellan, although still in Ohio, was given credit for the first Union victory of the war. It would lead to a series of defeats for the Confederacy that would eventually force General Robert E. Lee to give up any hope of securing Western Virginia for the Confederacy and propel George McClellan to command of the Army of the Potomac.[57]

Lee was desperate to jump-start the Confederate offensive in Western Virginia. He replaced Porterfield with General Robert S. Garnett. Garnett had graduated from West Point in 1841 and served with distinction during the Mexican War. He was Lee's adjutant general of Virginia state forces until June 6, 1861, when he was commissioned a brigadier general in the Provisional Army of the Confederate States. Lee sent Garnett to Huttonsville to reorganize Porterfield's shattered command. His mission was twofold – prevent the Union forces from gaining any further ground in Virginia, and attack the B&O Railroad. Perhaps no one during the entire war summarized better the value of the Baltimore & Ohio Railroad to the Union war effort than Robert E. Lee when he wrote to General Garnett, "The rupture of the (B&O) railroad at Cheat River would be worth an army to us."[58]

To keep the Union Army out of the Shenandoah Valley Garnett split his small force to protect the mountain passes at Rich Mountain and Laurel Hill. His men began to fortify these points in mid June. Over the next few weeks reinforcements arrived that doubled his force to nearly 6,000 men. McClellan responded by crossing the Ohio River at Parkersburg on June 21 in order to take charge of the next Union offensive in person. He concentrated four brigades at Philippi before moving against the two Confederate strongholds. As he advanced, he not only utilized the existing telegraph line running along the B&O tracks to inform his superiors in Washington City of his movements, but ordered a temporary line built along his route of march, a first in the annals of modern warfare. He also had two experienced telegraphers assigned to his headquarters staff to ensure the rapid transmission of information. The field operations of his telegraph service were ably administered by Mr. W. G. Fuller whom he named assistant superintendent for the Department of Ohio.[59]

McClellan's plan was to send General Morris with one brigade on a diversionary attack on Laurel Hill, while he led the main force against the Rich Mountain position. The battle of Rich Mountain was fought on July 11. Thanks to the aggressive actions of his unit commanders and overwhelming numbers, McClellan scored another victory. The casualty figures were beginning to inch up with a total of 74 for the Union and 92 for the Confederates. Within one hour of occupying the enemy's camp, McClellan was notifying his commander in Washington, General Winfield Scott, "We are in possession of all enemy works...Our success is complete and almost bloodless." As a group of Confederate prisoners were marching by his headquarters one of them exclaimed, "My God, Jim here's the telegraph!"[60]

Garnett realized that he could not hold his position at Laurel Hill and withdrew the night of July 11. His plan was to retreat along the turnpike through Beverly to Staunton. When misinformed that Union forces had already occupied Beverly, and thus had cut off his avenue of escape, he turned his column to the northeast and made for a pass in the mountains fifty miles away. The road he followed took him to within 15 miles of Oakland, Maryland, a station on the B&O's main line.

Aware of these movements, McClellan made one final attempt to cut off his retreat by again using the railroad as a tactical weapon. On July 12, he ordered General Hill at Grafton to use special trains to pick up his guard units from where they were stationed and shuttle them as quickly as possible to Oakland. From there they would march south and intercept Garnett's force before it could clear the mountain pass. In this instance, the new technologies failed him. The telegram was not delivered to General Hill until 11:00 a.m. the next day. Because the railroad guards were assigned fixed locations, they did not have the supplies or means of transportation for a field operation. Finally, cut off from the guiding hand of their boss, William Prescott Smith, the local B&O agents were overwhelmed with the complexity of the mission. Hill left Grafton with two small troop trains on the afternoon of July 14 and did not arrive in Oakland until a little before 10:00 p.m. The trains carried about one thousand men and three pieces of artillery but no horses to pull them. The rest of the men, wagons, and artillery horses did not arrive until the next day. By then General Garnett had been killed in a rear guard action at Corrick's Ford, but the majority of his men had made good their escape. Never again would the B&O fail an army commander when the means were at hand to complete the mission.[61]

McClellan's victory at Rich Mountain drove the Confederate forces back through the Allegheny Mountains and opened the Staunton-Parkersburg Turnpike as far as Cheat Mountain. By fortifying Cheat Mountain, McClellan was able to protect the vast number of counties that he had liberated from Confederate control and at the same time threaten a Union invasion of the Shenandoah Valley.

Lee left Richmond after the battle of Bull Run and arrived at Monterey on July 28. His mission was to coordinate the movement of three separate Confederate forces in an attempt to regain control of Western Virginia. Lee faced a combination of difficult terrain, bad weather and a shortage of supplies. More importantly, he lacked the formal authority to control the actions of his three field commanders. In September, an attempt to break the Cheat Mountain line failed as did the opening of a second front in the New River – Kanawha Valley region. Ordered to return to Richmond, Robert E. Lee left Western Virginia on October 30, 1861. He took with him three things he had not arrived with – a newly grown beard, a horse named Traveler, and the sobriquet "Granny Lee" for his lack of effectiveness.[62]

As Lee was coming west, Mc-Clellan was heading east. The First Battle of Bull Run had been fought on July 21 and the Union Army under General Irvin McDowell soundly defeated. A younger man was needed

General Robert E. Lee commanded the Virginia state forces in 1861. (D. C. T.)

to replace the ancient hero Winfield Scott. His prewar training, organizational skills and well-publicized victories in Western Virginia made George Brinton McClellan the ideal candidate. His liberal use of the telegraph to inform both his superiors in Washington and the press at large of those victories did not harm the growing reputation of the man some would call "a Young Napoleon." On July 22, McClellan received the following telegram at his headquarters in Beverly: "Circumstances make your presence here necessary. Charge Rosecrans or some other general with your present department and come hither without delay." With the main line of the B&O broken by Jackson at Martinsburg, McClellan was forced to take a train north to Wheeling and then cross the Ohio River. From there he would take a circuitous route through Pittsburgh, Harrisburg and Philadelphia before boarding a B&O train in Baltimore for the final segment of his journey to Washington City.[63]

The Baltimore and Ohio Railroad was truly the first front of the Civil War. Within ninety days of the firing on Fort Sumter, battles were fought and strategic points occupied that determined which side would ultimately control the railroad. Who controlled the B&O directly affected the loyalty of Maryland, the statehood of West Virginia, and the preservation of Washington as the nation's capital. To accomplish this, the first battles of the war were fought, the first soldiers and civilians were killed, and the advantages of using the telegraph and railroad in fighting a modern war were introduced. For the people who lived in Baltimore, Harpers Ferry and Grafton, these events would always mark the day the war came by train.

John Work Garrett, President of the Baltimore & Ohio Railroad Company. (*Loyal West Virginia*)

CHAPTER THREE

JOHN WORK GARRETT

John Work Garrett was born in Baltimore City on July 31, 1820, to Robert and Elizabeth Garrett. His father, the youngest of six children, had emigrated from Ireland with his family at the age of seven. In 1819, he opened his own trading company in Baltimore City, Robert Garrett & Company. The firm did much of its business with the farmers and merchants in Western Maryland, Western Virginia and the Ohio Valley. Understanding the potential for trade between this region and the Port of Baltimore, Robert Garrett became a primary investor in the Baltimore & Ohio Railroad.

John Work Garrett literally grew up with the B&O Railroad, having a chance as a boy to witness the laying of the first tracks and the inauguration of steam power with the "Tom Thumb." Educated at the Boisseau Academy in Baltimore and a preparatory school in Easton, Pennsylvania, he spent his summer months learning the family business from the ground up by working in his father's warehouse.[64]

In 1840, Robert Garrett invited his two sons, Henry, age 21, and John, only 19, to become partners in the firm and renamed it Robert Garrett and Sons. John's extensive travels in the west gave him an intimate knowledge of the people, geography, and products both needed and available in the region. This knowledge would serve him well when he entered the railroad business. [65]

The B&O opened service to Cumberland in 1842. Four years later, it began its assault on the Allegheny Mountains that would lead to its chartered destination, the Ohio River. The immense cost of tunneling and erecting bridges in order to close the track at Wheeling nearly bankrupted the railroad. With their business interests so closely aligned, the firm of Robert Garrett and Sons offered their considerable resources to help save the B&O. In return, John and his brother were named to the board of directors. In 1853, at the modest age of thirty-eight, John Work Garrett was elected president of the B&O Railroad.

He replaced Thomas Swann, who was elected mayor of Baltimore City in 1856 and governor of the State of Maryland ten years later.[66]

Shortly after the stirring events of John Brown's Raid in 1859, Garrett addressed an audience in Baltimore City during which he declared the position of the B&O Railroad should "the irrepressible conflict" come to pass. "It is a Southern line. And if ever necessity require – which heaven forbid! – it will prove the great bulwark of the border, and a sure agency for home defense." Two things deserve consideration when evaluating these remarks. First, Garrett, like his family's firm and many others in Baltimore City, enjoyed a decidedly Southern lifestyle. The means of which to support it came, for the most part, from the North and West. Second, no one at this time could have predicted that the state of Maryland, a slave state, and the western counties of Virginia, some of which contained the B&O's tracks, would have remained loyal to the Union. In the early days of the war, he had to overcome these remarks in order to prove his loyalty to the Union.[67]

Garrett's difficulties began early in 1861. Several states had already left the Union and, fearing Maryland and Virginia would follow suit, many shippers in the West transferred their business to the northern ports of Philadelphia and New York. With revenue being lost to his rival lines, Garrett took a bold step. He guaranteed his shippers against any loss resulting from a political or military action while in transit on the B&O Railroad. With the delivery times and freight rates in the B&O's favor, the railroad quickly regained the lost business and held it until the outbreak of hostilities.[68]

Garrett's next challenge came when a rumor began to circulate in April that the management of his railroad had refused to carry troops to defend the nation's capital. Garrett believed this to be the handiwork of his competitors at the Pennsylvania Railroad. He instructed his agents by telegraph, "Our company fully recognizes the present legal authorities State and National under which we live, and as common carriers propose to promptly and safely transport all passengers or freight that those authorities may desire…"[69]

Before these countermeasures could take effect, another set of circumstances put the B&O in a difficult situation. Following Lincoln's call for 75,000 volunteers on April 15, Governor William Dennison of Ohio arranged to move 800 men along the main line of the B&O to Washington. Two days later Master of Transportation William Prescott Smith was informed that approximately 2,000 soldiers would be arriving in Baltimore City via the PW&B and an additional 2,000 by the Northern Central. As a result, Garrett was forced to tell Governor Dennison that the demand for rail cars was so great that he would have to cancel the troop movement from Ohio. This in turn caused Dennison to doubt Garrett's true motives and he so informed the authorities in Washington.[70]

On April 18, the day after Virginia voted to secede from the Union, Garrett received a communication from the Mayor of Charles Town threatening to destroy the long bridge over the Potomac River at Harpers Ferry if he did not receive a guaranty that the B&O would not carry any Federal soldiers over its main line. This Garrett flatly refused to do. On the same day Virginia's Governor John Letcher, perhaps in remembrance of Garrett's "Southern line" speech, wrote to the B&O's president, "I desire that the Baltimore & Ohio Railroad Company shall pass no troops destined for any place in Virginia over their road. Virginia and Maryland are destined to be together and if troops are brought into our state or Maryland they may seriously embarrass us in both states. Pass none therefore over your road."

The very next day Garrett received the following letter, "It is my duty to inform you that all Republicans must be removed from your road…If they are not removed your road will be one continuous ruin." This was signed by a committee of "Fifteen Hundred Western Maryland Men." [71]

A more thorough and lengthy threat was delivered anonymously. "One hundred of us, Firm Respectable, Resolute men – have determined and Sworn to each other, to destroy '*every*' Bridge & tear up your Track on both lines of your Road – (Main & the Branch) between this City & their head points – If you carry another Soldier over either line of your Road after Saturday April 20th…This organization of ours extends from here to Grafton & Washington & your trains will be watched. Many of our committee know your personally… We have a large force ready to answer our calls." These anonymous threats could possibly have been ignored, but the next two directives clearly placed John Work Garrett in a situation that few men would have had the fortitude to endure. Secretary of War Simon Cameron warned Garrett that the movement of "rebel troops" over his line would be considered an act of treason. This was followed by a letter from Governor John Letcher of Virginia stating, "In the event that you allow Federal troops to be passed over your road, I will take possession of so much of said road as lies within this state." [72]

Garrett's only recourse was to ask Simon Cameron for enough troops to protect his railroad from hostile action by Southern forces. Cameron was not only the Secretary of War, but also a major stockholder in the Northern Central Railroad of which his son was the vice-president. It was known as "Cameron's road." At Harrisburg, the Pennsylvania Railroad transferred its long haul freight to the Northern Central for final delivery to the Port of Baltimore. The two railroads worked hand in hand and were the arch rivals of the B&O. Instead of looking at the B&O as the only direct rail link between the nation's capital and the loyal states, a connection that must be kept open at any cost, Cameron saw Garrett's predicament as a golden opportunity to destroy

Secretary of State Edwin McMasters Stanton. (D. C. T.)

his competition. He readily agreed to station troops along the Northern Central and the Philadelphia, Wilmington and Baltimore railroads but flatly refused to help Garrett.

Once General Benjamin F. Butler opened the route from Annapolis to Washington City, Cameron seized all the railroad equipment on the Annapolis and Elk Ridge Railroad and the B&O's Washington Branch for use by the Federal government. He called on Thomas A. Scott, vice-president of the Pennsylvania Railroad, to manage the operation. This was an obvious affront to Garrett as he was giving complete control of the B&O's track and equipment to a prewar rival. It was also the president of that same railroad, J. Edgar Thomson, that Cameron had sent to Baltimore on April 17 to coordinate the initial surge of troops to Washington. After the Pratt Street Riot Thomson suggested to Cameron that, "Maryland should feel the power of the General Government in a manner that will hereafter keep her quiet, if it does not make her loyal" and, "The War Department should at once destroy… the bridges on the main stem of the Baltimore and Ohio Railroad as high up as Harpers Ferry." How this would have aided the war effort, he did not say.[73]

On May 1, Garrett wrote to Simon Cameron and requested that the B&O be allowed to resume its passenger and mail service on the Washington Branch. The next day he received a curt reply to the effect that permission would not be granted until rail service was fully restored through Baltimore City. This was after the Pratt Street Riot and before Butler occupied Baltimore. It was also during this same period of time that Virginia state forces were allowing trains to run between Baltimore and Wheeling with minor disruptions. Finally, after Butler had broken the siege by occupying Baltimore City, a limited number of trains were allowed to transit the Washington Branch starting on May 16.[74]

Simon Cameron's blatant hostility to the B&O left the main line severed for six months, forcing an overflow of eastbound business onto the Pennsylvania and Northern Central lines. Eventually freight rates soared and consignments were refused due to lack of equipment while B&O trains sat idle in Baltimore. Shippers appealed to Washington for relief and asked the obvious question, what was the government doing to reopen the main line of the B&O? Finally,

Samuel M. Felton, the president of the Philadelphia, Wilmington and Baltimore Railroad and himself a victim of Cameron's discrimination, launched an attack in the newspapers that made public the unethical practices of the War Department. Lincoln could no longer ignore the obvious and replaced Cameron with Edwin McMasters Stanton in January of 1862. Garrett had endured a trying time. Now he could turn his attention to running his railroad and supporting the War effort.[75]

President Street Station of the Philadelphia, Wilmington and Baltimore Railroad was built in 1850. The domed end building still exists today and is one of three existing pre–Civil War train stations in Baltimore City. The other two are Camden Station and Mount Clare; both belonged to the B&O Railroad. (PW&BRR Guide)

CHAPTER FOUR

PHILADELPHIA, WILMINGTON AND BALTIMORE RAILROAD

The Philadelphia, Wilmington and Baltimore Railroad Company was organized in 1838 through the consolidation of three smaller lines that had previously been chartered to service these three primary cities. Samuel M. Felton was elected president of the line in 1851. When he took office, he was, like John Work Garrett of the B&O, faced with a high level of debt and a low return for the company's investors. A sound railroad man like Garrett, he immediately set about to reduce the corporate debt and through internal improvements make the PW&B a profitable railroad. Within ten years, he had replaced the original strap rail with heavy "T" rails and built a number of new stations and bridges. He also purchased a new steam ferry, the *Maryland,* to carry rail traffic across the Susquehanna River between Havre de Grace and Perryville. Constructed of iron and powered by steam, three sets of tracks were laid on the main deck of the boat. It could accommodate over twenty rail cars per crossing. The vessel it replaced was similar in design and the first of its type in the country. By 1861, the PW&B was operating 32 locomotives and 674 railcars.[76]

The strategic importance of the area served by the PW&B cannot be overlooked. Its 99 miles of main line connected the second largest city in the United States, Philadelphia, with the third largest city, Baltimore. It was the main route for troops and supplies moving from New York and New England to connect with the B&O in Baltimore. In between, Wilmington was both a port city and a center of manufacturing. Not only were the roundhouse and machine

THE WAR CAME BY TRAIN

Samuel Morris Felton was elected President of the Philadelphia, Wilmington and Baltimore Railroad in 1851. (Ralph Vincent)

shops of the PW&B located there, it was also the northern terminus of the Delaware Railroad, which ran nearly the length of the state of Delaware before crossing into Maryland as far as Salisbury. This was the only rail service available to the lower Eastern Shore counties until after the war. Of even greater importance was a number of powder mills located along the banks of the Brandywine River. Owned by the Du Pont Company, they provided half of all the gunpowder used by the Union Army during the war.[77]

After the Pratt Street Riot on April 19, 1861, government officials in Maryland ordered the railroad bridges north of Baltimore destroyed and the telegraph lines cut to prevent any additional troop movements through the city. As a result, portions of the 3,089-foot bridge over the Bush River, and the 5,238-foot bridge with a draw span over the Gunpowder River were burned. In the days that followed, Felton faced a number of problems similar to those of Garrett and the B&O. If Maryland left the Union, one-half of his railroad would be located in the Confederacy. Not sure of what the Marylanders would do next, Felton needed to find a way to rebuild his railroad and protect his repair crews.[78]

Militia units from Baltimore had also burned the bridges on the Northern Central Railroad. This meant that all the troops in Harrisburg would have to be transferred to Philadelphia and then sent south on the PW&B as far as Perryville, where they could board ships for Annapolis. To secure this route, General Patterson sent Colonel Charles P. Dare with detachments from two regiments to garrison Perryville and requested a Navy vessel to protect the ferryboat landing at Havre de Grace until a sufficient infantry force could be gathered to seize the tracks south of the Susquehanna River. Colonel Dare was the author of the PW&B's guide book and knew the location of every bridge and station by heart. Before his mission could be accomplished, the Spesuita Rangers, a militia unit from Harford County under the command of Captain B. H. Keen, attacked the Bush River bridge a second time and set fire to the draw span on the bridge.[79]

66

General Winfield Scott, the commanding general of the U.S. Army, was almost frantic to occupy Baltimore and reopen the rail lines between the North and the nation's capital. As late as May 5, his plans were thwarted by the fact that several of the newly formed volunteer regiments under General Robert Patterson's command were without uniforms, equipment, or even muskets with which to fight. Finally, on May 9, a second effort was made to avoid the Pratt Street gauntlet. A force of 775 men from the Seventeenth Pennsylvania Regiment, five companies of Regulars from the Third U.S. Infantry, and six guns of Sherman's Battery left Perryville on a steamer and sailed down the Chesapeake Bay. They were off-loaded at Locust Point near Fort McHenry and marched to the B&O's Camden Station without incident. From there they traveled west to Relay and then along the Union-held Washington Branch to reinforce the Capital. At the same time, Patterson ordered Colonel Dare to take his regiment, the Twenty-Third Pennsylvania, across the Susquehanna River and begin occupying stations and bridges between Havre de Grace and the outskirts of Baltimore City.[80]

Union soldiers were now guarding his line, but as with the B&O, Felton was forced to make repairs at his own expense. Not knowing how long the hostilities would last or if the Marylanders would attack again, Felton seized on a revolutionary idea to protect his track gangs by building the first armored rail car in military history. It was the invention of Rufus A. Wilder, the chief engineer of the Mine Hill Railroad who happened to be in Philadelphia on the day of the Pratt Street Riot. Felton was immediately impressed with the plans and arranged for its construction at the Baldwin Locomotive Works in Philadelphia.

At this time, Matthias Baldwin's company was the largest producer of locomotives in the world. His men worked in secrecy for two weeks. When completed, "The Philadelphia Fort on Wheels" as it was called, was 65 feet long and 9 feet wide. It was covered with half-inch iron boilerplate that made it immune to rifle fire. At one end, a 9-lb. Howitzer was mounted on an adjustable carriage that allowed it to be fired through portholes in three directions. The gun and crew were protected by retractable hatches similar to that of a naval war ship. The remainder of the car was lined with 50 loopholes to allow for the safe firing of infantry weapons. It could carry five gunners and up to 60 infantrymen. The car was sent to the Bush River to protect the crew rebuilding the bridge there. On the night of May 13, Butler occupied Federal Hill and the next day Baltimore's "period of armed neutrality" came to an end. The threat of attack rapidly diminished and Wilder's armored railcar was transferred to Northern Virginia where it was put into service on the Union controlled Orange & Alexandria Railroad.[81]

First armored rail car constructed during the Civil War. Known as the Philadelphia Fort on Wheels, it was built to protect PW&B track workers shortly after the Pratt Street Riot. (L.I.N.)

A second weapon that was used to protect the railroads north of Baltimore after the Pratt Street Riot was made of paper and not iron. On May 16, President Lincoln sent a letter to General George Cadwalader who was then in command of the Department of Annapolis stating, "Herewith you will receive a power to arrest persons…and hold them as prisoners though there should be demands by writ of habeas corpus." The next day Lincoln suspended the writ of *habeas corpus* along the railroad lines between Harrisburg, Philadelphia, Washington and Annapolis. Lincoln extended his constitutional authority without the consent of Congress. This suspension allowed the Army to arrest, without due process of the law, anyone considered a threat to the Union.

The first test of this extra-legal activity came with the arrest of John Merryman. Merryman was a lieutenant in the Baltimore County Horse Guards and had been ordered to burn the bridges of the Northern Central Railroad after the Pratt Street Riot. He was arrested at his home in the middle of the night by a detachment of Union soldiers and taken to Fort McHenry. No less a personage than Chief Justice of the Supreme Court Roger B. Taney of Maryland issued a writ of *habeas corpus* for his release. General Cadwalader refused to do so citing Lincoln's instructions. This resulted in a landmark legal case entitled *Ex Parte* John Merryman in which Chief Justice Taney rendered a five thousand word opinion that stated, in part, only Congress, and not the President of the United States, had the power to suspend the writ of *habeas corpus*. It further illustrates the importance of the railroads in sustaining the nation's capital and in turn the preservation of the Union.[82]

Besides the construction of the first ferryboat for railcars and the first armored railcar, the PW&B contributed to a third technology related to Civil War railroading – the hospital train. At the beginning of the Civil War little thought was given to the evacuation of large numbers of wounded from the battlefields. Freight trains took supplies to the front and the wounded were loaded into boxcars or placed on flatcars for the return trip. From the main supply base, they would be transferred by boat or passenger trains to U.S. General Hospitals in major Northern cities. Eventually, the interiors of boxcars and passengers cars were altered to improve the care and comfort of the patients being transferred.

In June of 1862, Dr. Elisha Harris, a member of the United States Sanitary Commission, presented his design for a hospital car to Quarter Master General Montgomery Meigs. The Sanitary Commission was a civilian organization founded in 1861 to provide care for sick and wounded soldiers. Their activities ranged from inspecting camps and hospitals to sending medical supplies and volunteer surgeons to supplement the Army's medical corps after major battles like Antietam and Gettysburg.[83]

General Meigs approved the plan and instructed the various railroads between Washington and New York City to begin altering existing passenger cars. He also ordered the USMRR to do the same thing at its shops in Alexandria, Virginia. Through the personal efforts of the PW&B's President Felton, the first car was completed early in October of 1862 by the PW&B. It was the very same car that had been abandoned by the Sixth Massachusetts Regiment on Pratt Street in Baltimore during the riot of April 19, 1861. The 51-foot long passenger car was fitted with upright posts to accommodate three tiers of berths. The genius of Dr. Harris's design was the fact that the patient never had to be moved from his stretcher. The soldier was taken from the field ambulance into the car and the poles of the stretcher inserted into huge rubber bands attached to the uprights. The rubber bands reduced the jolting effect of rail travel. When the train arrived at its destination city, the stretchers were unslung and the patient carried to the General Hospital.

The "Harris car" could carry up to 36 recumbent patients and had seats at each end for the nurses or attendants. The cars were equipped with a stove, water tank, supply locker and water closet (toilet). An added advantage over converted boxcars was that a surgeon could move from car to car to attend to the patients. The PW&B produced fourteen hospital cars during the war. They were initially introduced into service by being added to regular scheduled passenger trains.[84]

In 1863, Surgeon Robert O. Abbott, the Medical Director of the Department of Washington, ordered the construction of several complete hospital trains. Each train consisted of specially designed cars for the surgeon, the apothecary, a kitchen and ten ward cars. Variations of this design were used in both the eastern and western theaters. To signify that the hospital trains were carrying non-combatants, each locomotive and tender was painted scarlet and ran during the day with two yellow hospital flags on either side of the cowcatcher. Painted in large letters on the sides of each car was the inscription "U.S. Hospital Train." At night, it ran with three red lanterns hung beneath the headlamp. With a fleeting strand of chivalry during this first modern war, both sides honored the humanitarian purpose of these trains.[85]

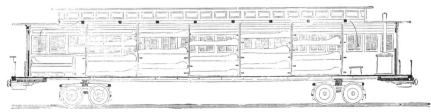

First hospital car constructed during the war. The PW&B rebuilt the passenger car that was severely damaged during the Pratt Street Riot to accommodate sick and wounded soldiers. (M&SHCW)

CHAPTER FIVE

UNITED STATES MILITARY TELEGRAPH

The Civil War is considered by many to be the first modern war. No two technologies complemented each other more and supported this theory better than the railroad and the telegraph. Professor Samuel F. B. Morse patented his electro-magnetic telegraph in 1837. It was not until 1843 that Congress approved an expenditure of $30,000 to test the process. The next year construction began on a line between Baltimore and Washington, DC. The wire was to be installed along the main line of the B&O Railroad as far as Relay and then the length of the Washington Branch to the Capital. The board of directors of the railroad had agreed to allow Professor Morse to run his line parallel to their tracks free of charge if he, in turn, allowed the railroad free use of the telegraph once it was in service. Even though the service was available, the B&O did not utilize the telegraph for controlling rail traffic until several years later. Once the dynamic was understood, a marriage of technologies took place. Other railroads readily allowed telegraph companies to string their lines along their tracks in return for free telegraph service.

Ironically, the first telegraph line was designed to be laid underground. It consisted of a lead pipe carrying an insulated copper wire much like the conduit systems of today. A special plowshare was designed to cut a trench two inches wide and twenty inches deep into which automatically dropped the lead pipe. The plowshare was cast in the molding room at the B&O's Mount Clare Shops. Sixteen oxen were required to pull the plow. Wire was laid between Baltimore and Relay without any difficulty. However, the Washington Branch was constructed of heavy ballast stone and the ingenious plowshare would not work. At this point the telegraph pole was invented and the communication link completed to the nation's capital. The first commercial telegraph service in the world was opened on May 24, 1844, when Samuel Morse tapped out the immortal message "What hath God Wrought?"[86]

During the Crimean War (1854-1855), the telegraph was used but only to connect the headquarters of the British, French and Turkish armies. Its limited success was observed by then-Captain George B. McClellan of the United States Army who would be the first to use the telegraph on the battlefield during his Western Virginia Campaign of 1861.[87]

By 1861, there were 50,000 miles of commercial telegraph lines in the United States. Most of this business was conducted by two major companies. The American Telegraph Company controlled the north-south traffic along the East Coast. The Western Union lines ran east and west all the way to California. The Federal Government relied wholly on these commercial companies to fill its telegraphic needs. The United States Army did not have a component to handle telegraphic communications.

As a railroad man, when Simon Cameron was appointed Secretary of War in 1861, he readily understood the potential of both the railroad and the telegraph in waging a war. This ensured the availability of these two technologies to the federal government from the very beginning of hostilities.

Cameron summoned Thomas Scott to Washington to manage the railroad and telegraph services for the Army. Scott, in turn, called on Andrew Carnegie and gave him the task of recruiting linemen and telegraphers for the newly formed United States Military Telegraph Corps (USMTC). Carnegie was at the time superintendent of the Pittsburgh Division of the Pennsylvania Railroad. He had begun his career as a messenger boy in a telegraph office and later attained the skills of an operator. He was considered an expert on railroad related telegraph operations. After the war, Andrew Carnegie became one of America's wealthiest men through his investments in the steel and railroad industries. Because of the situation in Baltimore, Carnegie was forced to go by rail to Philadelphia and then by water to Annapolis.

When he arrived in the capital, one of his first challenges was the fact that Congress had not yet passed an appropriation for the newly formed USMTC. Carnegie presented the problem to the president of the American Telegraph Company, Edward S. Sanford, and arranged for his company to supply funds and equipment to the USMTC until Congress could rectify the situation. The headquarters of the Corps were in the telegraph office of the War Department building which, in time, became a favorite haunt of President Lincoln.[88]

The creation of a Telegraph Corps required the employment of individuals with specific skills. Not only were they expected to rapidly transmit information but also to become adept at encoding and decoding messages. There were only about 2,000 telegraph operators in the United States in 1861 and approximately 100 of these were women. In addition to operators, linemen were needed to construct new lines and repairmen to keep them operational. Members of the USMTC were civilian employees of the government and exempt from military service. However, this did not keep them from being stationed on or near the battlefield. There were occasions when Corps employees were killed, wounded or captured along with the troops they were serving with. Because of their unique status, they were denied government pensions. After the war, Andrew Carnegie personally supported these men and their families if they fell on hard times.[89]

Thomas A. Scott was Vice President of the Pennsylvania Railroad before being appointed Assistant Secretary of War in 1861. (D. C. T.)

On April 22, 1861, Carnegie sent the following telegram.

> David McCargo,
> Supt. Telegraphs, Penna. Railroad Co., Altoona, Pa.
> Send four of your best operators to Washington at once, prepared to enter Government telegraph service for the war.
> (Signed) Andrew Carnegie
> 19 words paid, Govt.

The first four telegraphers hired were from the Pennsylvania Railroad and all four had considerable experience with scheduling trains. They were Samuel M. Brown, David Strouse, Richard O'Brien and Davis Homer Bates. They also took the Annapolis route to Washington. Strouse and Bates were assigned to the War Department Telegraph Office, Brown to the Navy Yard and O'Brien to the B&O's Washington Depot. David Strouse was appointed the first superintendent of the USMTC. In poor health when he arrived, he literally worked himself to death by November of 1861.[90]

During the first months of the war, an infrastructure for the USMTC did not exist and it had to entrust its communications to private companies. By the end of June, additional telegraph operators were hired and assigned to the following locations to insure the priority transmittal of government messages: W. H. Bauer and J. J. G. Riley at Camden Station; Jules F. Guthridge at Relay; William B. Kress and Crosby J. Ryan at Annapolis Junction; Samuel M. Brown and Jesse H. Bunnell at Annapolis; Jesse W. Crouse, O. H. Kinnaman and H. L. Smith at the Washington Depot.[91]

Operation of the military telegraph during McClellan's campaign in Western Virginia was equally well managed. On April 12, 1861, the same day Southern batteries opened fire on Fort Sumter, Governor Dennison of Ohio sent a request to Anson Stager, the General Superintendent of the Western Union Telegraph Company in Cleveland, to meet him in Columbus. At that meeting the Governor asked Mr. Stager to assume control of the telegraph service in Southern Ohio and work with then-Captain George B. McClellan who was about to be promoted to department commander. Stager readily agreed and travelled to Cincinnati to confer with McClellan. On May 14, McClellan was promoted to major general. On May 27, he officially appointed Stager superintendent of the telegraph lines in the Department of the Ohio.[92]

It will be remembered that in the opening weeks of the war that both rail and telegraph service were still operating along the main line of the B&O Railroad. Stager secured the services of Mr. T. B. A. David who managed the telegraph office in Wheeling, Virginia, and informed him that the Secretary of War was anxious to know what the Rebels were doing at Harpers Ferry. Mr. David and George M. Deetz, the telegraph operator at Cumberland, Maryland, devised a private code that allowed them to pass any tidbit of information on to the War Department. Stager also solicited the services of W. G. Fuller in Grafton. Fuller was the superintendent of the telegraph line that ran from Grafton, Virginia, to Cincinnati, Ohio. He was given the first official army cipher used by the telegraph during the war and put in charge of all government traffic between Grafton and Parkersburg. It was David and Fuller that collected the necessary supplies and managed to keep an active telegraph line apace of McClellan's advance from Grafton to the battle of Rich Mountain. In acknowledging their contribution to that victory, Mr. David was put in charge of all the telegraph offices in Western Virginia and Mr. Fuller for the construction and maintenance of the lines.[93]

When David Strouse died in November of 1861, Amasa Stone, a director of the Western Union Telegraph Company that employed Anson Stager before the war, recommended him to Secretary of War Cameron as a suitable replacement. On November 11, Stager was appointed a captain and assistant quartermaster in the Army and assigned to duty as superintendent of all the military telegraph lines in the United States. He was promoted to colonel in 1862 and brevet brigadier general for meritorious service on March 13, 1865.[94]

When first established in April of 1861, the USMTC was part of the Quartermaster Department of the U.S. Army. In January of 1862, it was placed under the direct control of the Secretary of War, and functioned independently of any other branch of the Army.

That the operations of the USMTC grew at a phenomenal pace is reflected in the statistics for 1861. At the end of October, there were 50 telegraph stations and 280 miles of line in operation. By the middle of November, this number had jumped to 106 telegraph stations and 1,136 miles of line. By 1865,

Photograph of Andrew Carnegie taken in 1861 when he was in charge of recruiting linemen and telegraphers for the USMTC. (L. C.)

the Corps had strung 15,000 miles of line with over 6,100 miles in service when the war ended. This included 73 miles of underwater cable.[95]

In 1866, the United States Military Telegraph Corps was incorporated into the United States Signal Corps. Its remaining employees became soldiers in the United States Army. On January 26, 1897, President Grover Cleveland approved an act that authorized the Secretary of War to issue certificates of honorable service to members of the United States Military Telegraph Corps or, if deceased, to their descendents. The act was specifically worded to prevent members of the Telegraph Corps from ever receiving a government pension.[96]

Telegraph office in the field. Wagons like this one equipped with telegraph instruments and a 100-cell battery allowed the USMTC to supply armies in the field with direct communications between their commanding general and his unit commanders. By the end of the war the Corps had strung 15,000 miles of line. (Miller's)

Chapter Six

The Burnt District

Slowly throughout the summer months of 1861, John Garrett regained possession of his railroad. First came Baltimore City and the Washington Branch with only a brief disruption of services and no physical damage. In the west, the Northwestern Virginia Railroad and the main line from Wheeling to Grafton were secured after the battle of Philippi in June. The minor damage inflected by Colonel Porterfield's men was quickly repaired. So, too, was most of the main line from Grafton to Cumberland. The greatest amount of damage was inflicted between Point of Rocks and Cumberland. Master of the Road John L. Wilson referred to this section of tracks as the "burnt district." The Confederates did not relinquish their death grip on Martinsburg until the following year. As a result, over 100 miles of track between these points were out of service until March of 1862, much of it having been destroyed or removed by the Rebels. The main line would not be fully operational between Baltimore and Wheeling until January 6, 1863, when an iron railroad bridge was completed at Harpers Ferry. And then the cycle of destruction resumed.[97]

During the first three months of the war, a number of Union generals were promoted or transferred and several new military departments established in the areas served by the B&O Railroad. Major General John A. Dix replaced General Patterson as commander of the Department of Pennsylvania and made his headquarters in Baltimore City. John Adams Dix was another old soldier fighting his last war. Born in 1798, he had fought the British in the War of 1812. He then became a lawyer, U.S. Senator and president of two different railroads. In the final days of the Buchanan administration, he was the Secretary of the Treasury. Lincoln commissioned Dix a major general of volunteers to rank from May 16, 1861. This made him the senior ranking volunteer officer in the Union Army during the entire war. Within his department were the states of Pennsylvania, Delaware, and most of the Maryland counties east of the Monocacy River. Brigadier General Rosecrans was officially named as McClellan's replacement and given command of the newly created Department of Western Virginia, which included all of the counties of Virginia between the Blue Ridge Mountains and the Ohio River.[98]

While recovering from the wound he received at the battle of Philippi, Colonel B. F. Kelley was promoted to brigadier general and assigned command of the Railroad Division with headquarters in Grafton. He was an ideal choice considering his prewar railroading experience and knowledge of the area. To Kelley fell the difficult and somewhat thankless job of protecting the main line of the B&O from Cumberland to Wheeling and the Northwestern Virginia Railroad from Grafton to Parkersburg. Kelley would spend the entire war in Western Maryland and the new state of West Virginia, always assigned to duties related to guarding the railroad. Robbed of any fame associated with a more notable battlefield, he was awarded the rank of brevet major general on August 5, 1864. Kelley died at his summer home in Oakland on July 16, 1883.[99]

The final link in the chain of commands between Baltimore and Wheeling was the Department of Harpers Ferry and Cumberland. Colonel Frederick W. Lander was promoted to brigadier general on August 6 for his gallant actions at the battles of Philippi and Rich Mountain. It was to be his command but he was wounded in a rear guard action at Edwards Ferry following the battle of

Ball's Bluff. On October 22, General B. F. Kelley received orders to move with his troops to Romney and assume command of the Department of Harpers Ferry and Cumberland until Lander was fit for duty.[100]

Romney was located on the Northwestern Turnpike where a covered bridge carried the turnpike over the South Branch of the Potomac River. Its strategic importance was similar to that of Philippi. Although the railroad did not go through the town, it circled around it for a distance of sixty miles. An enemy force in Romney would be located near enough to the main line to threaten any point between Oakland and Martinsburg. Conversely, the Union occupation of

Brig. Gen. Benjamin F. Kelly. (D. C. T.)

Romney would threaten Winchester and other points in the Lower Shenandoah Valley.

Kelley immediately began to concentrate his forces at New Creek Station 25 miles west of Cumberland. They consisted of a number of companies from three different Loyal Virginia regiments, the Fourth and Eighth Ohio infantry regiments and three pieces of artillery served by volunteer infantry detachments. There were also two companies of cavalry commanded by captains Keys and McGee. Kelley's plan was to attack Romney with his main force along the Northwestern Turnpike. At the same time, he ordered Colonel Thomas Johns to take his Second Maryland Potomac Home Brigade regiment from Patterson's Creek on the B&ORR and make a flank march that would enable him to enter the town from the east. His mission was to block the Winchester Road and cut off the Confederates' line of retreat. It was a replay of Kelley's Philippi battle plan. The two forces were to converge on Romney at 3:00 p.m.

When within three miles of their target, Kelley's advance was stalled by a battery of enemy artillery firing from the east side of the river. The guns were well placed in a cemetery on high ground that controlled the western approach to the town. Confederate infantry was also entrenched on high ground to cover the bridge and ford. Kelley put his ad hoc artillery units into action and the two sides battled it out at long range for about an hour. Unable to silence the enemy's guns, Kelley ordered his entire column of infantry to charge straight across the bridge and into the enemy's works. At the same time, his cavalry was ordered to gallop across the ford and under the bridge to maximize the shock value of the charge. It worked. After firing a few rounds the Rebel infantry threw down their guns and fled into the mountains. Their cavalry and artillery attempted to escape on the Winchester road but were so closely pursued by Keys' and McGee's companies that all their artillery and wagons were captured along with 300 stands of arms, camp equipment and about 100 draft animals. All of this was accomplished with the loss of only one man killed and twenty wounded.[101]

Colonel Johns' Marylanders failed to reach their objective. The One Hundred and Fourteenth Virginia Militia C.S. under the command of Colonel A. Monroe was guarding the bridge over the South Branch of the Potomac River. Monroe had his men remove a section of the flooring near their end of the bridge. When Johns' lead company reached the gap, they were caught in the open and forced to retreat after losing seven men. Shortly after the attack failed, the firing ceased in Romney and Johns correctly assumed the town had been captured. Not wishing to waste the lives if his men in an unnecessary charge he fell back to Old Town, Maryland.[102]

On the Confederate side, now a major general, Thomas J. "Stonewall" Jackson was assigned command of the Valley District in the Department of

Northern Virginia. On November 4, he received his orders and took the next train to leave Manassas Junction for Winchester, arriving that night. The old nemesis of the B&O was back for a third time. The next day he wrote a letter to the Confederate Secretary of War Judah P. Benjamin requesting a transfer of troops from the Cheat Mountain-Huntersville region of Western Virginia in order to better protect the area around Winchester.[103]

During the month of November, the B&O pushed work trains eastward out of Cumberland in an attempt to reopen the main line. Before making any progress, a second enemy of the railroad struck. Floodwaters took out a section of the B&O's 21st Bridge just west of Cumberland. Five flat cars positioned on the bridge to help hold it in place were also washed away. The same storm surge struck the line at George's Creek and carried away a number of iron hopper cars weighing four and a half tons each. It took eight days to repair the damage. On November 10, business resumed between Cumberland and all points west.

Four days later repairs were completed on the bridge over Patterson Creek. This allowed military trains to run between Cumberland and Green Spring Station, a distance of sixteen miles. The 26th and 27th were dedicated to repairing the South Branch Bridge. On the last day of November, a work train arrived with an ample supply of lumber at the Little Cacapon Bridge. A single span 131 feet long, it had been burned on June 18. Repairs were not completed until December 10. The next day the construction crew continued to move east. This section of line had been out of service for six months. In many places the banks had washed out, depositing dirt and rocks on the tracks. The debris was cleared and the work train continued on as far as the Great Cacapon. The bridge over this river had been burned on June 13. It consisted of two spans totaling 132 feet each. Repair work began on December 12 and was completed five days later. Rail service was now resumed between Hancock and Cumberland.[104]

On December 2, Jackson reported that B&O repair crews were rapidly working to replace the bridge over the Little Cacapon. He went on to state that, "With but comparative little exception both tracks (of the main line) have been by our Government taken up from Furnace Hill, near Harpers Ferry, to Martinsburg, and about 7½ miles of one of the tracks has also been removed west of Martinsburg." This was six months after Jackson had first occupied Martinsburg. Simon Cameron's plan not to protect the B&O Railroad was still paying dividends – for the Confederacy.

The availability of iron rails in the Confederacy was a critical issue from the very beginning of the hostilities. The average production of rails in the South before the war was about a tenth of that of the North. When the war began this number dropped to zero. The almost unlimited access to the B&O's

rails and equipment during the first year of the war was a godsend to the Southern railroads. The ever-efficient Captain Thomas Sharp was still managing the removal of B&O property as late as December of 1861. One section of the double line near Martinsburg was kept in place so it could be used for the removal of the other. Sharp repaired one of the previously damaged locomotives and used it to expedite track removal. General Jackson assigned him a detail of fifty militiamen to help with the project. At the same time, he ordered Colonel Turner Ashby, his cavalry commander, to move his headquarters to Martinsburg to ensure the protection of the work crews there. By the end of December, 37 miles of track between Harpers Ferry and Back Creek had been pulled up and the rails, fixtures and thousands of cross ties shipped south. Miles of telegraph wire were also taken.[105]

One example of how captured B&O rails were utilized by the Confederate Army was the Centerville Military Railroad. As the campaign season for 1861 came to an end in Northern Virginia, the Confederate Army established its winter quarters at Centerville. This was six miles northeast of Manassas Junction where the Manassas Gap and Orange & Alexandria railroads met. It was the Manassas Gap Railroad that had brought Jackson's brigade here the previous July to help win the First Battle of Bull Run. The two railroads could deliver an immense amount of supplies to the junction, but the harsh winter weather soon converted the wagon road into a muddy trough.

To relieve the situation, General Joseph Johnston ordered a rail line constructed between Manassas Junction and Centerville. Labor would be supplied by advertising for skilled workers in the Richmond papers and hiring slaves from the owners of nearby plantations. Lacking an experienced railroad man on his staff, he requested the services of Captain Thomas Sharp to manage the project. Where to get the rails was another problem. Realizing its scarcity, the directors of the Orange & Alexandria balked at loaning such a precious commodity to the Army. Captain Sharp had an extensive knowledge of what had been taken from the B&O. On December 22, he received permission from General Jackson to ship several miles of rails from a warehouse in Winchester to Manassas Junction. Construction began immediately, but was not completed until the beginning of February. From then until March 9, when Johnston was forced to abandon his position, the supplies flowed without interruption. Although of a short duration, it was the first military railroad constructed during the war.[106]

As soon as the Union Army occupied the Manassas Junction, Garrett sent his Master of Transportation, William Prescott Smith, to Manassas to look for material taken from the B&O. During the first year of the war, the B&O had suffered huge losses without any compensation from the Government. Garrett was anxious to recover every ounce of iron he could. Smith was emphatic that he could identify the rails that belonged to the B&O by the way their ends had been drilled to accommodate the "Trimble Splice." Trimble, who was now a general in the Confederate Army, had invented a splicing system before the war and sold a large quantity to the B&O.

Before any action could be taken, Quarter Master General Montgomery Meigs instructed the United States Military Railroad to remove the rails for its own use. Garrett was furious and wrote a letter to Secretary of War Stanton in protest. It is obvious that Garrett and Stanton were rapidly forming a sound working relationship. By direction of the Secretary of War, over 3,000 pieces of spliced rail were returned to the Baltimore & Ohio Railroad.[107]

Another interesting development in the latter part of 1861 was the marriage by necessity of the two prewar archenemies, the B&O Railroad and the C&O Canal. Specifically chartered as commercial rivals, it was the refusal of the C&O to allow the B&O to lay its tracks next to the canal at the base of Maryland Heights that forced the B&O to cross the Potomac River at Harpers Ferry and continue westward on the Virginia side of the Potomac River before reentering the state near Cumberland. It was along this very same section of track that the B&O sustained its greatest losses during the war.

During the year, a series of floods had ravaged the infrastructure of the Canal Company. It had also sustained considerable damage and disruption of trade due to military operations. Whether by design as in the case of the B&O, or indifference, the Government failed to compensate the C&O for losses sustained through enemy action or, at times, even pay for services rendered. At the same time, the demand for coal was ever increasing. With the main line severed and its custom-designed coal hoppers lying in heaps around Martinsburg, the B&O was limited to shuttling trains between the coal mines and Cumberland, the western terminus of the C&O Canal Company.

Desperate to gain revenue by whatever means available, an agreement was reached in September for the transfer of coal from canal boats to railcars. The B&O erected two horse-powered derricks at Sandy Hook, located a few miles below Harpers Ferry on the Maryland side of the Potomac River. Additional derricks were added as quickly as possible and their capacity rose to fifty carloads a day. The coal then moved by train to Baltimore and other points not serviced by the canal.[108]

Despite the fact that rail service had been restored between Cumberland and Wheeling, it did not mean that the trains moving along these tracks were not subject to attack by Confederate raiders. In the fall of 1861, a special train consisting of a single passenger car pulled by B&O Locomotive No. 201 was headed west to Wheeling when it was fired on by a small band of Rebels.

B&O Locomotive No. 201 and crew that escaped Rebel ambush near the Cheat River. (B&ORRM)

When the train stopped at the Oakland Station a warning was received by telegraph that an enemy force was moving to cut off the train at a point west of town and capture the dignitaries riding in the coach. To complicate matters, while taking on fuel and water, the fireman fell and broke his arm. By chance, a former B&O engineer was present and volunteered to take his place. As the special rounded a curve neared the Cheat River Bridge, the crew saw a group of Rebels tearing up a rail and piling logs and ties on the tracks. Fortunately the Rebels chose to rremove the inside rail. The quick thinking engineer pushed the throttle forward and the engine rumbled across the bare ties and burst through the obstruction before remounting the rail on the other side. At the same time, volunteer fireman flung a piece of firewood at the would-be train wreckers. Once past the danger zone, the engineer climbed onto the roof of his cab and, pulling a flask from his pocket, drank a mocking toast to his attackers, which was answered with a poorly aimed volley of gunfire.

The high-speed collision with the debris on the tracks damaged the pilot wheels, shattered the headlight and dented the smokebox and cylinder casings but the special was still able to complete its run to Wheeling. Later in the war, the brave engineer of No. 201 was shot and killed while operating a locomotive for the United States Military Railroad.[109]

Near the end of November, John W. Garrett attempted to bypass Secretary of War Simon Cameron in an attempt to get protection for his railroad. Thanks to Cameron, the official Government position as related to the B&O Railroad was to do nothing. Any help Garrett received in protecting his repair crews or guarding the bridges was the result of cooperation by local Army of-

ficers whose decisions were based on duty and common sense and not a wish
to enhance the profits of the Pennsylvania Railroad. Garrett communicated
to Reverdy Johnson, then a member of the Maryland House of Delegates,
that men and construction materials were being held in reserve and that they
would immediately be committed to repairing the road in the "burnt district"
as soon as the Army would give his crews the protection they needed. It was
hoped that Johnson would relay the message to his contacts in Washington.
He also sent J. H. Sullivan, an agent of the B&O Railroad in Bellaire, Ohio,
to Washington to discuss the matter with General McClellan and Treasury
Secretary Salmon P. Chase. Before anything could come of these conferences,
Jackson launched a winter campaign designed to keep the 25-mile gap on the
main line between Harpers Ferry and Back Creek from being closed.[110]

CHAPTER SEVEN

THE RAILROAD BRIGADE

Immediately after the Pratt Street Riot, all of the railroads within the state of Maryland were unprotected. General B. F. Butler was the first Army officer assigned the duty of protecting a rail route to the Capital. The Department of Annapolis was established on April 27, 1861. Its boundaries were task specific – 20 miles either side of the Annapolis & Elk Ridge Railroad from Annapolis to Annapolis Junction and from Annapolis Junction to the Capital along the Washington Branch of the B&O. The department's headquarters was the city of Annapolis. When Butler occupied Relay on May 5, his authority was extended to the entire length of the Washington Branch. Following his successful but unauthorized occupation of Baltimore City on May 13, he was relieved of command. Major General George Cadwalader was ordered to assume command of the department two days later, with headquarters in Baltimore City. Throughout the Summer and Fall of 1861 newly recruited regiments continuously flowed through the department. Some were temporally assigned to guard a bridge or train station before being ordered further south.

On July 19, the boundaries of the department were expanded and Major General John Adams Dix assumed command of the newly established Department of Maryland with headquarters in Baltimore City. The units assigned for special duty became known as the Railroad Brigade. This unit is not to be confused with Railroad Division commanded by General B. F. Kelley. When Colonel John C. Robinson took command of the brigade in November of 1861, it consisted of three regiments – the Tenth Maine, Sixtieth New York and the First Michigan. Robinson had been the commander of Fort McHenry during the turbulent times in April and held the fort until Butler occupied Baltimore. A year later, he was promoted to brigadier general and fought in all of the campaigns of the Army of the Potomac until severely wounded in

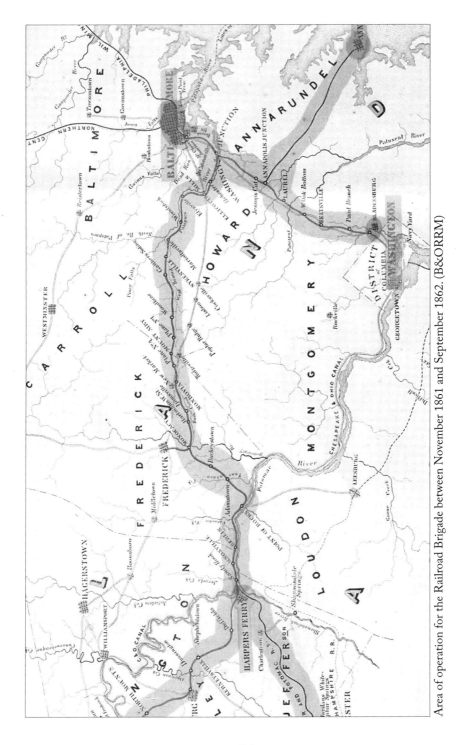

Area of operation for the Railroad Brigade between November 1861 and September 1862. (B&ORRM)

the left knee at the battle of Laurel Hill in 1864. The wound caused the removal of his leg and ended his career as a field commander. In 1894, General Robinson was awarded the Congressional Medal of Honor for his gallant conduct at the battle of Laurel Hill.[111]

The Tenth Maine arrived at the President Street Station of the PW&B in Baltimore on October 8. It went into camp at Patterson Park on the east side of the city and remained there until November 4, when it was transferred to Relay. Relay was located nine miles southwest of Baltimore where the Washington Branch was connected to the main line by the Thomas Viaduct. A fort, later containing five pieces of artillery, was under construction. Company B was

Major General John A. Dix. (D. C. T.)

stationed in the fort and 100 men a day were assigned to help in its completion. It was named Fort Dix in honor of the department commander General Dix. Another company was detailed to guard the viaduct and the passenger bridge that ran below it. The rest of the regiment was drilled on a daily basis.[112]

On November 9, the Sixtieth New York Regiment arrived and in a pouring rain pitched its tents next to the Maine regiment. The regiments in the brigade were then assigned as follows: the New Yorkers would guard the main line of the B&O from Relay east to Baltimore and west to Ellicott's Mills; the Tenth Maine the Washington Branch from Relay to Annapolis Junction; and the First Michigan from there to Washington, DC.[113]

In the Maine regiment's sector, a specially assigned train, B&O Locomotive #31, dropped off companies at two-mile intervals. Within the company's area, sentries were posted a quarter mile apart. John Mead Gould served in the Tenth Maine. He kept a journal that was later published as a regimental history. At this time the lower Potomac was blockaded by Confederate batteries lining the southern bank of the river. This forced a tremendous amount of freight and troop movements onto the Washington Branch of the B&O. Gould was astonished that so many trains could run on the single track between Relay and Washington without a collision. "I learned from the engine driver that all extra movements are done by telegraph which with the fact that passenger trains rarely "Book" (as he called it) more than 25 miles an hour even when late makes it…safe."[114]

The New York regiment was distributed as follows: Company B was sent up the line to Ellicott's Mills; Company K was stationed in Fort Dix; Company F, where the tracks crossed the Washington Turnpike one mile from camp; Company D, Mount Clare Station; Company C, Camden Station; and Company I went to Locust Point. The remaining companies of the regiment pitched their tents at Relay where they drilled and acted as a reserve force. On October 27, this camp and the regiment's headquarters were relocated to Jackson's Bridge near the Baltimore City Limits in order to put them closer to the center of their line of operation. In January, these companies moved into permanent barracks, which gave them a good deal of comfort for the balance of the winter. The others fared far better than their predecessors at Valley Forge. Company I, at Locust Point moved into the unoccupied St. Charles Hotel. Company D, at Mount Clare took over one of the B&O's engine houses. Company H, at Camden Station was assigned the upper level of a building occupied by the Union Relief Association. The other companies built comfortable wooden barracks near their duty stations.[115]

The commanding officer, Colonel William B. Hayward, issued detailed instructions to his company commanders regarding their assignment to the Railroad Brigade. The following is an excerpt from the November 20 circular. "In Moving your officers and men from one position to another, in cases requiring the use of a passenger train, you will see that they confine themselves to the Accommodation, known as the Ellicott's Mills Train. As this passes over your part of the line four times daily, in each direction, at good intervals it ought to afford sufficient facilities for your objects. It is desired that you will not stop any other passenger trains…unless upon some very urgent necessity."[116]

That working on or guarding the railroad was a dangerous job was illustrated by an event that occurred when the Sixtieth New York Regiment was stationed at Relay. On the night of December 11, 1861, their camp was alarmed by the sound of a nearby explosion followed by a whistling sound that resembled the flight of an artillery shell or mortar bomb. The unknown object landed only a few feet behind a corporal and his guard making their rounds. When no explosion followed, the corporal sought out the object and discovered it to be a piece of locomotive boiler-flue about three feet long and weighing over ten pounds. A group of officers and men then began to make their way along the tracks to find the origin of its flight. The chaplain of the regiment, Richard Eddy, recorded what they found.

"While going down the side of a deep cut through which the road here passes, I came upon the body of a man, horribly mutilated... He had evidently been blown into the air, and to such an elevation that coming down feet first, both legs were driven into the mud to some distance above the knees. The man had on a soldier's uniform, but we never learned what regiment or state he belonged to. The locomotive, one of the kind called "camel back" lay upon the side of the track, a wreck. Fragments of it were strewn in every direction, some to the distance of four hundred feet. The engineer was found two hundred and sixty-four feet from the track, having been thrown... through the top of a large tree, breaking off in his passage limbs of the tree three inches in diameter. The dome of the engine, weighing at least eight hundred lbs., was found twenty-five feet beyond the engineer. The fireman remained at the tender, but was so badly scalded that he survived but a few hours. Capt. Ransom was standing with one foot on the step of the engine, having got on only a few moments before... He was thrown on the side of the track, but received no injury. A most surprising escape!"[117]

The regiments assigned to railroad duty during the winter months enjoyed excellent Thanksgiving and Christmas dinners thanks to their close association to the means of its delivery and well established camp sites. In February, a number of changes took place in the brigade. General McClellan and his staff passed through Relay with a trainload of pontoons followed by others carrying infantry and batteries of artillery. McClellan observed with satisfaction as a pontoon bridge was laid across the Potomac River and Harpers Ferry reoccupied by the Union Army. At the same time, the operational limits of the Railroad Brigade were expanded westward. Colonel Robinson pulled five companies of the Tenth Maine off the Washington Branch and sent them up the main line to guard points from Ellicott's Mills westward. On March 8, four more companies were redeployed as far up as Monocacy Junction to relieve those of the First Michigan so that regiment could be consolidated at Annapolis Junction.[118]

In March of 1862, Colonel Dixon S. Miles assumed command of the Railroad Brigade. Dixon Miles was one of the many Maryland born Regular Army officers who remained loyal to the Union when the Civil War began. At the tender age of fourteen, he entered the United States Military Academy at West Point. Upon graduation, he was commissioned a second lieutenant and sent to various posts on the frontier. During the war with Mexico in 1846-1848, Miles led the Seventh U.S. Infantry in a number of engagements winning promotions to major and lieutenant colonel in only four months.

When the Civil War began Miles was a full colonel and in command of the Second Infantry Regiment. Since the army was short of Regulars, he was given command of a division as General Irwin McDowell prepared for his

Camp of the Tenth Maine Regiment at Annapolis Junction, winter 1861. (USAMHI)

march "On to Richmond." On July 21, 1861, the First Battle of Bull Run was fought. Miles' Fifth Division was held in reserve and saw very little action that day. During the retreat to Washington, he was accused of being drunk and soon relieved of his command. A court of inquiry found no justification for the claim but the damage to his reputation was irreversible.[119]

When Miles first took command of the brigade, he made his headquarters at Relay. On March 17, he issued General Order No. 18 that required his officers to give their full cooperation to the conductors on the railroad. This was very different from the attitude exhibited by Simon Cameron. By the spring of 1862, the Union Army had control of Harpers Ferry and was pushing its way south and west. At the same time, the Department of Maryland, still under the command of General Dix, had evolved into the Middle Department with the specific responsibility of protecting the B&O, PW&B and the Northern Central railroads. These two events caused a realignment of the duties performed by the Railroad Brigade. The eastern most station to be guarded by the brigade was now Relay. At the direction of General McClellan, Miles transferred his headquarters to Harpers Ferry on April 7.[120]

On March 28, the Tenth Maine Regiment transferred to Harpers Ferry and its companies were redistributed along the Winchester and Potomac Railroad. Sergeant Major John Gould was sent in advance of the regiment to find quarters for his commanding officer, Colonel George Beal. Gould boarded a passenger train at 9:00 a.m. and was surprised to see that the new Secretary of War, Edwin McMasters Stanton, and a number of ladies from Washington were passengers. Gould detailed his journey in a letter home, which revealed the extent of the destruction wrought on the area during its extended occupation by Confederate forces. At Sandy Hook he noted, "The rebels made rather a poor thing of destroying the bridge. They succeeded in burning the wood and tumbling the iron work over board but failed to destroy or injure a single pier. They tried to break a pier by cutting a hole through the bridge and running off an engine against it. The engine however fell through too quick and instead of striking the pier as they intended went down to "pot" and is there now…" He went on to describe his first impression of Harpers Ferry. "It … was a town of some note, but the ruin, absolute devastation now in its place is beyond anything I ever dreamed of…" In referring to the U.S. Arsenal he wrote, "In a building near the bridge are thousands of gun barrels, burnt, bent or welded together into piles of a dozen." In searching for a house for the colonel he declared, "I felt perfectly sick at the sight. As we climbed the hill through every species of filth, we found houses in every degree of mutilation."[121]

On May 20, Miles reported the troop strength and distribution of units

HEAD QUARTERS
RAILROAD BRIGADE

Relay House, 17th March, 1862.

General Order,
No. 18.

Every Officer and all Pickets of the Brigade will, when required,

GIVE AID AND ASSISTANCE

To Conductors on the Railroad,

To Preserve Order in the Trains; and to Apprehend and Retain in Custody any Disorderly Person guilty of Infraction of Law,

To be dealt with as a Court may determine; the circumstance to be reported to these Head Quarters without delay.

D. S. MILES,

Col. 2d Inf., Comdg. R. R. Brigade.

General Order No. 18 issued by Colonel Miles while his headquarters were at Relay, Maryland. (HFNHP) serving in the Railroad Brigade to General Dix. It is obvious from this report that Miles merely had his headquarters at Harpers Ferry and was not the post commander at this time.

Location	Officers	Enlisted men	Total
Harpers Ferry (Headquarters)	3	0	3
Winchester	35	843	878
Charlestown	30	672	702
Sir John's Run	35	853	880
Opposite Williamsport	7	194	201
Relay	34	852	886
Beltsville	28	384	412
Ellicott's Mills	3	97	100
Monocacy Bridge	32	648	680
Totals	207	4,543	4,750 [122]

On May 23, Stonewall Jackson made a surprise attack at Front Royal, Virginia, which forced Major General Nathaniel P. Banks to abandon his position at Strasburg and retreat through Winchester to the Potomac River. Harpers Ferry was very likely the next target. Colonel Miles began to summon reinforcements and ordered six companies of the Sixtieth New York along with headquarters, staff, and band to join him at Harpers Ferry "immediately." The regiment arrived at Sandy Hook at 3:00 a.m. the next morning. Here it stayed until the following day when it marched across the railroad bridge and through the town to Bolivar Heights and where it went into a line of battle facing the Charles Town Road.[123]

When the Secretary of War was informed of Jackson's return to the Lower Valley, he immediately began shipping reinforcements from Washington by train to Harpers Ferry. These included 3 heavy guns and 300 sailors from the Washington Naval Yard. Brigadier General Rufus B. Saxton arrived on May 25 and assumed command of the defenses of Harpers Ferry. A West Pointer, he had served on McClellan's staff in Western Virginia. Saxton was shocked to find but a single company of infantry guarding Harpers Ferry. The rest of Miles's men had been siphoned off by General Banks to defend Winchester. Troop trains continued to arrive and Saxton's garrison soon swelled to 8,000 soldiers and sailors. Colonel Miles served as Saxton's chief of staff.

Having driven Banks out of Winchester, Jackson sent the Stonewall Brigade to probe the defenses of Harpers Ferry. The Rebels captured Charles Town on May 28 and then maneuvered around the town for two days before launching a surprise attack on Bolivar Heights, and then disappearing into the darkness. Threatened by three different Union formations, Jackson was forced to retreat back up the Valley and recalled the Stonewall Brigade. General Saxton left Harpers Ferry on June 2, and Colonel Miles resumed the dual offices of post commander and that of the Railroad Brigade. On April 25, 1893, Saxton was awarded the Congressional Medal of Honor for "Distinguished gallantry and good conduct in the defense of Harpers Ferry." Colonel Miles would garner no such recognition.[124]

On June 9, 1862, Major General John E. Wool assumed command of the Middle Department. Born in 1784, Wool was the oldest officer to serve on active duty in either army. He ended the War of 1812 as a colonel and was a brigadier general during the war with Mexico. When the Civil War began, the now Brevet Major General Wool was 77 years old and in command of the Department of the East.

Secretary of War Stanton issued the following orders on June 17. "That the military protection and defense of the Baltimore and Ohio Railroad east of Cumberland to the city of Baltimore, and the railroad between Harpers Ferry and Winchester, is especially assigned to the command of Maj. Gen. John E. Wool. Officers on the line of that road will report to him." The responsibilities of the Railroad Brigade now extended almost one hundred miles west of Harpers Ferry. Prior to this, Colonel Miles had exhibited a degree of inde-

pendence. Five times between June 4 and June 6, he reported directly to the Secretary of War on the condition of the B&O bridges in the area he commanded.[125]

With Jackson's corps now part of the Army of Northern Virginia, combat operations along the railroads were reduced to small raids by local Confederate cavalry units. By order of the War Department the Winchester and Potomac Railroad was repaired and operated by the B&O. A direct supply line for the garrison at Winchester, it became a favorite target of the Rebel Raiders. On August 28, a train consisting of two passenger cars and a mail car was traveling from Harpers Ferry to Winchester when it was attacked

Major General John E. Wool. (D. C. T.)

about midway between Summit Point and Wade's Depot by a detachment of thirty men from Company A of the Twelfth Virginia Cavalry commanded by Lieutenant Milton Rouss. When the Rebels heard the train approach, they quickly placed a barricade across the tracks. When it was 100 yards from the obstruction, they opened fire and the startled engineer drifted the train into the barricade and stopped. A second group of raiders rushed to the back of the train and jammed the wheels so it could not be reversed. Then the Confederates hastily climbed aboard the train and captured eight Union soldiers, the engineer and some civilians. Additional firing took place in the mail car and the Adams Express agent, Mr. Lacor, was severely wounded in the thigh when he tried to escape.

Having secured the train, the passengers were taken off and the mail car thoroughly searched. The Adams Express safe was opened and $4,000 taken along with some other valuables. In a mail pouch, dispatches from General Pope to General White were found and sent to General Stonewall Jackson. Their search complete, the cars were set on fire and the locomotive detached from its tender. After heating the boiler to the bursting point, the raiders sent the unmanned locomotive down the line at full throttle in the hopes of causing a collision. With no additional fuel, it ran out of steam about three miles from Winchester. The civilians were released and the prisoners taken to Mount Jackson.[126]

On September 4, Lee's army began to cross the Potomac River and concentrate around Frederick, Maryland. Before he could advance any farther north, he would have to remove the threat to his line of communications by eliminating the garrison at Harpers Ferry. Having once commanded the post, Stonewall Jackson was the likely choice to command the expedition. As Confederate troops advanced on Martinsburg, Brigadier General Julius White transferred his force of 2,500 Union soldiers to Harpers Ferry, swelling the ranks there to over 13,000 men. Although outranking Colonel Miles, he chose not to assume command of the post.

Jackson surrounded Harpers Ferry with six infantry divisions and opened fire on September 13. The key position to the defense of the town was Maryland Heights. After a day long battle with Confederate General Lafayette McLaws's division, Colonel Thomas Ford, the Union commander on the Heights, ordered a general withdraw without consulting Colonel Miles. The next day the Confederates hauled rifled cannon to the tops of Maryland and Loudon Heights and commenced shelling the Union troops on Bolivar Heights. Miles managed to hold out one more day, giving the bulk of his cavalry a chance to escape. On the morning of September 15, Jackson renewed the bombardment with devastating results. After a council of war in which his

Colonel Dixon H. Miles, last commander of the Railroad Brigade. (D. C. T.)

brigade commanders voted unanimously to surrender, Miles issued the order to his men to show the white flag. For some reason, one Confederate battery continued to fire and a shell exploded just behind where Miles was standing. A piece of shrapnel ripped the flesh from his left leg.

At Harpers Ferry, the Confederate Army captured 12,700 men, 73 cannon and 200 wagonloads of supplies. It was the largest surrender of U.S. forces until the fall of Bataan at the beginning of World War II. As at Bull Run, Miles was made the scapegoat for the Union disaster caused by poor decisions made in Washington. Based on the report issued by the Harpers Ferry Commission, it is obvious that had he not been killed in action, Colonel Miles would have been court martialed for "…the shameful surrender of this important post."[127]

Colonel Miles died the day after he surrendered Harpers Ferry and with him died the Railroad Brigade. Most of the units assigned to the Railroad Brigade west of Frederick City had been either transferred to General Nathaniel Banks' command in May or captured in the surrender. The one exception was the Fifty-Fourth Pennsylvania Infantry. This regiment was commanded by Colonel Jacob Campbell. Campbell made his headquarters at Sir John's Run and distributed his 900 men along a fifty-six mile stretch of B&O track between the Back Creek and South Branch bridges. The only other units left were those stationed between Monocacy Junction and Relay. In time, they became part of the Third Separate Brigade. Part of the Defenses of Baltimore, this brigade was responsible for guarding the B&O Railroad between Baltimore City and Frederick, and the Washington Branch between Relay and Annapolis Junction.[128]

CHAPTER EIGHT

UNITED STATES MILITARY RAILROAD

In April of 1861, Thomas A. Scott, Vice President of the Pennsylvania Railroad, was appointed Assistant Secretary of War and given the responsibility of managing the railroad and telegraph services required by the Federal Government. In the opening months of the war, Scott took control of the Annapolis & Elk Ridge Railroad and the Washington Branch of the B&O Railroad. The Regular Army had never fought a war using the railroad before and had no internal component to manage rail operations. The seizure of these lines was the beginning of the United States Military Railroad (USMRR).

As mentioned before, many of the generals and government officials called from civilian life to manage the war to preserve the Union were experienced railroad men. They were supported in their endeavors by their Commander in Chief, Abraham Lincoln. Lincoln himself had considerable experience with the legal aspect of railroading, having been counsel for or against thirteen different railroads in a total of 142 cases. Three of these were considered landmark decisions. The most notable being the *Hurd v. Rock Island Bridge Company* that established the precedent that railroads had the legal right to bridge navigable rivers. Another involved the Illinois Central one year before George McClellan was appointed the company's chief engineer in 1857.

Lincoln was also a firm supporter of the Transcontinental Railroad. Despite a series of Union defeats, he signed the Pacific Railroad Bill on July 1, 1862, which allowed for the construction of the Transcontinental Railroad to begin in 1863. It is this author's opinion that had Lincoln lived, he would have considered the signing of the Railroad Bill second only to that of the Emancipation Proclamation. It is little wonder that Lincoln was the first President of the United States to use the railroad as a political tool when he arranged

Colonel Daniel McCallum Director and Superintendent of the USMRR. (N. A.)

to travel through nine states on the way to his inauguration or that he delivered one of his most enduring speeches from the rear of that train where he gave his farewell address to the people of Springfield, Illinois.[129]

The Railways and Telegraph Act of January 31, 1862, empowered the President to seize and operate any railroad or telegraph company's equipment for use in the war and place its management and employees under control of the military. Due to their ready cooperation and inherent efficiency, the Northern railroads were allowed to operate under their peacetime management with only minor exceptions. The main mission of the USMRR was to repair and operate captured Southern lines in support of the Union Army. The first example of this was in 1861 when Army engineers laid seven miles of track from the B&O's depot in Washington across the Long Bridge to connect with the Orange & Alexandria Railroad in Alexandria, Virginia. Prior to this, all passenger and freight traffic between these two cities passed over the Long Bridge in wagons.[130]

The two names most often associated with the success of the USMRR are McCallum and Haupt. Daniel C. McCallum was appointed Director and Superintendent of the United States Military Railroad on February 11, 1862, with the rank of colonel. Two years later, he was transferred to the Western Theater and appointed General Manager of all railroads under government control in the departments of the Cumberland, Ohio, Tennessee and Arkansas. On September 24, 1864, he was awarded the rank of brevet brigadier general. McCallum emigrated from Scotland with his parents and settled in Rochester, New York. He learned the business of railroading from the bottom up while working for the New York and Erie Railroad. In 1854, he became the general superintendent of that line. Originally, the USMRR came under the direction of the Quartermaster Department commanded by Brigadier General Montgomery C. Meigs and was limited to railroads in the Eastern Theater. Later McCallum was ordered to report directly to the Secretary of War Edwin

Stanton. In 1864, his authority was extended to the Western Theater and he took what had been learned in the Army of the Potomac and applied it to supporting Sherman's Atlanta Campaign. Although well qualified, McCallum did not at first take an active part in field operations. He remained in Washington. Focused on the "big picture," he coordinated the efforts of Northern lines and expedited deliveries with equipment manufacturers – especially locomotives.[131]

In the Spring of 1862, General McClellan moved the Army of the Potomac south to initiate his Peninsula Campaign. General Irwin McDowell was given command of the newly formed Department of the Rappahannock. His mission was originally to protect the Capital in McClellan's absence and later to open a second front against the Confederate capital by advancing south along the Richmond, Fredericksburg and Potomac Railroad. When Confederate General Johnston withdrew south to confront McClellan, every bridge on the RF&P between the Aquia Creek depot and Fredericksburg had been destroyed and three miles of track removed. In order to allow General McDowell to concentrate an army of 40,000 men at Fredericksburg, the RF&P would have to be repaired in the shortest possible time. The Quartermaster Department was wholly incapable of performing this task.

On April 22, 1862, Secretary of War Stanton sent a telegram to Herman Haupt, one of the most accomplished railroad engineers in the country, to come to Washington. Herman Haupt had entered the United States Military Academy at the age of thirteen and graduated in the class of 1835. After serving only three months in the Army, he resigned his commission and became a surveyor for a number of small railroads. In 1840, he went to work for the York and Wrightsville Railroad where he became fascinated with the theory and application of bridge construction. In 1851, he published the internationally acclaimed thesis *The General Theory of Bridge Construction*. At this time, he was the Superintendent of the Pennsylvania Railroad. One of his subordinates was the future Assistant Secretary of War Thomas A. Scott. In 1861, Haupt applied for the

General Herman Haupt, Chief Construction Engineer of the USMRR. (L. C.)

99

same position but was turned down, obviously, because he no longer worked for the company and Simon Cameron was hiring only his own people. Haupt's last prewar assignment was as Chief Engineer and Contractor for the Hoosac Tunnel in Massachusetts. The tunnel became a political boondoggle and was a great distraction for him during the war.

When Haupt arrived in Washington, Stanton requested that he proceed to Major General McDowell's headquarters on the Rappahannock River and evaluate the engineering required to reopen the RF&P as far as Fredericksburg. Having requested the instructions in writing, Haupt replied in kind. "I have considered your request and will go immediately…I have no military aspirations, and am particularly averse to wearing the uniform; would prefer to perform the duties required without military rank… Pay I do not require or care about." Stanton readily accepted, believing it to be a short assignment. On April 29, Haupt landed at Aquia Creek with a steamer full of men and materials for the rebuilding of the line to Fredericksburg. It was soon evident that Stanton had picked the right man for the job. His first notable accomplishment was to construct a bridge over the Potomac Creek in only nine days. When President Lincoln viewed the structure he exclaimed, "That man Haupt has built a bridge four hundred feet long and one hundred feet high across Potomac Creek, on which loaded trains are passing every hour, and upon my word, gentlemen, there is nothing in it but beanpoles and cornstalks." Realizing his services would be needed for an indefinite period; Haupt was commissioned a colonel on May 28, and appointed Chief of Construction and Transportation in the Department of the Rappahannock.[132]

Haupt's next major contribution to the Union war effort was to establish a Construction Corps that was specifically trained and equipped to repair and, if necessary, destroy a railroad. Initially labor was supplied with details from nearby infantry regiments that were neither trained nor interested in the manual labor required to do such work. Haupt was one of the first Army officers to seize upon the potential of using runaway slaves, known as Contrabands, as a labor force. The Military Act of July 17, 1862, allowed for the employment of persons of "African Descent" at a rate of $10.00 per month. Haupt put hundreds of these men to work who were all too familiar with manual labor and eager to work without the threat of a master's lash. Also, by creating a permanent "Corps," he was able to create an efficient work force, both black and white, that was highly skilled in the tasks required to construct a railroad. By the end of the war, the Construction Corps of the USMRR employed approximately 10,000 men.[133]

The farsighted Haupt established in Alexandria a complex similar to the B&O's Mount Clare Shops. Here he not only repaired USMRR locomotives

General Haupt used escaped slaves to create a highly efficient Construction Corps. (N. A.)

and railcars, but collected equipment and supplies for rapid deployment when necessary. Haupt also designed a prefabricated bridge system with interchangeable parts that could be adapted to any situation.

On September 5, 1862, Herman Haupt was promoted to brigadier general for "exceptional and meritorious service" during General Pope's failed advance into Northern Virginia. He refused to accept the promotion or pay, but wore the uniform and signed his correspondence as a general officer. Haupt's reason for wishing to remain a civilian was so he could be present when required for the litigation of the Hoosac Tunnel project. Despite his many contributions to military railroading, his refusal to accept two offered commissions eventually led to his dismissal by Secretary of War Stanton on September 14, 1863. Because of his training and organizational skills, the Army's railroad continued to function at a high level. By the end of the war, the United States Military Railroad controlled 2,000 miles of track – more than England and France combined at that time – and operated 6,330 cars and 419 locomotives. Besides converting captured railroads to the standard 4 feet 8.5 inches, it constructed two of its own lines: the seven-mile connection between Washington, DC, and Alexandria, Virginia; and the City Point & Army Line to support the siege of Petersburg. Never one to remain idle, Haupt published a 310-page book entitled *Military Bridges* in 1864.[134]

Herman Haupt's first accomplishment as chief construction engineer for the USMRR was to replace the bridge over Potomac Creek. When viewed by President Lincoln, he declared "…there is nothing in it but beanpoles and cornstalks." (Miller's)

CHAPTER NINE

THE WINTER WAR

As the major armies of both sides suspended operations for the winter months of January and February 1862, the area between Harpers Ferry and Cumberland remained active. General Stonewall Jackson, the newly appointed commander of the Valley District, was not content to sit out the winter at his headquarters in Winchester. Never one to limit his military ambitions, Jackson proposed a plan to the Confederate Secretary of War, Judah Benjamin, for the liberation of Western Virginia from Union control. At the same time, he would permanently disable the B&O west of Cumberland. Reinforced by his beloved Stonewall Brigade and three others under the command of General William W. Loring, he planned a winter campaign that would first drive General Kelley's force out of Romney and thus secure Winchester and the Lower Shenandoah Valley from Northern aggression. Then he would go after the region occupied by McClellan's forces the previous summer. "I deem it of great importance that North Western Virginia be occupied by Confederate Troops this winter." wrote Jackson.[135]

Jackson's advance on Romney got underway on an unseasonably mild New Year's Day, 1862. That night the weather turned bitter cold and the realities of a winter march in a mountainous region quickly set in. During the first week of the new year, Jackson's shivering warriors burned the B&O's water station at North Mountain, and captured Bath (now Berkeley Springs), Alpine Station and Sir John's Run. On January 4, Confederate forces consisting of two regiments and a section of artillery from Shumaker's battery engaged Union troops guarding the railroad bridge over the Great Cacapon. The guard detachment consisting of only 80 men held out for two days before they were forced to retreat. The Rebels then burned the trestling on the Great Cacapon Bridge and two houses owned by the B&O Railroad. A second attempt was made to disable the C&O Canal by causing a breach in Dam #5. Also on January 5, the main Confederate force halted on the south bank of the Potomac River opposite the town of Hancock. Jackson demanded an immediate surrender or threatened to bombard the town. Only the timely arrival of a Union force under the command of Brigadier General Frederick W. Lander saved the town from capture or destruction.[136]

Not willing to throw his forces across the river against a reinforced enemy, Jackson continued his advance on Romney. General Lander also went to Romney to take command from the ailing General Kelley. Not fully recovered from the wound he had received at Philippi, he was forced to return to Cumberland to recuperate. Lander did not feel he had sufficient force to hold Romney and evacuated the town on January 10. Two companies from the Seventh Virginia Cavalry entered it the next day. It was not until January 15 that the main Confederate column arrived. Jackson wanted to continue the invasion but his men were spent. Their continuous exposure to the harsh elements and a lack of transportation for food and camp equipment made it impossible to go any further.[137]

On January 23, Jackson returned to Winchester with the "Stonewall" Brigade. He left General Loring to hold Romney with his Army of the Northwest. By now, the town had changed hands several times and many of its buildings had been either damaged or completely destroyed. With a shortage of shelter and supplies, Loring and his men were not happy about being ordered to stay at this frigid outpost while Jackson's men returned to the relative comforts of Winchester. At the urging of his officers, Loring sent a request to Jackson to relocate his command for the winter. Jackson disapproved the request but sent it up the chain of command to the War Department. When Secretary Benjamin issued an order to return Loring's brigades to Winchester, Jackson was outraged at what he considered unwarranted interference with his command and threatened to resign from the Army. This he was talked out of, but the evacuation of Romney was allowed to take place the first week of February. Before leaving, the Confederates burned the covered bridge over the South Branch of the Potomac River. On February 5, a Union force under the command of General Lander reoccupied the town. Then General Lander fell ill due to an infection related to his wound received at the battle of Edwards Ferry. He died on March 2. Command of his division was then given to Brigadier General James Shields.[138]

That the Baltimore and Ohio Railroad was now wholly engaged in the war to preserve the Union was demonstrated by a resolution approved by the board of directors in January. "RESOLVED, that the display of the American Flag as heretofore at prominent stations of the Company, be approved and that as the Company regains possession of its Road the National Flag shall be displayed at its principal Stations and shall so continue until otherwise ordered by the Board."[139]

In November of 1861, George B. McClellan had replaced General Winfield Scott as General in Chief of the Armies of the United States. From his headquarters in Washington, he viewed the war in Virginia as one continuous front and the Lower Shenandoah Valley as the far right flank of that front. The key point, both offensively and defensively, was Harpers Ferry. It was an ideal location from which to launch a northward invasion and as long as it was in Confederate hands, the main line of the B&O could not be operated from end to end. Conversely, its occupation by Union forces was a direct threat to Winchester and all Confederate resources in the Shenandoah Valley. It would also allow for the construction of a bridge to replace the one Jackson had destroyed in May of 1861.[140]

A career politician, Nathaniel P. Banks was elected Speaker of the House of Representatives in 1856 and governor of the state of Massachusetts two years later. Seeking to mobilize the New England states in the likelihood of a civil war, President Lincoln appointed him a major general of volunteers in January of 1861. General Banks was placed in charge of the Department of Annapolis in June of 1861 where he was undoubtedly introduced to some of the key personalities of the B&O Railroad as well as the absolute necessity of keeping Maryland in the Union. It was Banks who ordered Colonel John R. Kenly of the First Maryland Infantry U.S. to arrest the Baltimore City Police Commissioners on July 1. The following September he was directed by the Secretary of War to arrest the Maryland State Legislature when it met in a special session in Frederick.[141]

When General Patterson was relieved of his command for failing to keep Joe Johnston from reinforcing Beauregard at Manassas, Banks was named his replacement and given com-

Major General Nathaniel P. Banks. (D. C. T.)

mand of the short-lived Department of the Shenandoah on July 25. Banks agreed with Johnston's assessment that Harpers Ferry could not be held without a much larger force and transferred his three brigades to the north side of the Potomac, preferring to control the town from the safety of Maryland Heights. Thus, Harpers Ferry became a no man's land for the remainder of the year. To protect the B&O repair crews in the area, General McClellan gave Banks the responsibility of guarding the various river crossings between Sir John's Run and the mouth of the Monocacy River. From his headquarters in Frederick City on January 18, Banks reported to Major General McClellan that, "There are now upon our line between Point of Rocks and Hancock nine regiments and twelve guns devoted to this duty."[142]

McClellan's reoccupation of Harpers Ferry required a two-step approach. First, he would have to construct a bridge across the Potomac River that would allow him to move men and supplies into Virginia in sufficient numbers to repel a Confederate counter strike. Then he would begin constructing a new railroad bridge that would once again carry the B&O's trains between Maryland and Virginia. Army engineers surveyed possible crossings opposite Williamsport and Harpers Ferry before recommending a site 100 yards up river from the previously destroyed railroad bridge. It would be a complex operation. First, a standard pontoon bridge would be laid in order to establish a bridgehead on the Virginia side of the river. Then a much more substantial bridge 800 feet long would be constructed using canal boats. The larger canal boats would increase the strength of the bridge and enable the rapid crossing of wagons and artillery and eventually bridge building components. President Garrett was elated at the prospect of reopening his main line and offered to deliver sixty canal boats then in the possession of the B&O for use in the project. General Banks would provide the necessary soldiers to protect the operation.[143]

McClellan arrived at Sandy Hook on February 26 to take personal charge of the operation. The next day he reported to Secretary Stanton that the engineers had completed the first pontoon bridge and that 8,500 infantry supported by eighteen pieces of artillery had already crossed and were occupying the high ground around Harpers Ferry. Work on the canal-boat bridge was scheduled to begin the next day. Unfortunately for McClellan it would never happen. At the last minute, the engineers discovered that the lift-lock they were going to use to transfer the canal-boats from the canal to the river was too narrow by a mere four to six inches to allow the boats to enter. When McClellan reported the disappointing news to his superiors in Washington, Stanton responded with the obvious question, "If the lift-lock is not big enough why not make it big enough?" McClellan was forced to explain that the lock and flood gates would

General Banks' Division crossing the Potomac River on a pontoon bridge at Harpers Ferry February 26, 1862. (L. I. N.)

have to be completely rebuilt and that that would take longer than actually rebuilding the railroad bridge.[144]

Although an embarrassment for McClellan, the lack of a canal-boat bridge did not delay the operation for long. On March 4, work began on the new railroad bridge. Everywhere within the "burnt area" there was a great deal of activity. Banks pushed his men past Harpers Ferry and occupied Charles Town. On February 28, McClellan ordered Brigadier General James Shields, now in command of General Lander's old division, to advance on Martinsburg from Hancock. At the same time, General Alpheus S. Williams was to cross the Potomac River with his brigade at Williamsport and join forces with Shields. Greatly outnumbered, Jackson was finally forced to give up Martinsburg after occupying the town for ten months. In order to keep additional troops from being transferred to McClellan's main army, General Johnston had ordered Jackson to occupy the attention of General Patterson but cautioned him to balance his actions between showing a bold front and not becoming engaged in a battle he could not win. To this end, Jackson remained in Winchester until the night of March 11. Having transferred all of his supplies to Strasburg, he hoped to launch a surprise attack under the cover of darkness that would delay Banks' advance for a few more days. Due to a mix up in the positioning of a wagon train containing rations for his soldiers, he was forced to cancel the attack and abandon the town without firing a shot.[145]

On March 2, the commands of Shields and Williams passed through the now abandoned Martinsburg and marched south to join forces with General Banks. On March 12, the Union Army entered the strategically important town of Winchester and gained complete control of the Lower Shenandoah Valley. The next day the three commands were unified under Banks and designated the Fifth Corps of the Army of the Potomac. General Williams assumed command of Banks' old division.[146]

No longer threatened by Confederate forces, all the resources of the B&O Railroad could now be applied to repairing the main line. During the downturn of business caused by the numerous disruptions in service, management had wisely determined not to lay off any of its workers. Instead, they were reassigned to repairing and building locomotives and rail cars, and stockpiling construction materials so that as soon as access was gained to a damaged section of track, it could be repaired in the shortest possible time. Had this not been done, experienced men would have been forced to seek employment elsewhere or drawn into military service. When the main line was finally restored, there would be an ample supply of labor and equipment to carry the freight.[147]

McClellan considered the construction of a new bridge at Harpers Ferry a top priority. On March 7, he wrote to Garrett in an abbreviated fashion, "It is most important that the rr. Bridge at H.F. should be completed with the least possible delay." Still winter, the frigid temperatures and stormy weather made the task even more difficult. Efforts to raise the trestles were frequently hampered by heavy rains and frozen ropes. The Harpers Ferry railroad bridge was completed on the night of March 18. Remarkably, the feat had been accomplished in only fourteen days.[148]

At the same time the bridge over the Potomac River was under construction, other crews were pushing to replace the track between Harpers Ferry and Martinsburg. On March 4, a team of experts arrived to oversee the project. They were W. C. Quincy, Acting Master of Road; Thomas Haskett, Supervisor of Bridges; Benjamin Uncles, Supervisor of Water Stations; and four track supervisors. Not wishing to wait for the bridges to be completed, large cables were stretched across the river. Barges laden with heavy timbers were drawn across to the Virginia side to replace the line of woodwork 1,620 feet in length on the iron trestling that ran along the side of the arsenal grounds. These were followed by others carrying rails, track fixtures and crossties, all of which had to be hoisted up from the river to the bluff above.

With the Lower Shenandoah Valley free of Confederate troops, repair trains could now move east on the main line toward Martinsburg without fearing an attack. The bridges at Sleepy Creek and Cherry Run were repaired by March 5. That same day, Assistant Master of Road W. E. Porter arrived with a crew at Back Creek where he found a gap in the bridge 130 feet long. He immediately ordered a wire suspension bridge to be constructed as a temporary measure. Five days later trains were crossing on the suspension bridge and work was under way for a permanent replacement. Once they could cross Back Creek Bridge, track gangs pushed on as fast as possible, reaching Martinsburg on March 14.

On March 19, the new tracks had been completed next to the arsenal at Harpers Ferry and the crews were working their way toward Martinsburg. The gap was finally closed on March 29 and full service resumed on the main line the next day with almost 800 cars passing over it between Baltimore and Grafton. Now the wisdom of retaining its workers paid off. Had the management of the B&O taken the normal course of action and laid people off, it never would have had the manpower or equipment to accommodate the abrupt increase in demand. Ever the businessman, John Work Garrett announced a rate reduction on freight moving from west to east to coincide with the reopening of the main line. Merchants in the Ohio Valley who had been forced to pay higher prices to the Northern Central-Pennsylvania Railroad monopoly were only too happy to return their business to the B&O. In the annual report for 1862, Garrett was able to report that the revenue for the months of July and August were the highest in the history of the company.[149]

Now that the trains were running again, it was time to tabulate the damage caused by Jackson and his fellow Rebels on the B&O. The double-tracked section between Harpers Ferry and Martinsburg was out of service from the last week of May 1861, until March 30, 1862, with additional attacks taking place all along the line from Cumberland to Parkersburg resulting in numerous bridges being damaged or totally destroyed. The epicenter of this destruction was the rail yard at Martinsburg. The machine shops and water station were burned. Fourteen locomotives and tenders, 83 rail cars and valuable parts from nine additional engines were taken south along with 36 miles of track. In the same area, 42 locomotives and 386 cars were damaged or destroyed and 102 miles of telegraph lines removed or rendered inoperable. Thirty-six bridges on the main line had been damaged or destroyed, some more than once.[150]

A remarkable amount of work was accomplished during the month of March 1862. Not only was the main line put into service but sidings added along the single-track section to accommodate the anticipated surge in wartime traffic. Water stations were rebuilt at several points between Harpers Ferry and Patterson Creek and telegraph service fully restored. The next great challenge was to salvage and repair as much of the rolling stock as possible. An example of the problems faced by the company are shown in a letter written to President Garrett by William Prescott Smith on March 12. "I found six of our Camel Engines at Duffield with all their wheels under them…All of the main and parts of the side connections have been carried away with all the brasswork, consisting of various parts. Their houses or cabs are gone." These engines were taken to the Mount Clare Shops in Baltimore where they were repaired and put back into service.[151]

An additional task was given to the B&O by the War Department. The same day that General Banks occupied Winchester, he informed General Randolph B. Marcy, McClellan's Chief of Staff, that he intended to reopen the Winchester and Potomac Railroad as soon as possible. Secretary Stanton declared the W&P a U.S. Military Railroad and placed it under the protection of the United States Army. He further directed the B&O to complete any necessary repairs and "…submit expenditure to this Dept." Garrett's response in a letter to Stanton dated March 18, reveals that a positive working relationship was rapidly developing between these two powerful men. "The Harpers Ferry bridge is completed and an engine has just passed over it from Maryland to Virginia. Our engineers advise that our men have rendered secure three bridges and trestled another on the Winchester road, and that trains will run to Charles Town to-morrow. The work east of Martinsburg and west of Harpers Ferry is progressing rapidly, and within a week, we hope to open the entire line. I have pleasure in announcing these facts to you, to whose comprehensive and vigorous arrangements for the protection of the road (B&O) we are so much indebted for the opportunity of accomplishing this work, of such great importance to the whole country."[152]

The spring of 1862 saw the first grand offensive of the Army of the Potomac. Major General George B. McClellan transferred his near perfectly trained, organized, and equipped army of over 100,000 men from the environs of Washington, DC, to Fort Monroe at Hampton Roads, Virginia. His plan was to advance up the peninsula formed by the James and York rivers and attack Richmond from the east. A second force under the command of General Irvin McDowell was to move south from Fredericksburg. In order to keep McDowell from being reinforced, Jackson returned to the Lower Valley and attacked General Shields' division on March 23, at a small village a few miles south of Winchester named Kernstown. Although Jackson was beaten by a superior force, his only defeat during the war had the desired results. President Lincoln, fearing for the safety of the Capital, delayed the transfer of a number of divisions to McDowell at Fredericksburg. Banks pursued Jackson up the Valley as far as Harrisonburg. Then, believing Jackson was no longer a threat, he slowly moved back down the Valley to Strasburg. Unknown at the time, the battle of Kernstown was an inauspicious beginning to one of the most brilliant series of maneuvers in military history. It became known as The Shenandoah Valley Campaign and made Stonewall Jackson a legend.[153]

Convinced Jackson was no longer a threat, Shields's division was transferred to Fredericksburg. Banks, with a force of approximately 10,000 men occupied Strasburg with a small reserve at Winchester. Unbeknown to Banks, Jackson was heavily reinforced. After defeating General John C. Fremont at the battle of McDowell, he marched south undetected through the Luray Valley and attacked a small force at Front Royal commanded by Colonel John R. Kenly of the First Maryland Infantry Regiment. Kenly fought a delaying action which allowed Banks to withdraw his main force to Winchester. On May 25, the First Battle of Winchester was fought. Banks was defeated and fled to Martinsburg. Here he established a rear guard while his wagon trains and main force crossed the Potomac River at Williamsport. At 5:00 p.m., the last of Banks' men abandoned Martinsburg. The B&O employees on duty there were forced to follow suit. Three days later Jackson's raiders burned the trestling on the Opequan, Pillar and Back Creek bridges. The Back Creek and Opequan bridges were repaired on June 6. The Pillar Bridge at Martinsburg was completed on June 8, and regular service resumed between Harpers Ferry and Wheeling. Fortunately, the main line was not occupied to the extent it had been during Jackson's previous offensive operations. All repairs were completed within fourteen days.[154]

When notified of Banks' defeat, Lincoln cancelled the advance from Fredericksburg and ordered McDowell to send 20,000 men to the Valley to trap Jackson. At the same time, Jackson was focused on removing the prisoners and supplies he had captured at Winchester and avoiding the approach of three different Union commands. After sending the Stonewall Brigade to probe the defenses of Harpers Ferry, Jackson led a withdrawal up the Valley, defeating two more Union divisions in the process. Following the battles of Cross Keys and Port Republic, the Union forces retreated down the Valley and Jackson allowed his men a few days of much needed rest. Summoned by General Robert E. Lee to join forces on the peninsula in opposing McClellan's advance on Richmond, he marched his army out of the Shenandoah Valley on June 18.

With Jackson gone the B&O Railroad was free from attack by the Confederate Army for most of the summer. However, a second enemy remained and was every bit as destructive as the "Mighty Stonewall." It was the weather. Throughout the month of April, heavy rains and snow caused severe flooding along the Potomac River and its tributaries. As mentioned before, a temporary bridge had been constructed with great difficulty at Harpers Ferry and began carrying traffic on March 19. Whenever threatened by high water, it was a common practice to place heavily laden rail cars on the bridge spans to hold them in place. On the morning of April 22, the river was running at full flood stage. At 11:30 a.m., the two spans nearest the Maryland side were swept away along with fourteen carloads of coal. Four hours later a canal boat was lifted out the canal by the high water and hurled against the bridge taking out another section and dropping ten more coal cars into the river. By 8:00 p.m., most of the remaining spans had been washed away along with thirty-six carloads of coal. Because of the floodwaters, it was a week before construction could begin on a new bridge. During this same period, several other bridges between Harpers Ferry and Cumberland were damaged or swept away by floodwaters.

The second bridge at Harpers Ferry was completed on May 4. Four hundred loaded cars passed over it the same day. Flash flooding between June 5 and June 7 completely destroyed this bridge. On May 9, crews began trestling the river from both sides. On June 15, the third bridge at Harpers Ferry was completed. While it was being built, a fourth bridge was being fabricated at the Mount Clare Shops. Known today as the Bollman Truss, it was made of iron and revolutionized the process of bridge building. As each section was completed, it was shipped to Harpers Ferry and one by one, the wooden spans replaced with iron. Most of this work was completed by the middle of August.[155]

Chapter Ten

THE FIRST
INVASION

During the summer months of 1862, the war moved as far away from the B&O Railroad as it would get and then slowly returned to again threaten the main line between Monocacy Junction in the east and Grafton in the west. During the respite, track gangs worked to replace the second track west of Martinsburg. At the same time crews worked to salvage as many of the railcars as possible from the rivers and streams to which they had been consigned by Confederate soldiers or washed away in the floods. In mid July, rails were laid from the main line to the edge of the Opequan River to allow crews to retrieve the coal cars that had been run off the tracks the previous year. The cars were sent to the Mount Clare Shops for salvage or repair.

In June, unusually heavy rains fell throughout the Allegheny and Blue Ridge mountains causing considerable flooding along the Shenandoah and Potomac Rivers. On the B&O, the trestlework on the Great and Little Cacapon and Back Creek bridges was again damaged but repairs were completed the next day. On the Winchester and Potomac, things were much worse. The bridge one mile above Harpers Ferry was swept away on the night of June 4 severing the supply line used to feed General Sigel's division at Winchester. Repairs did not commence until three days later when the water level receded.[156]

During the previous two months, General McClellan advanced methodically up the peninsula with the Army of the Potomac and was now close enough to Richmond to hear the church bells ring. On the last day of May, General Johnston launched a counter attack that caught McClellan by surprise. In the fighting near Fair Oaks, Johnston was wounded and General Robert E. Lee assumed command of the Confederate Army on June 1. He fought a series of battles beginning on June 25 that became known as the Seven Days Battles. The end result was to drive McClellan's army back down the peninsula and save Richmond. During the next two months, Lee marched and fought his newly-formed Army of Northern Virginia from Tidewater Virginia to the Banks of the Potomac River.

Meanwhile, McClellan had fallen out of favor with the Lincoln administration for his failure to capture Richmond. Major General John Pope was transferred from the Western Theater to Washington and given command of the newly-formed Army of Virginia. To supply manpower for this new organization Pope ordered Brigadier General Jacob D. Cox to transfer half of his force then stationed in the Great Kanawha Valley of Southwestern Virginia to Washington. Fortunately, the main line of the B&O had been fully restored and the railroad's management was able to show the government what could be accomplished if the Army provided it with the necessary protection. General Cox led his division of 5,000 men, 1,100 horses, 270 wagons, and 12 pieces of artillery to a point thirteen miles east of Charleston, Virginia. From there steamboats carried them up the Ohio River to Parkersburg. While the troops labored through the August heat, B&O employees arranged for their transshipment east. Nearly 400 railcars with their required complement of engines and tenders were assembled. The first troops arrived in Parkersburg on August 21. As fast as the steamers were unloaded the soldiers were transferred to waiting trains that carried them down the Northwestern Virginia Railroad to Grafton. From there they took the main line of the B&O to Relay and the Washington Branch to the nation's capital. By special arrangement entire trains, less the locomotives, were transferred to the United States Military Railroad at the Long Bridge for shipment to their final destination in Virginia. Moving within sight of each other, the troop trains traveled over 400 miles in approximately 40 hours. This long distance troop movement was a complete success. Cox's entire infantry force passed through Parkersburg in only three days, followed by the wagons and horses as fast as the steamboats arrived. Later in the war, the B&O participated in troop movements on a much larger scale.[157]

Having defeated the newly-formed Union army under the command of Major General John Pope at the battle of Second Manassas (Bull Run), Lee informed President Jefferson Davis on September 3 that it was time to invade the North. His reasons were both numerous and cogent. A major victory in Union territory coming on the heels of the previous two would certainly hurt Northern morale. By showing the world that the South had the capacity to wage an offensive war, it was possible that foreign countries would recognize the Confederate States of America as a new nation. Many at this time still believed that Maryland was only waiting for an opportunity to throw off the yoke of "Northern aggression" and add its star to the Confederate banner. As soon as his army crossed the Potomac River, Lee hoped to gain a significant number of Maryland recruits. Finally, the two contending armies with tens of

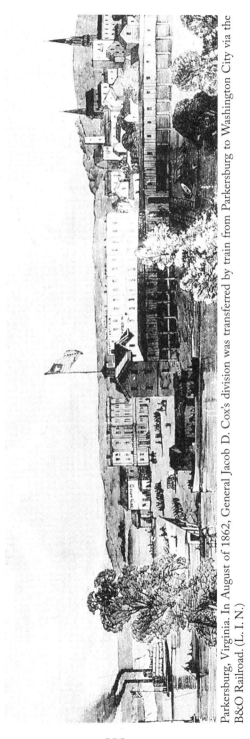

Parkersburg, Virginia. In August of 1862, General Jacob D. Cox's division was transferred by train from Parkersburg to Washington City via the B&O Railroad. (L. I. N.)

thousands of animals and nearly 200,000 men combined, were a constant drain on the Northern Virginia farmers. Acres of grain, timber, and herds of cattle were being consumed at a prodigious rate. Every day that Lee could transfer the war out of Virginia was important for conserving natural resources and allowing the farmers to harvest their fall crops.[158]

Lee's decision to cross the Potomac River from Leesburg and move west to Frederick City was well suited for the operation he planned in Maryland. Whoever commanded the Union Army after Pope's defeat at Second Manassas, would be forced to move his men north of the Potomac to shield Washington from attack and west away from its extensive fortification if he wished to repel the invaders. This not only removed the bulk of the Union Army from Northern Virginia but also opened the main line of the B&O between Martinsburg and Harpers Ferry to another round of destruction. By positioning his army at Hagerstown, Lee could establish a line of communication south through the Shenandoah Valley to Winchester and threaten to invade Pennsylvania by moving up the Cumberland Valley to Harrisburg. Harrisburg was both the state capital and a major rail center for the Northern Central Railroad. Such a threat could not be ignored and Lee hoped to lure the Union Army into a battle of his choosing. Like any other military plan, success ultimately depends on the enemy doing what you want them to do. Unfortunately for Lee, that did not happen.

As the Confederate Army surged towards the Potomac River during the first week of September, Union General Julius White held Martinsburg with a force of 2,500 men, and Colonel Dixon Miles commanded both the Railroad Brigade and the defenses of Harpers Ferry with a force of over 11,000. Following the defeat of General Pope at Second Manassas, George McClellan was called on for a second time to lead a field army. Fully aware of the vulnerability of the two garrisons, McClellan ask the new General in Chief of the Union Army, General Henry Halleck, to evacuate the two threatened points and transfer the garrisons to his Army of the Potomac. Halleck refused and sent orders to Colonel Miles to hold out, "...to the latest moment."[159]

Halleck's decision doomed both the garrison at Harpers Ferry and Lee's invasion of Pennsylvania. Lee could not afford to have a large Union force astride his line of communication to Winchester. He would have to delay his march north until he could eliminate the threat. It was in response to this situation that Lee issued the now famous Order #191 that sent Stonewall Jackson with six of Lee's nine divisions to capture Harpers Ferry on September 10. Lee went to Boonsboro with Longstreet and the balance of his army to await the fall of Harpers Ferry. General J.E.B. Stuart was ordered to cover the rear of the army with his cavalry division and hold Frederick City for as long as possible.

Lee was counting on McClellan's penchant for moving slowly and methodically to give him the time he needed to complete the Harpers Ferry operation and regroup his army. McClellan pulled together the wreckage of Pope's army with the returning units from his failed Peninsula Campaign and took the field with a reconstituted Army of the Potomac in only four days. His mission was twofold. First, stay between the Federal Capital and Lee's army. Second, seek out and destroy the Army of Northern Virginia. By September 13, McClellan was at Frederick with his main force. It was on this same day that two soldiers from the Twenty-Seventh Indiana Regiment found the "Lost Order" #191. Now McClellan was not only closer than expected, he had the precise knowledge of what Lee planned to do.[160]

The next day McClellan moved with overwhelming strength against a thin line of Confederates defending three passes along the South Mountain range. The fighting continued until after dark before all three passes were seized. As he had in Western Virginia the year before, McClellan kept the telegraph near his headquarters. When the fighting ended at South Mountain, the lines were extended to Boonsboro on September 15 where telegraphers W. J. Dealey and J. D. Tyler, having passed out of Harpers Ferry with some paroled prisoners, reported for duty. The next day the line was advanced through Keedysville to provide service for the army's headquarters. A second line was connected with Hagerstown which enabled McClellan to coordinate supply shipments from Harrisburg. At 1:20 p.m. on September 17, he wired General Halleck, "Please take military possession of the Chambersburg & Hagerstown Railroad (C.V.RR), that our ammunition and supplies may be hurried up without delay. We are in the midst of the most terrible battle of the war – perhaps, of history."[161]

Lee withdrew to the town of Sharpsburg where he waited for Jackson to complete his mission and reunite the army. Harpers Ferry fell on September 15. Jackson left General A. P. Hill and his division to handle the details of the surrender and marched through the night to join Lee. On September 17, McClellan launched a series of attacks that turned the quiet farmland of Washington County, Maryland, into the scene of the bloodiest day in American military history. Nearly 23,000 men were killed, wounded, or reported missing. Despite the terrible carnage, Lee remained on the battlefield that night and the next day. When McClellan failed to attack, Lee polled his generals as to the feasibility of counter-attacking. All said no, and the Army of Northern Virginia withdrew that night. McClellan followed the next day but only as far as Shepherdstown. There the campaign ended.

During the Antietam Campaign the main line of the B&O was again severed. When the Confederates occupied Frederick, Maryland, on September 7, they gained control of several miles of the main line east and west of the Monocacy River and the spur running into the city of Frederick. The next day the iron suspension bridge consisting of three spans, each measuring 115 feet in length, was blown up and the water station at Monocacy Junction destroyed. Tracks along the main line and spur were torn up and the station at Monrovia burned.

Prior to the battle of Antietam, Jackson's forces once again occupied Martinsburg and Harpers Ferry. On September 13 the Pillar Bridge in Martinsburg was again destroyed. Harpers Ferry was surrendered on September 15. During its brief occupation by Confederate forces considerable damage was done to the B&O. The newly installed Bollman Truss sections three and four of the Potomac River Bridge were blown up as was the iron span on the Winchester & Potomac line. The tool house, carpenter shop, and blacksmith shop were burned. The Rebels exhibited every manner of destruction for the company's rolling stock. Twenty-four boxcars were burned. Three gondola cars were run into the river. Two crane cars were thrown into the C&O Canal. B&O Locomotive No. 30 was set on fire and left hanging in the trestlework at the west end of the Potomac River Bridge. B&O Locomotive No. 166 was also burned.[162]

During the fighting and immediately after the battle of Antietam the B&O Railroad was of limited service to the Union Army as supply trains from Baltimore were backed up east of the Monocacy River. The one place where McClellan could gain some resupply by rail was at Hagerstown. Because of the long past legal battle between the B&O Railroad and the C&O Canal, the B&O had been forced into Virginia at Harpers Ferry and bypassed Hagerstown before reentering the state near Cumberland. The only line servicing Hagerstown in 1862 was the Cumberland Valley Railroad. The Cumberland Valley was chartered in 1831. It originally ran from the Susquehanna River to Chambersburg. By the outbreak of the Civil War, it had extended service north to Harrisburg and south to Hagerstown. By 1849 much of the track was in need of repair. Rather than replace its rails, the company opted in 1851 to purchase two small engines with a single drive wheel. The "Pioneer" and the "Jenny Lind" were only capable of pulling three-car trains but this was sufficient for the needs of the company at the time. Just prior to the Civil War, the Cumberland Valley began to upgrade its track in order to handle longer trains and bigger engines.[163]

As McClellan's army approached Sharpsburg, the only way to send him supplies by rail from Washington was over a circuitous route that began with the Washington Branch of the B&O and ended with the Cumberland Valley Railroad in Hagerstown. On the night of September 17, Colonel O. N.

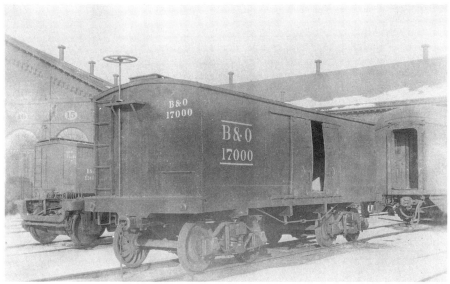

Iron boxcars like this one were used to carry ammunition during the Civil War. (B&ORRM)

Lull, the superintendent of the CVRR, received a telegram from the Secretary of War stating that a badly needed supply of ammunition would be leaving Washington and he was to expedite its delivery to the Army of the Potomac. The train left the Washington Depot at 8:00 a.m. the next day. It consisted of four iron B&O boxcars. At Baltimore, the cars were transferred to the Northern Central that took them to Harrisburg. At Harrisburg Superintendent Lull assigned the company's fastest locomotive, the CVRR Locomotive "Judge Watts," to pull the train and selected Joseph Miller to be the engineer and Henry Ward as fireman. Having previously cleared the tracks, Lull instructed his engineer to make the run to Hagerstown as fast as he could. At 10:44 a.m., the special left the Bridgeport yard and never slowed down until it reached Newville. The train passed through Mechanicsburg and Carlisle at 60 miles per hour. At Newville a ten minute stop was necessary to cool the journal boxes that contained the axle bearings. Then it was full throttle all the way to Chambersburg where the train again stopped to take on water and cool the journal boxes. From Chambersburg the ammunition train did not stop until it reached its final destination at 12:42 p.m. on September 18. From Harrisburg to Hagerstown, Joseph Miller and the "Judge Watts" completed their 74-mile run in one hour and fifty-eight minutes. From Hagerstown, a wagon train took the ammunition to the Army of the Potomac.[164]

The Antietam Campaign represented the first time during the war that

Northern railroads, other than the B&O, would take part in supporting a Union field army during active operations. Herman Haupt, the brilliant Chief of Construction and Transportation for the United States Military Railroad, sent one of his able assistants, W. W. Wright, to take charge of the Cumberland Valley line between Harrisburg and Chambersburg. He instructed all of his agents to allow the companies then being utilized to use their own personnel to operate the railroads unless they proved inefficient. Only then would the USMRR assume military control of the lines and equipment required to support the Army.

On September 18, Haupt conferred with President Garrett and Master of Transportation William Prescott Smith of the B&O to establish a supply route for McClellan's army as long as it remained in Western Maryland. Supplies from the Washington, DC, area would move along the main line of the B&O. Supplies from the north would be carried by the Northern Central to Bridgeport, near Harrisburg, where they would be transferred to the Cumberland Valley Railroad. The CVRR would then run them south via Chambersburg to Hagerstown. From there wagon trains would distribute the supplies to the Army of the Potomac. The B&O was equal to the task but the York and Cumberland, a much smaller line, was forced to borrow both personnel and rolling stock from the Pennsylvania Railroad to meet the demand. To facilitate the movement of supplies, Haupt ordered all private sidings emptied and halted all non-military traffic until further notice. At Hagerstown, he found half a dozen trains stranded and the main line blocked with unloaded freight cars. Haupt immediately seized control of the line between there and Chambersburg and put one of his agents, J. D. Potts, in charge. On his way back to Baltimore, he found 200 loaded freight cars that had been stranded on the B&O sidings near Monocacy Junction for a week. He immediately ordered the freight unloaded and the cars returned to service.

On September 23, Garrett informed Haupt that the B&O was not able to meet its demands because other lines were not returning their empty freight cars. To remedy this problem Haupt sent two experienced dispatchers from Virginia to canvas the rail yards of the Pennsylvania, Northern Central, and several smaller connecting lines and expedite their return to the Baltimore & Ohio Railroad. Realizing the importance of reopening the main line, he went to Harpers Ferry the next day to check on the progress of the new Potomac River Bridge. He quickly determined that the work force was too small and the supply of building materials inadequate for the task. Haupt sent a telegram to his headquarters in Alexandria ordering his Construction Corps to report to Harpers Ferry with 150,000 feet of timbers he had accumulated for just such an emergency. [165]

On September 26, disaster struck on the Cumberland Valley line. During the pending invasion of its state, the Twentieth Pennsylvania Militia regiment had been called into service and sent to Hagerstown to perform guard duty. The crisis having passed, it was returning home to Harrisburg via the CVRR. The morning was foggy and the engineer kept his speed down to seven miles an hour as he approached the town of Bridgeport, which was just across the Susquehanna River from Harrisburg. At the same time a second train had been dispatched from Bridgeport and was heading south on the same track. The two collided head on just outside of Bridgeport. Without warning, the militiamen were thrown about the cars or landed in a heap along the roadbed. Nearly a hundred men were killed or injured in the accident. Although never given the credit, they, too, could be considered casualties of the Antietam Campaign.[166]

As far as the railroads were concerned, the Antietam Campaign made two facts apparent that would have a definite impact on the outcome of the war. First, unlike Southern railroads burdened with the states' rights issue, a large number of Northern lines could come together quickly and efficiently to achieve a single purpose, and second, the generals and government officials running the war were finally giving the B&O all the support and protection they could.

The battle of Antietam was a turning point in the war. The first great invasion of the North had been turned back. If not outright defeated on the battlefield, Lee's return to Virginia was victory enough for Lincoln to issue the Emancipation Proclamation. By expanding the purpose of the war from preserving the Union to also abolishing slavery, Lincoln all but eliminated the possibility of European intervention on the side of the Confederacy. The issue of Maryland was also settled. Lee had received only a few hundred recruits at best and a less-than-enthusiastic welcome from the pro-Union towns in Western Maryland. To be sure, there were a large number of Marylanders who would fight for the Confederacy until the bitter end, but the majority of the state's population would remain loyal to the Union.

One thing different about the battle of Antietam was the fact that it was the first time that a Union Army in the East found itself in possession of a major battlefield. When Union soldiers entered the abandoned Confederate lines on September 19, the true extent of the death and destruction around the town of Sharpsburg became apparent. The bodies of 3,600 dead soldiers littered the landscape while most of the 17,000 wounded awaited medical attention. Every barn, farm house, and outbuilding was pressed into service as a makeshift hospital. The rural nature of Washington County provided few buildings suitable for long term care of the wounded. By wagon and ambulance, they were conveyed along the National Road to Frederick City. Quickly that city exhausted its supply of public buildings suitable for housing the wounded. It then became the mission of the B&O to transfer thousands of sick and wounded soldiers as well as Confederate prisoners of war by train to Baltimore. By the end of 1862, five U.S. Army General Hospitals were opened in Baltimore City and Fort McHenry was utilized as a prisoner of war camp.

Prisoners began to accumulate immediately after the battle of South Mountain. On September 16, Captain Mattison of the Twelfth New Jersey Infantry Regiment, at the time part of the Railroad Brigade, placed his men aboard two eleven-car trains at the Ellicott's Mills station and proceeded to Monocacy Junction. From there they marched into the city of Frederick where they received 1,700 Confederate prisoners from the Army of the Potomac's provost marshal, most of whom had been captured in the fighting two days earlier. Mattison's men marched their prisoners back to the Junction where the two trains were waiting to take them to Baltimore. The Rebels' train ride ended at Camden Station. From there they were marched to Fort McHenry and turned over to the garrison there.

The New Jersey boys returned to their camp at Ellicott's Mills where 8,000 paroled Union prisoners arrived on September 20. They had been captured during the siege of Harpers Ferry and marched into town along the National Road. The next day, four companies from the Twelfth under the command of Major Davis were assigned to escort the Union POW's to Camp Parole in Annapolis. Left behind were about 500 sick and wounded men that were sent to by train to the hospitals in Baltimore.[167]

CHAPTER ELEVEN

AFTER
ANTIETAM

The battle of Antietam took place on September 17, 1862. The next day both armies held their ground and waited for the other to make a move. That night the Confederate Army crossed back into Virginia at a ford near Shepherdstown. McClellan sent his cavalry and the Fifth Corps in a pursuit that was beaten back a day later. Lee remained near Martinsburg for several days before retreating south as far as Winchester. This gave the Southern forces yet another opportunity to damage the main line of the B&O between North Mountain and Harpers Ferry, a distance of thirty-five miles. McClellan made no effort to follow Lee's army into Virginia. Instead, he concentrated on protecting the border of Maryland from further invasion. He sent two army corps to reoccupy Maryland Heights and Harpers Ferry and a third to Williamsport. The rest of his army remained encamped around the original battlefield while McClellan sought supplies and replacements before taking the offensive.[168]

While the soldiers of the Army of the Potomac recovered from the Antietam Campaign, employees of the B&O set about repairing the latest damage. On September 15, a repair crew arrived at the Monocacy Bridge. The area around the bridge had been a campsite of the Confederate Army during its brief occupation of Frederick and was littered with the remains of dead animals and other types of garbage. Once this debris had been buried, the crew began to build a new bridge. The original structure had been of iron and rested on two stone piers about thirty feet above the river. The Rebels had poured gunpowder into the cores of the iron casting and had simply blown the bridge off its piers. The new bridge was made entirely of wood and completed in only five days. The reconstruction train then moved up the line to Harpers Ferry where on September 25, the work crews commenced removing the damaged cars, engines and iron bridge sections that had been wrecked during the latest

Confederate engineers blew the iron Monocacy Bridge off its stone piers before leaving Frederick in September of 1862. This view shows the iron trusses installed at the end of the war. (B&ORRM)

Confederate occupation. The bridge over the Potomac River had once again been destroyed but the piers remained intact despite the fact that the Confederates tried five times to blow them up.[169]

Henry Kyd Douglas was a Marylander from Washington County who served on the staff of General Stonewall Jackson. In his post-war memoir, he described how the Confederates attacked the B&O while encamped at Martinsburg. "…details were sent out to tear up the Baltimore and Ohio Railroad from Hedgesville to Halltown…the ties burned, the rails bent by fire and warped out of all use, small culverts, bridges, and water tanks destroyed, as well as all telegraph lines…" He then went on to pay the B&O repair crews the ultimate compliment. "After all it was a waste of time and energy, for when we left we were hardly beyond the sound of a steam whistle before the road was filling the air with the noise and smoke of countless trains…Four times during the war I saw the futility of trying to stop them."[170]

Lincoln and Stanton were not satisfied with McClellan's sealing the border between Maryland and Virginia. They wanted him to seek out and destroy the Army of Northern Virginia. Lincoln feared that McClellan would spend the remaining good weather months planning the perfect offensive operation and then go into winter quarters as he had when first given command of the Union armies. At the end of September, Lincoln determined to go to the Antietam battlefield for two reasons. First, he would personally thank the soldiers of the Army of the Potomac for their valiant service to the nation. Second, he would meet with General McClellan and try to persuade him to attack Lee before the end of the campaign season. John Work Garrett was asked to arrange the trip and invited to accompany the President in recognition for his services to the Union war effort.

Garrett arranged for a special train to take the President and a select number of dignitaries to Western Maryland and back. It left the Washington Depot at around 6:00 a.m. on October 1, and traveled the length of the Washington Branch to Relay where it entered the main line. Passing through Ellicott's Mills, Monocacy Junction and Point of Rocks, it stopped on the Maryland side of the Potomac River opposite Harpers Ferry. From there the President and his entourage crossed the river on a pontoon bridge. On the first day, the President toured the ruins of Harpers Ferry and reviewed the troops of the Second Corps then garrisoning the town. The next day he reviewed the Twelfth Corps in Pleasant Valley before proceeding to McClellan's headquarters on the battlefield. For the next two days, Lincoln reviewed the troops and visited the wounded. He also met with McClellan and his generals to discuss strategy. Early on the morning of October 3, Lincoln invited his friend, Ozias Hatch, to walk with him through the still sleeping tent city of soldiers. When they arrived at the top of a hill overlooking the vast encampment, Lincoln spoke, "Hatch, Hatch, what is all of this?" His friend responded, "Why Mr. Lincoln, this is the Army of the Potomac." Lincoln remained silent for a moment and then replied, "No, Hatch, no. This is McClellan's bodyguard." The "Young Napoleon" had commanded his last army. On November 5, Lincoln informed General Halleck, "By direction of the President, it is ordered that Major General McClellan be relieved from the command of the Army of the Potomac; and that Major General Burnside take command of the Army."[171]

On the last day, Lincoln and his guests toured the South Mountain Battlefield and then traveled in Army ambulances to Frederick City where Garrett had a special train waiting at the B&O Station on South Market Street to take the group back to Washington. From the rear of the passenger car Lincoln made a brief address to the large crowd that had gathered to see off the Chief Executive.[172]

While the Army of the Potomac remained encamped along the Potomac River, Confederate cavalry units continued to strike at the B&O and other nearby railroads. On October 2, Colonel John D. Imboden led his First Virginia Partisan Rangers in a raid against the bridge over the Little Cacapon River. John Imboden was a lawyer in Staunton, Virginia, before the war. As a captain, he commanded the Staunton Artillery and helped capture the Harpers Ferry arsenal in April of 1861. In the spring of 1862, the Confederate Congress authorized the formation of partisan units. Partisan units usually operated independent of regular army formations in what today would be called special

President Lincoln addresses a crowd in Frederick City from the rear of the special train that will return him to Washington after his visit to the Antietam Battlefield. (B&ORRM)

operations. The most famous of these partisan bands was Mosby's Rangers led by the "Gray Ghost" himself, John Mosby. In 1863, Imboden was promoted to brigadier general and given command of the Northwestern Brigade that was in its self a semi-independent unit that specialized in attacking the B&O Railroad.[173]

At this time, the Fifty-Fourth Pennsylvania Infantry Regiment was guarding a fifty-six mile section of track between Back Creek and the South Branch of the Potomac. Its commanding officer, Colonel Jacob M. Campbell, established his headquarters at Sir John's Run and maintained contact with far flung units via the telegraph. Company K was detailed to guard the Little Cacapon Bridge. Early on the morning of October 4, Imboden's men approached the company's fortified camp hidden in a dense fog and charged over the unmanned entrenchments just as the company was attending roll call. After a brief skirmish, Captain Edmund R. Newhard surrendered his command. About thirty of the Union soldiers managed to escape. Imboden's men set fire to the bridge, water station, and camp equipment and then moved on to nearby Paw Paw Station where they captured a second company in its entirety. When his scouts reported a train approaching, Imboden burned the second camp, cut the telegraph line and retreated with his prisoners and 175 captured Austrian muskets.[174]

On October 10, General J.E.B. Stuart crossed the Potomac River at McCoy's Ferry with a force of 1,800 men divided equally under the command of General Wade Hampton, Colonel William "Grumble" Jones, W. H. F. "Rooney" Lee and four (4) pieces of artillery under the command of Captain John Pelham. Their mission was to burn the Cumberland Valley Railroad bridge over the Conococheague Creek near Chambersburg and capture as many horses as possible from the farmers of Southern Pennsylvania. Their route took them through the towns of Mercersburg and St. Thomas.[175]

They arrived at their objective just after sundown and the town was surrendered by 8:00 p.m. Upon entering the town, the three commands separated to perform their prearranged tasks. Sentries were posted and the telegraph lines cut. Jones headed north to burn the railroad bridge only to find out that it was constructed of iron and not wood. Lacking any tools or explosives, he was forced to leave it standing. Buglers sounded assembly at 4:00 a.m. the next day. Horse catchers and pickets swarmed back into Chambersburg. Before leaving the town, Stuart's men cleaned out the railroad warehouse of hats, boots and anything else they could carry on a horse. In a separate warehouse, they found the ammunition from General Longstreet's ordnance train that had been captured when the Union cavalry escaped from Harpers Ferry a month earlier. This would soon be put to use in an unexpected way. At 8:00 a.m., Stuart led his command out of town. Colonel Matthew C. Butler, commander of the Second South Carolina Cavalry was put in charge of the rear guard with orders to burn the railroad depot, machine shops and government warehouses. Several rail cars of the Cumberland Valley and at least one locomotive, the "Pioneer," were either damaged or destroyed. Within an hour's time, a great pillar of smoke was rising above Chambersburg as the Confederate rear guard trotted off to join the main column. When the citizens of the town attempted to put out the flames, the exploding shells from Longstreet's ordnance train kept them at bay.[176]

Realizing that the Union forces would be expecting him to return by the same route, Stuart first moved east and then south, passing through Cashtown and Fairfield before crossing the Maryland state line. From there he passed through Emmitsburg and Libertytown before crossing the main line of the B&O near New Market. Stuart eventually crossed the Potomac River at White's Ford, about fifty miles south of where he started the raid. A lively skirmish took place between the Union and Confederate cavalrymen but Stuart's entire force made it safely back into Virginia along with 1,200 captured horses.[177]

In mid-October, a new wave of destruction was unleashed on the B&O's property in Martinsburg. The polygonal engine house, the half engine house, machine shops, warehouse, and telegraph office were all burned. The coal bins,

The Cumberland Valley Railroad's "Pioneer" was damaged during J.E.B. Stuart's raid in 1862. (B&ORRM)

sand house, blacksmith shop, and water station were also destroyed. Approximately thirty-eight miles of main track and sidings were torn up. Colonel James L. Lane of the Twenty-Eighth North Carolina Infantry recalled his brigade being complimented by General Jackson for destroying ten miles of track near the North Mountain Depot. "...the men amused themselves when rails on burning ties were red-hot by tying 'iron cravats' around adjacent trees. The depot was not burned at this time because the wind would have endangered private property." A touch of chivalry still remained but not for long.[178]

Not all damage to the railroad was inflicted by the weather or the Rebels. On October 29, a train consisting of twenty-three cars loaded with hay was crossing on the Harpers Ferry Bridge when loose hay sifted its way down through the iron trestling in to the cooking fires of some government workers below. The train soon caught fire and was run across to the Maryland side where it burned itself out but not before all the cars were destroyed. Over 500 feet of woodwork on the bridge was also burned.[179]

In November, Major General Ambrose E. Burnside transferred the Army of the Potomac from its camps in Rectorstown, Virginia, to the Rappahannock opposite Fredericksburg. Lee was forced to recall Jackson's Corps from the lower Shenandoah Valley to oppose this latest move against Richmond. On December 13, Burnside ordered his army to cross the river and threw it against Lee's well entrenched lines on the high ground behind the city. The slaughter was horrific and the Union Army suffered 12,653 casualties, the Confederates less than half that number. As soon as Jackson's men withdrew from the lower Valley, repair crews swarmed in from both the east and west to repair the latest round of damage. It was not until Christmas Day that civilian and military trains were again able to run west as far as Martinsburg. After a disruption of over four months, full service was restored to the main line on January 7, 1863.[180]

Before the year ended, there was a command change associated with guarding the railroad. On December 17, Major General Robert C. Schenck was ordered to relieve Major General Wool as commander of the Middle Department and the Eighth Army Corps. So hated was Wool by the citizens of Baltimore that one city paper proclaimed, "…almost any change…would have been hailed with acclamations."

Schenck had no military training and owed his rank to several years in Congress and the diplomatic corps. To his credit, he served in the field until wounded at the Second Battle of Bull Run. On December 22, he received the following instructions from the Secretary of War: "Your command covers the Baltimore and Ohio Railroad from Baltimore to the Ohio River. The protection of the road and its reconstruction is an important duty entrusted to you. General Kelley's command is subordinate to you, and you will employ such means and force as you deem proper to ensure the reconstruction and maintenance of the road."[181]

VOL. V.—No. 236.] NEW YORK, SATURDAY, JULY 6, 1861. [SINGLE COPIES SIX CENTS. [$2 50 PER YEAR IN ADVANCE.

Entered according to Act of Congress, in the Year 1861, by Harper & Brothers, in the Clerk's Office of the District Court for the Southern District of New York.

Front page of *Harper's Weekly* depicting the Wheeling statehood convention held on June 11, 1861. (Richard Wolf Collection)

CHAPTER TWELVE

WEST VIRGINIA

The aggressive action taken by the Union Army during the Spring of 1861 not only secured a vast section of the Baltimore and Ohio and the Northwestern Virginia railroads, it drove the Virginia state forces out of a region that had voted decidedly against secession. This allowed the citizens of these far western counties of Virginia to begin the process that ultimately led to statehood. It was an extremely complex legal process that would take two years to complete.

By 1860, Virginians living between the Atlantic Coast and the Shenandoah Valley were united economically and politically by a system of railroads, canals and turnpikes, as well as a significant investment in slavery. The residents of those counties lying west of the Allegheny Mountains resented the lack of internal improvements and considered themselves under-represented in the State Legislature. The difficult terrain precluded the pursuit of plantation agriculture or the application of slavery on a large scale. Businessmen engaged in mining, lumbering, and the newly-developed oil industry looked to the north and west to market their products and the B&O Railroad as their delivery system.

The long simmering animosity between the Trans-Allegheny, Piedmont and Tidewater regions of Virginia was exemplified in the 1840 Virginia State ordinance that made it a treasonous offense for anyone to discuss statehood in Western Virginia. The tipping point came on April 17, 1861, when the Virginia convention passed an Ordinance of Secession by a vote of 88 to 55. Most of the dissenting votes came from delegates representing the western counties, some of whom had to flee for their lives after voicing their protests.[182]

The First Wheeling Convention was held May 13-15. Direct action was hindered by the fact that the statewide referendum to approve Virginia's Ordinance of Secession was not scheduled until May 23. Realizing the referendum was a mere formality, the delegates agreed to wait until after the

Francis Pierpont. He was recognized as the Union Governor of Virginia by President Lincoln in 1861. (*Loyal West Virginia*)

measure had passed so that they would be on firm ground when confronting secession.[183]

The Second Wheeling Convention opened on June 11. Ninety-three delegates were in attendance representing thirty-two of the far western counties. To achieve statehood, its proponents would need to clear a number of legal hurdles and gain the support of the Lincoln administration. The greatest of these was Article IV, Section 3, of the United States Constitution, which states in part that new states may be admitted by Congress into the Union, but that no state shall be formed or erected within the jurisdiction of any other state without the consent of the legislatures of the states concerned as well as the Congress. In short, only the legislature of Virginia could approve the creation of a new state within its borders.

Their solution to this dilemma was as brilliant as it was bold. Acting on Lincoln's belief that secession was unconstitutional and therefore illegal; the delegates in Wheeling declared that the governor and all other government officials in Richmond had abdicated their offices by joining the Confederacy. On June 19, the Second Wheeling Convention passed an ordinance that created a reorganized government for the state of Virginia and elected Francis Pierpont Governor the next day. John S. Carlile and Waitman T. Willey were elected to fill the vacancies in the U.S. Senate. Those members currently serving in Congress from the region retained their seats. Lincoln, always cautious not to give the Confederacy any official recognition and at the same time eager to add support for his war measures both on the battlefield and in Congress, agreed and recognized Francis Pierpont as the legal governor of Virginia.

A formal acknowledgement of Pierpont's authority came in a letter from Secretary of State Simon Cameron on June 25, 1861.

"Hon. John S. Carlile, Wheeling, Va.:

Sir: As the President has now been appealed to by his excellency Governor Pierpoint to aid in repelling the Southern marauders and their confederates from Virginia, you are requested to take your instructions from him in organizing forces in Virginia for that purpose, and the company and field officers of the troops now or hereafter to be organized will be commissioned by him.

Allow me to tender to you my sincere thanks for the patriotism, intrepidity, and intelligence which have characterized your intercourse with this Department in the trying times during which you have aided its efforts." [184]

Next, the delegates had to acquire a mandate from the general population for the creation of a new state. A referendum was scheduled to take place October 24, with balloting for or against an "ordinance of dismemberment" from the state of Virginia and the selection of delegates for a Constitutional Convention should the question pass. The bill authorizing the referendum specifically designated thirty-nine counties to be included and invited others to participate in the process. The vote was by any measure overwhelmingly in favor of a new state: 18,408 for and 781 against.

The Constitutional Convention convened in Wheeling on November 26. At stake was approximately 25% of Virginia's land mass, 32% of its white population, and nearly all of its mineral resources. One of the first items of business was the selection of a name for the new state. Kanawha, a reference to the Kanawha Valley through which both the Great Kanawha River and the

James River and Kanawha Turnpike traverse in the southern portion of the state, was first put forth. Wishing to retain a portion of their original identity, Western Virginia was considered before West Virginia was finally agreed on.

The delegates were then confronted with their most serious challenge – to define the borders of the state they wished to create. The Ohio River settled the matter in the west and the straight as an arrow Pennsylvania state line supplied the eastern boundary for the panhandle counties of Marshall, Ohio, Brooke and Hancock. Although the mountain range that had long separated the two Virginias would appear to have been the default answer, attempts were made to add or subtract on both sides of the Allegheny range. At this point, a non-geographical element was thrust into the debate.[185]

The Baltimore and Ohio Railroad was a mainstay in the economic life for many of the western counties. Its iron rails linked the region with markets in the Ohio Valley and the port of Baltimore. Over the years, it brought both immigrants and employment to the very people that sought independence from the Old Dominion. Unfortunately, its main line did not conform to a strict delineation by the Allegheny Mountains. It crossed the Potomac River at Harpers Ferry in the lower end of the Shenandoah Valley and traveled along the south bank of the river through Martinsburg and crossed back into Maryland about eight miles east of Cumberland. From there it ran west through Oakland and re-entered Virginia near Cranberry Summit. The state of Virginia and the Confederate government had already demonstrated a willingness to destroy what it could not possess. On September 15, 1862, Governor John Letcher declared in a message to the Virginia Legislature, "The Baltimore and Ohio railroad has been a positive nuisance to this state, from the opening of this war to the present time; and unless its management shall hereafter be in friendly hands, and the government under which it exists be part of the Confederacy, it must be abated…"

Both John Work Garrett and the founding fathers of West Virginia knew the B&O must be kept beyond the influence of the Confederacy both during and after the war. Peter G. Van Winkle was both a delegate from Wood County and president of the Northwestern Virginia Railroad. He continuously stressed the economic importance of the B&O Railroad on the mountain counties and the need for an uninterrupted connection between West Virginia and Maryland. Gordon Battelle of Ohio County put a finer point on it. He expressed a desire "…to have every rod of the great improvement within the limits of this new state." To achieve this, counties east of the Allegheny Mountains, whether they had voted for secession or not, would have to be included in the new state. Thus, the counties of Pendleton, Hardy, Hampshire, Jefferson, Berkeley and Morgan, due to their particular association with the B&O Railroad, were to become a part of the new state of West Virginia and its southeastern boundary to be adjacent to the state of Maryland.[186]

One final issue needed to be resolved before applying to the Federal government for admission to the Union and that was slavery. While only 5% of Virginia's slave population resided in the western counties, it was legal and the Valley counties were from the other side of the mountain. Berkeley, Jefferson and Morgan were heavily invested in the "Peculiar Institution." To abolish slavery without adequate compensation would alienate these three critical railroad counties as well as the minimum number of slaveholders elsewhere in Western Virginia. The delegates side-stepped the issue by declaring that future importation of slaves would be prohibited.[187]

The Constitution now in its final form, a referendum was held for its approval. On April 3, 1862, the document was accepted in the fifty counties that would compose the new state of West Virginia by a vote of 18,862 to 514. On May 29, Senator Waitman Willey, one of the new senators of the Restored Government of Virginia, introduced a bill authorizing West Virginia's statehood. The bill quickly became a victim of the debate between the immediate and gradual emancipation of slaves. It must be remembered that at this time Lincoln had not yet issued the Emancipation Proclamation. Senator Willey then introduced an amendment that specified the terms for gradual emancipation which was accepted, and the bill moved to the House of Representatives where it languished for six months before coming to the floor. It passed on December 10 and was sent to the President for his signature. Lincoln delayed his approval as he once again reviewed the legality of the entire process. Attorney General Edward Bates considered it unconstitutional and warned that such activity could spawn divisions in other states that Lincoln hoped to return to the Union in one piece. This was not too farfetched, as similar circumstances existed in eastern Tennessee and western North Carolina.

On January 1, 1863, The Emancipation Proclamation took effect. At the same time, President Lincoln announced that he had signed the West Virginia statehood bill the day before. The great irony was that a slave state was admitted to the Union at the same time slavery was abolished in the Confederacy.[188]

With statehood now in their grasp, the delegates met once more in Wheeling on February 12 to approve the gradual emancipation amendment and set March 26 as the date for a public referendum on the amendment which passed by a vote of 28,453 to 572. Lincoln issued a proclamation setting June 20, 1863, as the date West Virginia would become the thirty-fifth state in the Union. On May 28, an election was held to choose a governor, state legislature and other officials necessary prior to statehood. Arthur Boreman of Wood County was elected the first governor of West Virginia.[189]

Arthur I. Boreman, the First Governor of the State of West Virginia. (*Loyal West Virginia*)

While the Mountaineers' spirit was the ultimate driving force behind the statehood of West Virginia, it is fair to say that the Baltimore & Ohio Railroad was a major supporter and contributing factor to their success. When the state's Legislature met for the first time, it commissioned an artist to design the official state seal. The reverse side of the Great Seal of West Virginia contains a depiction of the Tray Run Viaduct near Rowlesburg. One of the most famous bridges ever built by the railroad, it is a fitting acknowledgement of the relationship between the People of West Virginia and the B&O Railroad.

CHAPTER THIRTEEN

THE JONES-
IMBODEN RAID

The B&O Railroad started the year 1863 off on a positive note. Most of the damage incurred during the Antietam Campaign had been repaired by the first week of January. On January 5, Major General Schenck, the new commander of the Middle Department, reported directly to President Lincoln, "The last rail was laid, completing the reconstruction of the Baltimore and Ohio Railroad, to-day. Trains will run through from Baltimore to Wheeling to-morrow." This was the first time the main line had been fully operational since September 5 of the previous year.[190]

That the Federal Government was now committed to protecting the B&O Railroad and its connecting carriers is reflected in the number of troops assigned to that duty within the Middle Department's Eighth Army Corps as of January 10, 1863.

Railroad Division – Brigadier General Benjamin F. Kelley

First Brigade – Colonel James A. Mulligan
23rd Illinois, Maj. Charles E. Moore
14th West Virginia, Col. Andrew S. Core
15th West Virginia, Lt. Col. M. McCaslin

Ringgold Bat. PA Cavalry, Capt. G. Work

Mulligan's IL Battery, Capt. John Rourke

Second Brigade – Colonel N. Wilkinson
6th West Virginia, Maj. John H. Showalter
11th West Virginia, Lt. Col. Daniel Frost
15th West Virginia, Co. G, Capt. S. F. Shaw
Wheeling City Guard, Capt. R. Hamilton

Third Brigade – Colonel Robert Bruce
2nd MD Potomac Home Brigade – Lt. Col. Porter
1st West Virginia, Lt. Col. J. Weddle
2nd MD Potomac Home Brigade, Co. F,
Capt. Summers
Washington Co, PA Cavalry,
Capt. A. J. Greenfield
6th West Virginia Inf. Co. C, Capt. T. A. Maulsby

Maryland Brigade – Colonel John R. Kenly
1st Maryland, Colonel Nathan T. Dushane
4th Maryland, Lt. Col. R. N. Bowerman
6th Maryland, Colonel George R. Howard
7th Maryland, Lt. Col. Charles E. Phelps

3ʳᵈ WV Cavalry, CO. H, Lt. W. H. Flesher
1ˢᵗ West Virginia Light Artillery

8ᵗʰ Maryland, Col. Andrew W. Denison
1ˢᵗ MD Cavalry Co. H & I, Maj. C. H. Russell
Baltimore Light Artillery, Capt. F. W. Alexander
17ᵗʰ IN Battery, Capt. M. L. Miner
6ᵗʰ NY Heavy Artillery, Col. William H. Morris

Defenses of Baltimore

First Separate Brigade – Brig. Gen. Lockwood
1ˢᵗ MD Eastern Shore, Col. James Wallace
2ⁿᵈ MD Eastern Shore, Lt. Col. E. E. Massey
Independent Cavalry Co., Capt. W. P. Smith
Purnell Legion Cav., Co. A, Capt. R. E. Duval

Second Separate Brigade. Gen. W. W. Morris
18ᵗʰ Connecticut, Col. William G. Ely
129ᵗʰ New York, Col. Peter A. Porter
150ᵗʰ New York, Col. J. H. Ketcham
151ˢᵗ New York, Col. William Emerson
Purnell Legion (MD) Cav., Capt. T. Clayton
5ᵗʰ New York Artillery, Col. S. Graham
2ⁿᵈ U.S. Artillery, Battery I, Lt. Thomas Grey
175ᵗʰ PA Militia, 2 companies

Defenses of the Upper Potomac

1ˢᵗ New York Cavalry, Colonel A. T. McReynolds
54ᵗʰ Pennsylvania, Colonel J. M. Campbell
Maryland Potomac Home Brigade Cavalry, one company, Capt. William Firey
12ᵗʰ Illinois Cavalry, Lt. Col. Hasbrouck Davis
12ᵗʰ Pennsylvania Cavalry, Col. Lewis B. Pierce
14ᵗʰ Pennsylvania Cavalry, Col. J. M. Schoonmaker
Nevin's Pennsylvania Battery, Capt. J. I. Nevin

Troops Not Brigaded

Frederick, Maryland, Col. S. H. Allen
3ʳᵈ Delaware, Lt. Col. S. H. Jenkins
Purnell Legion, Lt. Col. B. L. Simpson

Relay, Maryland
138ᵗʰ Pennsylvania, Col. C. L. K. Sumwalt

Monocacy Bridge
14ᵗʰ New Jersey, Col. William S. Truex

Fort Delaware, Lt. Col. D. D. Perkins
Pennsylvania Marine and Fortification
Artillery, Battery A, Capt. J. S. Stevenson

Annapolis, Maryland, Col. J. F. Staunton
67ᵗʰ Pennsylvania, Lt. Col. H. B. Burnham
Purnell Legion Cav., Co. B, Capt. Watkins

P.M.F.A., Battery B, Capt. F. von Schilling
Independent PA Battery, Capt. S. Mlotkowski
Independent PA Battery, Capt. John J. Young

Point of Rocks, Maryland
13ᵗʰ Pennsylvania Cav., Col. J. A. Galligher

York, Pennsylvania
Patapsco (MD) Guards, Capt. T. S. McGowan[191]

During the year, great efforts would be made by the Federal government to protect the B&O Railroad and on more than one occasion, great efforts would be made by the Confederate government to destroy it. The first of these was known as the Jones-Imboden Raid.

During the first two years of the war, the greatest amount of damage to the B&O was done along the tracks between Harpers Ferry and Cumberland. For the most part, the area west of Cumberland remained secure once McClellan had won the battle of Cheat Mountain on July 11, 1861. Several aborted efforts were made to attack the bridges at Rowlesburg that General Robert E. Lee had proclaimed, "...would be worth an army to us. (if destroyed)", and General George B. McClellan had ordered held, "...at all hazards."[192]

Rowlesburg is a perfect example of the effect the railroad had on counties in Western Virginia. In 1847, the B&O's chief engineer for the division, James Rowles, opened an office near a hamlet named Vicksburg. Two years later construction began on the main line that was to run westward to Grafton. The track crews completed their work as far as the Cheat River on Christmas Day, 1851. The next phase of construction would require the bridging of the Cheat River and the scaling of Laurel Mountain.

Most railroad bridges at this time were wooden trestles built upon stone piers. The B&O, always on the cutting edge of railroad development, utilized the talents of three of the world's leading engineers to design and build three, state-of-the-art bridges to traverse the hostile terrain. Benjamin Latrobe, Jr. selected the crossing points. Albert Fink designed an iron and wood truss bridge to cross the Cheat River. It consisted of two spans totaling 312 feet in length with a wooden roof to protect the structure from the weather. Then, traveling along the western slope of the Cheat River Canyon, two deep ravines formed by Tray Run and Buckeye Run had to be crossed. Fink answered the challenge by building the first two iron trestled railroad bridges in America. The Tray Run Viaduct was 445 feet long and stood 58 feet high. It is the likeness of this bridge that the State of West Virginia chose to put on the reverse of its State Seal. The Buckeye Run Viaduct was 350 feet long and 46 feet high. The iron for these structures was manufactured by the B&O at its Mount Clare Shops in Baltimore. Wendel Bollman also assisted on the project. He perfected the Bollman Truss Bridge that was fabricated in sections and used to replace the bridge at Harpers Ferry.

The first train crossed these magnificent structures a year to the day after the tracks were laid, December 25, 1852. Rapidly, the small hamlet of Vicksburg became the important railroad town of Rowlesburg. The B&O built a depot there with a 1,320 foot siding in 1853. On February 27, 1858, the town of Rowlesburg was incorporated and named for the B&O's chief engineer James Rowles.[193]

The genesis of the Jones-Imboden Raid was Captain John H. McNeill. Born in Moorefield, Virginia, he had moved to Missouri in 1848 to farm and raise cattle. When the war began, he returned to his native state and recruit-

Trestle work of the Tray Run Viaduct near Rowlesburg, West Virginia. Note the blockhouse in background. (B&ORRM)

ed a company of partisans known as McNeill's Rangers. During the winter of 1862, McNeill presented a plan to General John Imboden for the destruction of the B&O's prized bridges at Rowlesburg. McNeill thought that the flaw in the previous attempts to destroy the bridges was that the attack force was either too large to move swiftly or too small to defeat the static defenses forces guarding the railroad. McNeill wanted to lead about 600 men in a quick strike effort to bring down the bridges.[194]

Imboden was impressed and sent Captain McNeill to Richmond to present his plan to Secretary of War James A. Seddon. Seddon was likewise impressed but would not sanction the raid without the approval of Major General Samuel Jones who commanded the Department of Western Virginia. Jones also approved the plan but declined to commit any of his regiments to the project. He did offer an engineering officer and a team of specialists with their tools to facilitate the destruction of the bridges. McNeil's next stop was at the headquarters of Brigadier General William E. "Grumble" Jones, commander of the Valley District and the famed Laurel Brigade.[195]

"Grumble" Jones was a well-educated man, having received a master's degree in art from Emory and Henry College before entering West Point in 1844. In 1852, while returning to his duty station on the West Coast, his new bride was swept overboard in a

Brig. Gen. John D. Imboden. (USAMHI)

Brig. Gen. William E. "Grumble" Jones. (USAMHI)

violent storm off the coast of Texas. He never recovered emotionally from her loss and resigned his commission in 1857 to take up farming the Shenandoah Valley where he was born. When the war began, Jones was elected captain of Company D, First Virginia Cavalry and later became colonel of the regiment when J.E.B. Stuart was promoted to brigadier general. Jones and Stuart mixed like water and oil and the two soon parted ways. Jones's next assignment was to replace the recently killed Turner Ashby in command of the Seventh Virginia Cavalry Regiment. This proved to be a better fit and he was promoted to brigadier general and given command of the Laurel Brigade in October of 1862.[196]

At Jones's headquarters near Harrisonburg, Captain McNeill gave his final rendition of the plan to General Jones along with its endorsements by President Jefferson Davis, Secretary Seddon, and the others. Jones gave his approval as well, but the simple plan to get in and get out was about to get a lot more complicated.

While Captain McNeill was making his rounds, General Imboden considered the possibility of destroying the B&O Railroad and reclaiming the western counties for the Confederacy. On March 2, he wrote directly to Robert E. Lee, giving him an outline for a far more expanded operation. "The objects aimed at are, first, the destruction of all the bridges and trestling on the Baltimore and Ohio Railroad, from the bridge across the Youghiogheny River, at Oakland, as far as Grafton; and secondly, the defeat of the enemy's forces at Beverly, Philippi, and Buckhannon, and then to enlist in our army the young men of the northwest, and endeavor, if possible, to hold that section of country long enough to overthrow the local government, of which four-fifths of the people are heartily tired…I believe these objects can be accomplished with a force of 2,500 to start with, and 1,500 stand of arms to put in the hands of the recruits I know will join me…" He went on to explain that as soon as the enemy was pressed in the direction of Winchester, General William E. Jones should threaten Romney, New Creek, and Cumberland. At the same time, he (Imboden) would send a mounted force of 500 men to Oakland to burn the railroad bridge there. This would prevent any reinforcements from being sent west from Cumberland by train. These men would then cross the Cheat River and destroy the important bridges at Rowlesburg. With the bridges destroyed, the only threat to this force would come from Beverly and Buckhannon. "…I propose now that two days before my cavalry leave Moorefield for Oakland, I will march from this point on Beverly with my infantry and artillery, and attack that place the same day my cavalry crosses Cheat River."…"Being joined by my cavalry at Buckhannon or Weston, much of the Northwestern Railroad might be destroyed in a few days, and with a general destruction of these roads and bridges will end, I believe, the occupation of the northwest by the enemy, at least for some months to come…" The thought of disrupting the Constitutional referendum for West Virginia's statehood and the bitter memories of his "Granny Lee" days in 1861 may well have brought a smile to the Rebel chieftain's face when he contemplated the feasibility of such a plan.[197]

Lee approved the plan on March 26 and notified General "Grumble" Jones of his part in creating a diversion against Romney. Jones responded three days later with a counter proposal that he take his entire command to Rowlesburg via Moorefield and Oakland and that Imboden assume the secondary role by attacking Beverly with his infantry and Grafton with his cavalry. Once united, they would present a much stronger force against any Union counterattack. Such a plan would also ensure that Jones got a bigger share of the glory. Lee accepted Jones's recommendations and ordered the operation to commence on April 15. As a final touch, General Samuel Jones was to provide a diversion in the Kanawha Valley to prevent any Union forces from being sent from that area to repel the raid.[198]

Before the raid began, General Kelley's Railroad Division was officially designated the First Division, Eighth Army Corps on March 27, and "…charged especially with the protection of the Baltimore and Ohio Railroad from Monocacy Bridge to the Ohio River." Kelley was given command of all six brigades stationed within his area of operation by General Schenck in an attempt to unify the command structure along the main line of the B&O. [199]

Bad weather delayed the start of the raid until April 20. On that day, Imboden led his Northwestern Virginia Brigade, some 1,800 men strong, out of the Valley on the Staunton-Parkersburg Turnpike. By the end of the next day they were at Hightown where three units from General Samuel Jones's department reinforced the column. Imboden now had over 3,300 men including 700 cavalry. A drenching rain slowed their progress as they climbed over the mountain range and into the soon-to-be-state of West Virginia.[200]

Imboden's first action took place at Beverly. At a point several miles from the town, he divided his force in order to advance up both sides of the Tygart Valley River. Imboden led his infantry and artillery units up the east bank of the river for a direct assault on the town. The cavalry, led by the Eighteenth Virginia Regiment under the command of his brother, Colonel George Imboden, proceeded up the west bank with orders to surround the town and cut off the Yankee's escape route to Buckhannon. Advancing through a fog on the morning of April 24, Imboden encountered a force of over 800 men with two pieces of artillery from the Fourth Separate Brigade commanded by Colonel George R. Latham of the Second West Virginia Infantry. Latham made a personal reconnaissance with his two companies of cavalry and was surprised to find the Rebels so far west of where they were supposed to be.

Latham put his men in a strong defensive position just south of the town and waited. By now, the fog had cleared and Imboden was able to see that a frontal assault would be very costly. He ordered his men to engage the enemy at long range and sent a third force on a flank march to cut the road to Philippi. George Imboden's cavalry force struck first and drove in Latham's left flank. When informed of the situation, Latham drew back his main force and retreated on the Philippi Road before that, too, was blocked. Despite the daylong battle, losses were slight on both sides. Upon entering the town, the Confederates put out the fires started by Latham to destroy his abandoned supplies. Captured were horses, wagons, weapons, and an abundance of food – all welcome acquisitions for the always-needy Rebels.[201]

Major General Benjamin S. Roberts commanded the Fourth Separate Brigade in B. F. Kelley's Railroad Division. His particular area of responsibility was the area between Grafton and the Kanawha Valley. From his headquarters at Buckhannon in Upshur County, he received a steady stream of rumors concerning a Rebel build up in the Shenandoah Valley, but scouts and patrols found no tangible evidence. The information was dutifully sent up the chain of command and summarily ignored. When Colonel Latham informed him of the situation at Beverly, the general advised Latham to fall back to Philippi. Now with proof that some form of an invasion was under way, General Kelley reluctantly sent reinforcements from Grafton. Meanwhile, Roberts ordered a concentration of his troops at Buckhannon. His defense force soon swelled to 2,500 men when the Second, Third and Eighth West Virginia regiments joined his Twenty-Eighth Ohio Infantry along with Ewing's Battery from Pittsburgh. Fearing a large Confederate force was in the area, Roberts evacuated Buckhannon without firing a shot and retreated to Clarksburg on April 27.[202]

Imboden received false information that General Schenck had transferred six brigades to protect the railroad. Believing himself outnumbered, he ordered a retreat. That night he received a report that Roberts had abandoned Buckhannon. Realizing that Roberts would never retreat with reinforcements near at hand, he immediately ordered an advance on Buckhannon. The Confederates entered the town on the morning of April 29.[203]

From his headquarters at Lacey Springs in Rockingham County, General "Grumble" Jones issued orders on April 20 for the units designated to go on the expedition to meet him that evening at Cootes's Store. From there the raid would begin the next day. Jones's command represented the very flower of Confederate forces in the Shenandoah Valley at this time – four Virginia cavalry regiments plus two battalions and the man who first proposed the raid, Captain John McNeill, with his band of Partisan Rangers. The Maryland Confederates were also well represented with the First Infantry Battalion, the First

Cavalry Battalion and the four guns of Captain William H. Griffin's Baltimore Light Artillery. Finally, there was Captain R. Preston Chew's Battery of the Stuart Horse Artillery and pack train of mules carrying blasting powder to be used on the bridges at Rowlesburg.[204]

Jones's men trotted out of camp at 9:00 a.m. the next day and camped that night at Brock's Gap, a distance of fifteen miles. Fair weather turned foul as the expedition broke camp in a severe rainstorm the next day. After passing over Little North Mountain, they camped that night in the Lost River Valley, some twenty miles southeast of Moorefield. On April 23, they crossed over Branch Mountain and camped at Moorefield. Jones had hoped to cross his entire command over the South Branch River that night but the constant rains had caused the river to flood beyond the possibility of fording it. Time was his greatest enemy. He must get to Rowlesburg before his movements were discovered and the bridge guards reinforced. Jones made a difficult decision. He would send his slow-moving infantry and artillery back to the Valley.

The next day he struck out with 2,500 mounted troops and the mule train to cross the South Branch River at Petersburg. There he was disappointed to learn that the river was still overflowing its banks and the crossing would be quite difficult. Despite every precaution, several horses and riders were drowned and many more forced to turn back because of the current. In all about 300 men were left stranded on the near bank of the river and ordered to return to their camps in the Shenandoah Valley. Jones proceeded on with the main column, having lost a third of his strikeforce before he ever made contact with the enemy.[205]

Jones's first combat situation arose at Greenland Gap with a small, but determined, force consisting of ninety men of Company G, Twenty-Third Illinois Infantry and thirty-four men of Company of A, Fourteenth West Virginia. The Union soldiers had taken refuge in two strong wooden structures and blocked the only way through the gap. Lacking his artillery, Jones was forced to launch several frontal attacks that proved costly to his men and consumed several more precious hours. Leaving the Gap at 11:00 p.m., Jones pushed his men throughout the night. Crossing the Maryland State line, they halted at Red House on the Northwestern Turnpike early on the morning of April 26. Not only had Jones lost time and men at Greenland Gap, he had lost the element of surprise. Union forces up and down the main line of the B&O were put on alert and on April 25, Schenck advised Kelley, "The attempt may be to dash in on Rowlesburg and the Cheat River trestles…Look out for that."[206]

Defending Rowlesburg at this time was a detachment from the Sixth West Virginia Infantry Regiment under the command of Major John Showalter. The Sixth Regiment consisted of 14 companies with a strength in 1862 of

1,483 officers and enlisted men and may well have been the largest regiment in either army. It was formed in August of 1861 with the original designation Sixth Virginia Regiment U.S. The regiment was recruited for the express purpose of guarding the Baltimore & Ohio and Northwestern Virginia railroads. Its commander was Colonel Nathan Wilkinson who made his headquarters in Wheeling. The companies were assigned to guard numerous bridges, depots and hundreds of miles of track between the Ohio River and Oakland, Maryland.[207]

After a short rest at Red House, Jones divided his force in order to strike the B&O at several places at once. Colonel Asher W. Harmon of the Twelfth Virginia Cavalry was ordered to take out the bridge at Oakland, Maryland. A much smaller force was sent to burn the bridge at Altamont. Each time one of these bridges was destroyed, Kelley's ability to send a pursuit force from Cumberland was hampered. Jones then proceeded on towards his prime targets at Rowlesburg with the remainder of his command, about 1,200 men and the mule train. To defend the town and bridges, Major Showalter had a total of 250 men from companies F, K, L and O of the Sixth Virginia Regiment U.S.[208]

To enter the town, the first order of business for Jones was to capture the 339-foot covered bridge that carried the Northwestern Turnpike over the Cheat River. This was done by sending two men galloping up to the bridge and disarming the sentries before they could fire a warning shot. Then Colonel John S. Green led his Sixth Virginia Regiment across the bridge and took up a position where the St. George and Rowlesburg Turnpike met the road they were on. Jones then crossed the bridge and issued his attack orders to Green. Two hundred men under the command of Captain Octavius Weems of the Eleventh Virginia were to cross a nearby ridge and attack the first bridge. Taking advantage of the diversion, Green was to lead his regiment down the Rowlesburg Pike, followed by the Seventh Virginia, and charge into the town. Any Union defensive positions encountered on the outskirts of town were to be bypassed and left for the Seventh Regiment to deal with. Jones would remain near the covered bridge with the remainder of his force and reinforce either party as needed.

It had been a quiet Sunday morning up until this time when a civilian named John Wheeler burst into the Methodist meetinghouse and announced that the Rebels were attacking the town! The service abruptly ended as everyone rushed out to see for themselves. Major Showalter formed his men in a line of battle that stretched from the west end of the railroad bridges to the River Hotel. The railroad embankment provided a ready-made entrenchment. His meager force was augmented by a number of civilian volunteers. Everyone knew the value of the bridges to the army and the new state of West Virginia.

Showalter also sent a detachment to guard the Buckeye Run Viaduct and another composed of soldiers and civilians under the command of Lieutenant William R. McDonald of Company I, to man a line of rifle pits (Civil War foxholes) overlooking the turnpike about a mile outside of town.

Weems proceeded over the ridgeline but for some reason left most of his command to guard his rear and moved against the bridge with only about thirty men. They were surprised and driven off by a larger force of Unionists. Ironically, Weems did not bring up his reserves but simply withdrew to his starting point. Jones's first attack had failed.[209]

As Weems's men climbed over the mountaintop, Colonel Green advanced along the turnpike. When the Virginians entered a narrow pass about one mile from the town, Lieutenant McDonald's detachment of soldiers and civilian volunteers, numbering about forty in all, opened a punishing fire on the gray cavalry. Rather than charge past as ordered, Green retreated a safe distance and ordered a company of his men armed with carbines to dismount and advance on foot to try and drive the Yankees out of their rifle pits. When a second detachment threatened to outflank him, McDonald simply withdrew to a new position a little closer to town. When Jones arrived on the scene, he was furious to learn that both attacks had failed. Although he outnumbered his enemy four to one, he had not yet come to grips with their main line of defense. Furthermore, he was running out of food for both his men and horses and the clock was running on just when Union reinforcements would show up. Reluctantly, he called off the attack and set off to reunite his force with Harmon's command. He was also anxious to open communications with Imboden. Jones sent Lt. Colonel Marshall and the Seventh Virginia to Independence to destroy the two-span iron bridge over Raccoon Creek. The engineering detail with its mule-borne explosives was finally given a chance to show what it could do. Marshall then continued on to Newberg, a town on the main line east of Grafton. Here his men destroyed the B&O's machine shop, engine house, rolling stock and several hundred feet of track. Jones kept the main column moving until midnight on April 27, before making camp a few miles north of Independence. The next day he was joined by Harmon's command.[210]

Following the attack on Rowlesburg, two employees of the B&O, J. C. Sullivan and J. B. Ford, moved up the main line to Wheeling and reported to Garrett and Smith on April 28 that they had moved all the equipment from Grafton north except two engines. One was left at Grafton with six cars and the other at Mannington. In an attempt to move as much of the company's equipment as possible out of harm's way they ordered Colonel Wilkinson to have all freights and machinery from the Parkersburg Railroad at Grafton sent up the line to Wheeling. They went on to suggest that Jones's return to

Morgantown was done to cause panic in Wheeling and his real aim was to by-pass Mulligan's brigade in Grafton and destroy the bridge at Fairmont before moving west to attack the Parkersburg line... a remarkably accurate prediction.

In a second telegram sent later that day, the two men reported that two bridges had been burned near Burton by civilians and that Colonel Nathan Wilkinson of the Sixth West Virginia Infantry had panicked and burned the bridge near Clarksburg because he thought Grafton had been captured. They went on to state, "Bridge builders and materials, with a force of 200 or 300 guards, ...will be sent out tomorrow to rebuild the burned bridges ..."[211]

When Jones first entered the state of Maryland, he sent Colonel Asher W. Harmon with his Twelfth Virginia Regiment and Lt. Colonel Brown's First Maryland Battalion to Oakland to destroy the railroad bridge there that crossed over the Youghiogheny River. They were accompanied by Captain McNeill's Rangers to act as guides. A smaller force under Captain Edward H. McDonald was sent to burn the bridge at Altamont, twelve miles east of Oakland. Once their missions were accomplished, the two detachments were to make their way towards Morgantown via Kingwood with the idea of rejoining the main force at some point along the way.

As Captain McDonald approached Altamont with Company G of the Eleventh Virginia, he heard a train approaching from the east and quickly hid his men along the tracks near the station. To their delight, a ten-car stock train chugged to a stop and the entire crew dismounted and quickly disappeared into a nearby saloon. The Virginians wasted no time in seizing the train and began to search the cars for what they hoped would be a valuable haul. The first few cars proved to be empty but finally two were found to contain bags of oats. The winners this day were the men's horses that had been on short rations since the raid began. Each horse was allowed to eat its fill and their rider took away as much as he could carry.

McDonald then ordered his men to start tearing up the tracks running east towards New Creek. He planned to put the engine in reverse and demolish the train by running it into the railless roadbed. Being short of experienced railroad men, the regimental surgeon, Doctor John Daily volunteered to be the engineer. With a full head of steam in the boiler, he shoved the throttle forward and leaped out of the cab. To everyone's amazement, the train took off in the opposite direction towards Oakland. The raiders then mounted up and headed west to find Harmon's command.[212]

Colonel Harmon left Gorman, Maryland, at 5:00 a.m. on April 26, with a force of between 600 and 700 men. They swept the area for horses and supplies as they approached Oakland. The town was defended by Company O of the oversized Sixth West Virginia Regiment. The company consisted of fifty-nine men commanded by Captain Joseph M. Godwin and was known as the Groundhog Company because of the men's fondness for hunting the subterranean creature. Being a Sunday, many of the men were attending services at St. Mark's Lutheran Church and only a single sentry, Private Cornelius Johnson, guarded the road leading into town. Private Johnson was surprised and captured by a Rebel cavalryman after firing a warning shot that no one in the town heard. As he approached, Harmon sent units to surround the town to prevent anyone from escaping. Apparently, none of Oakland's 300 or so residents were aware that the raid was in progress and the sight of Rebel cavalrymen on the streets of their town was a total shock. Harmon paroled his prisoners and destroyed their weapons. Then he ordered his men to burn the station and any other associated railroad property. A second detachment was sent to burn the 180-foot-long bridge over the Youghiogheny River. This was a single span structure known as a Fink's Suspension Bridge was was made of iron with wooden trestles. It sat thirty feet above the river. The bridge was set on fire and the woodwork between the abutments was destroyed.

Harmon's Confederates left Oakland the same day they arrived and headed west towards Cranberry Summit, the next stop on the main line of the B&O just west of the Maryland state line. Shortly after their departure, a second unexpected event was witnessed by the town's people. A train approached from the direction of Altamont and slowly passed by the station without stopping. Anyone who happened to look up took notice that it had neither an engineer, fireman or conductor on board. The unmanned train continued on at a diminished rate of speed until it became entangled in the wreckage that was once the Youghiogheny Bridge. A construction train arrived two days later and put the engine back on the tracks before commencing to repair the bridge. They also reestablished telegraph service as far west as Rowlesburg. [213]

At Cranberry Summit, (present day Terra Alta, WV), Harmon's men brushed aside a small force of home guards as they charged into the town. A few stores were robbed and the water station and engine house burned. Then the column continued its march westward. The next day Harmon occupied Kingwood long enough to feed his men and search for horses. Then he headed toward Morgantown. On the same day, April 27, the supervisor of trains at Grafton, W. P. Willard, took a locomotive out to ascertain how much of the line was still in service. After surveying the damage at Cranberry Summit, he was making the return trip to Grafton when he was pursued by Rebel cavalry. Fortunately for Willard, the iron horse was the faster of the two.[214]

Morgantown was the county seat of Monongalia County and decidedly pro-Union. By now its citizens were fully aware that a raid was in progress. Unfortunately, there were no military forces available to defend the town. At around 1:00 p.m. on April 27, Captain Frank Bond and one man from the First Maryland Battalion C.S. rode into town under a flag of truce and accepted the surrender of the town. Major Brown then occupied the city with his battalion until Harmon arrived later in the day. The plan was to join forces at Morgantown but Harmon had not heard from Jones since they separated at Red House. Uneasy about spending the night in the hostile city, Harmon led his men out of town near sundown and rested his men for a few hours before pressing on to Independence where he found Jones's camp. During their rest stop, Captain McDonald and his Altamont detachment joined them.

With his entire command reunited, Grumble Jones needed to plan his next move. He could either continue on westward in hopes of linking up with Imboden, which in all likelihood is what the Yankees were expecting him to do, or go north, back through Morgantown and possibly as far as Uniontown, Pennsylvania. The latter move would certainly confound his enemy and at the same time take some of the sting out of his failure to capture Rowlesburg.

Jones's men broke camp at dawn on the morning of April 28 and with the First Maryland in the lead, prepared to make a return visit to Morgantown. By 10:00 a.m., the Marylanders went charging back into town for a second time. Their stay was brief and Jones led his men through the town and across the Monongahela River on a suspension bridge that partially collapsed under the weight of their transit.[215]

What Jones did not know at the time was that his appearance at Morgantown caused an explosion of widespread rumors and panic from the Lower Shenandoah Valley to Wheeling. On April 30, General Kelley relayed a report he had received from Colonel Mulligan to General Halleck. Mulligan's report contained a synopsis of the original plan Imboden had sent General Lee on March 2. "May I suggest you call the attention of the General-in-Chief to the probable fact of this being a grand combined movement to destroy the road effectively and recover West Virginia"[216]

Although Major Showalter had received some reinforcements, he knew he was still outnumbered by Jones and with the B&O's bridges taken out above and below Rowlesburg, he was cut off from further resupply. Showalter decided to save his command and abandoning arguably the three most valuable bridges in America at that moment, marched to the safety of Morgantown. Moving virtually in the wake of Jones's raiders, his men were treated as conquering heroes. Their arrival at Morgantown on the night of April 29 was considered a reason for rejoicing by its citizens there. Their elation was short-lived, however. When Showalter received a report that a large enemy force was again advancing on Morgantown, he decided to abandon that place as well and seek safety in, of all places, Uniontown, Pennsylvania. Leaving Morgantown on the night of April 30, Showalter marched his men hard and arrived in Uniontown at 1:00 p.m. on May 1. Here he received orders from Governor Pierpont to stay put. Disregarding the instructions of the Provisional Governor of Virginia, he left Uniontown by train for Pittsburgh. From there he took the steamer *Starlight* down the Ohio River and arrived at Wheeling at 7 p.m. on May 2. The next morning Major Showalter received orders from an unhappy Major General Schenck to return to Rowlesburg, "My object is to have you return as rapidly as possible to the Baltimore and Ohio Railroad at the point from which you left." Showalter dutifully ordered his men onto a train and headed out of Wheeling bound for the point from which they had left four days earlier.[217]

Anxious to fill the void left by Showalter's unauthorized departure, Schenck ordered troops sent from Kenly's command at Harpers Ferry. Brigadier General John R. Kenly commanded both the Maryland Brigade and the garrison at Harpers Ferry. A Mexican War veteran and general in the pre-war Maryland Militia, he was promoted to brigadier general by President Lincoln for his delaying action at Front Royal which allowed Banks to escape from Strasburg in May of 1862. Kenly sent 820 men from the Fourth and Seventh Maryland Infantry regiments west by train on April 27. Proceeding cautiously through Altamont, the troop train was halted the next day by the burned bridge at Oakland. Colonel Edwin H. Webster of the Seventh Maryland was in command of the expedition. Leaving the companies from the Fourth Regiment to protect Oakland, he marched out of town the next day with his men and arrived in Rowlesburg on April 30. Webster placed his men in defensive positions around the town and bridges and waited for reinforcements.[218]

Upon leaving Morgantown, Jones abandoned the idea of invading Pennsylvania and continued on the natural arc of his raid, heading southeast towards Fairmont where a costly iron bridge carried the B&O over the Monongahela River. His unexpected return to Morgantown had in itself caused considerable panic north of the state line. The occupation of Fairmont would also put him due north of Grafton, where the Northwestern Virginia Railroad joined the main line of the B&O. Its rail yard and machine shops made it a high priority target. To protect Grafton, Schenck sent Mulligan's First Brigade on April 28, followed by the First and Eighth Maryland regiments, and Miner's Indiana battery from Kenly's command at Harpers Ferry.[219]

Defending Fairmont was another mixture of home guard and militia units. They were joined by two companies of the One Hundred Sixth New York and forty-five men from the Sixth West Virginia Cavalry, numbering in all less than 350 men. Jones approached the town with the Twelfth Virginia Regiment, the Maryland Battalion and McNeill's Rangers on the right side of the road and the Sixth and Eleventh Virginia regiments on the left. The Seventh

Virginia would bring up the rear and act as a reserve. He ordered his flank commanders to charge through the town and seize the railroad bridge on the other side. Colonel Harmon led the units on the left through Coal Run Hollow where some of the outnumbered Yankees managed to get off a scattered volley before retreating to the west end of the bridge where they rallied behind Lieutenant Jackson Moore and his men from the Sixth West Virginia. At the same time, Colonel Green led his two regiments through the town with orders to cross the suspension bridge at Madison Street. From there he was to march down the east bank of the river and attack the east end of the B&O's bridge.[220]

When the Confederate cavalry appeared in overwhelming numbers, many of the defenders in the hollow, led by Major Festus Parish of the Twelfth West Virginia, made a break for the suspension bridge to the north. Once across, they managed to tear up thirty or forty feet of flooring before the Rebels caught up with them. At the same time, some of Parish's men took shelter in a foundry building on that side of the river. Each time the Confederates charged across the bridge and attempted to replace the missing planks, they were met with a withering fire that dropped at least one Rebel into the water below. After holding their position for about an hour, Parish's men began to run out of ammunition and withdrew downriver to the eastern approach of the railroad bridge. About eighty men crossed over to the west bank and joined in the final defense of the bridge. Many others, acting independently, hid in the woods that lined the river and fired at the charging Confederate cavalrymen as they rode by. Jones' entire command was now in position at both ends of the bridge and prepared for a final assault when the Union forces wisely agreed to surrender. It was nearly 11:00 a.m. and the uneven contest had lasted almost three hours.[221]

Just as the victors were collecting their prisoners, a train approached the south end of the bridges from Grafton. It carried two companies of infantry led by Major Moore and two brass-barreled cannons mounted on a flat car from Battery L, of the First Illinois Light Artillery commanded by Lieutenant John McAffee. The train came to a stop and, with cannons firing, the infantry leaped out and deployed in the direction of the bridge. The train then backed up to the safety of a deep cut. Some of the gray cavalrymen exchanged their carbines and pistols for recently captured muskets and engaged this newly arrived enemy at long range. Still having the advantage of numbers, others were sent to gain their flanks and the relief force was driven back to the cut where they boarded the train and made good their escape having lost one man killed and thirteen wounded.[222]

The morning had been spent fighting. Now it was now time for Lieutenant Williams to destroy another bridge. Captain John Henderson, who was a civil engineer before the war, commanded the work detail. The Fairmont Bridge consisted of three 205-foot spans and was the largest iron bridge on the main line at that time. It was constructed with tubular columns resting on stone piers. Williams attempted to take out the piers by placing three kegs of powder in three different places. The resulting explosion was loud but did no damage to the bridge. Williams then put the Sixth Virginia Regiment to work loading the bridge with heavy timbers and additional rails to add pressure on the super-structure. He then set fire to the timber and ignited a second series of powder charges. When the smoke cleared from the bottom, the piers and columns remained intact, while the superfluous timbers burned out of control from end to end. Captain Henderson then suggested that they pour gunpowder directly into the iron tubes where the energy of the charges would be contained. By the time the third series of charges had been prepared the sun had gone down. Although less spectacular than the previous two, the resulting explosion was far more effective. The costly B&O Railroad bridge at Fairmont was torn apart and fell into the Monongahela River.

While in control of the town, Jones paroled 222 prisoners and tended to his own wounded. The search for horses and supplies went on unabated. Fairmont happened to be the home of Francis Pierpont, governor of the re-organized state of Virginia. He and his wife had wisely left town prior to the arrival of the Confederate cavalry. The irate Rebels wanted to burn his house but General Jones prohibited it. They were given a margin of satisfaction by

The Fairmont Bridge consisted of three 205-foot spans and was the largest iron bridge on the main line of the B&O Railroad. (L .C.)

being allowed to burn his personal library and the law library he was creating for the new state of West Virginia.[223]

At 10:00 p.m. on April 29, Jones's Brigade marched out of Fairmont. It had been a long, hard day, and Grumble only marched his men a few hours before he let them make camp. Before noon the next day, they had traveled south into Harrison County. Jones now hoped to capture Clarksburg, the largest Union supply base in western Virginia. When he was within five miles of his objective, he learned that the city was garrisoned by a force of 5,000 men. The tired, depleted condition of his men and the lack of artillery made its conquest unlikely. As a consolation prize, he sent the First Maryland Battalion under Major Brown to capture Bridgeport. Charging into the town, the Marylanders received a stinging volley from a company of home guards hidden along the railroad tracks that killed one man and wounded the major. Despite the surprise encounter, Brown's men quickly gained control of the town and captured about forty soldiers and sixteen employees of the railroad.

Jones wasted no time in issuing orders for the destruction of B&O property in the area. He sent a detachment of the Eleventh Virginia to burn a bridge east of town and ordered White's Battalion to form a picket line two miles out on the road to Clarksburg and at the same time tear up the nearby tracks. The demolition engineer, Lieutenant Williams, was assigned the task of burning some trestles near the town. Another group of soldiers drove a freight locomotive and a single car into a stream. Jones then moved on in the direction of Philippi, making camp after dark.[224]

On May 1, Jones entered Philippi. Not being a railroad town, his troops gave their undivided attention to gathering horses and supplies. This part of the raid had been quite successful and he had amassed a herd of about 500 captured horses and cattle, not counting the broken down horses his men had exchanged for serviceable mounts. In order to streamline his command for the final stage of the raid, he ordered the Sixth Virginia to escort the captured herd to Beverly. With them went the sick and wounded and all who felt unable to keep up. With a much shorter column, Jones rode off the same day towards Buckhannon. After making camp that night he continued on the next day and had the good fortune to encounter one of Imboden's men.[225]

The same day the Confederates entered Philippi, Imboden sent his brother's regiment, the Eighteenth Virginia Cavalry, to Weston in hopes of making contact with Grumble Jones. When Colonel Imboden reported back that he was not there, General Jones ordered his command to fall back to Buckhannon in preparation for a return to the Shenandoah Valley. The next day a courier arrived with the news that Jones was only six miles away. He was followed a few hours later by the general himself. It would be the first time in twelve days that the two officers had made contact. After a brief discussion, the decision was made to unite their forces and move on Clarksburg. That same afternoon the Rebel raiders trotted out of town in the direction of Weston. Camping for the night just short of their objective, they entered the town the next morning. As soon as the surrounding roads were picketed, the seizure of supplies and horses began. Jones rested his recently combined command for two days and recalled the Sixth Virginia from Beverly to add strength to the proposed attack on Clarksburg.[226]

Clarksburg was truly a prize to be sought after. It was both the largest Union supply depot in Western Virginia and a major rail center for the B&O. Besides a number of well-stocked warehouses, there was a corral containing hundreds of horses and mules and tons of hay. Jones figured that if the garrison was anything like equal numbers to his command, he could be successful. To defeat a large Union force and capture Clarksburg would be the crowning victory of the campaign. Unfortunately for Jones, the numbers were not nearly equal. He soon learned that the union forces under Roberts and Kenly numbered 5,000 men in fortified positions supported by twelve pieces of artillery. The movement against Clarksburg was canceled.

Despite their disappointment, the two Rebel generals did not lose their offensive edge. Jones decided to again split his command. He would move west with his command and attack the Northwestern Virginia Railroad whenever and wherever possible. Imboden would move south and hold open an escape route through Nicholas County. At the same time, all the captured property and sick men that had been collected at Beverly and Buckhannon were ordered to Monterey in the Shenandoah Valley. Imboden left Weston on May 6. Included in the column was a wagon carrying his aged parents, George and Isabella, who had moved there from the Valley in 1855.[227]

Jones again divided his force in order to hit as many targets as possible in the shortest amount of time. Colonel Harmon led his Twelfth Virginia along with the Eleventh Virginia and White's Battalion to attack West Union. General Roberts responded by sending Colonel Latham with his Second West Virginia Union Infantry Regiment from Clarksburg by train to protect key points on the Northwestern Railroad. Latham left three companies at Salem and took his remaining six to West Union where he received an additional company of the Eleventh West Virginia from Parkersburg. Latham put his men in a strong defensive position and awaited the approaching enemy. When Harman arrived on the afternoon of May 6, he determined these lines too strong to attack with the force he had. Instead, he skirmished with Latham's men while sending a force under Captain Foxall Dangerfield to burn two small bridges at nearby Smithton. His men also captured a herd of cattle before retreating after nightfall. The next day Harmon occupied the small town of Harrisville where he captured and paroled a company of home guards. Then his men wrecked the post office and newspaper before heading out on the Parkersburg turnpike for several miles before going into camp near Cairo, a station on the Northwestern Virginia Railroad, where he caught up with Jones the next day.[228]

Jones left Weston on the morning of May 6 with the rest of his command and headed west on the Parkersburg Turnpike. After a grueling two-day march, he arrived at Cairo. Jones quickly captured the town without firing a shot. Lieutenant Williams immediately went to work, and using the last of his powder kegs, destroyed three sixty-foot bridge sections over the North Fork of the Hughes River. He then turned his attention to a series of short railroad tunnels. With help of Company A, detailed from the Thirty-fifth battalion, he packed cordwood that had been soaked in coal oil between the wooden supports and the rock walls of the tunnels. The cordwood was then ignited and the ensuing flames consumed the wooden supports, causing the tunnels to collapse. Before leaving, Jones burned a nearby sawmill to prevent it from being used to repair the damage and made camp a few miles down the turnpike where Harmon rejoined him the next day.[229]

The Jones-Imboden Raid was about to reach its geographic limits in a spectacular fashion. Jones left Cairo on the morning of May 9 and marched a short distance towards Parkersburg before turning southwest. His final objective was Burning Springs in Wirt County. A company from the Eleventh Virginia preceded the main column and entered the town around 10:00 a.m. followed by Jones that afternoon. News of the Rebels approach caused a general panic among the population that now numbered 6,000. Many sought to hide horses and other valuables while others fled down river towards Parkersburg.

The nation's petroleum industry was barely four years old and Burning Springs was located on top of one of the largest shallow oil deposits ever discovered. Overnight this sleepy town of 100 people located on the Little Kanawha River became part of the largest oil-producing region in the world. Close to one hundred steam-operated wells produced an average of 250 barrels a day of high grade oil. The barrels were loaded on flat boats and shipped down river to Parkersburg for processing into kerosene and lubricants. The B&O was a primary customer for the latter. The sight of such a modern industrial complex must have been a bewildering experience for many of the Confederate cavalrymen who knew only a life on the farm before the war.

Mr. Val Rathbone was both a resident of the town and a major investor in the oil business. When Jones arrived, Rathbone offered him a substantial amount of cash not to destroy the oil fields, with the caveat that the money would have to come from Parkersburg. "Grumble" declined to wait for the bribe and, in all probability, realized that no amount of money the Unionist offered would equal the economic impact the destruction of the oil facilities would have. He ordered every means of production, storage and transportation destroyed. No engineering talent or explosives were required. Only an open flame applied to the raw petroleum – its natural properties being the catalyst for its own destruction. Wells, storage tanks and warehouses were set on fire. As storage facilities collapsed, waves of burning oil flowed into the Little Kanawha River and traveled downstream threatening to ignite the town of Elizabeth eight miles away. Flat boats laden with full barrels of oil were set on fire and cut adrift. They gently moved with the current until their cargos erupted in a violent explosion that covered the surface of the river with fire from one bank to the other. Over it all a plume of thick black smoke rose a mile into the sky fed by hundred foot flames and visible from as far away as Parkersburg. Jones's men rode away that night leaving a perfect vision of hell behind. Oil production did not resume until 1865. Four days later Jones reunited his command with Imboden at Summerville.[230]

While resting his men at Summerville, Grumble Jones received a communication from General Samuel Jones in Lewisburg. Oblivious to the worn-out condition of Jones's men, he proposed a joint operation against Charleston – the future capital city of West Virginia. The offer was declined and the march home began on the morning of May 15. It would take Imboden ten days to reach his home base near Staunton in the Shenandoah Valley. Jones arrived at his headquarters near Harrisonburg on May 23.[231]

The Jones-Imboden Raid was one of the largest operations of its kind during the Civil War and specifically designed with the B&O Railroad in mind. In roughly a month's time, Imboden's brigade marched 400 hundred miles and Jones's 700 miles. The two brigades captured about 3,300 head of cattle and perhaps as many as 2,000 horses. Many of the horses taken were used to offset the huge number that died or were abandoned due to the constant marching and lack of food. Imboden, as Lee had done in 1861, misjudged the sympathy of the people in the western counties for the Confederate cause. Any recruits gained were equal at best to the number lost in killed, wounded and desertions. The indiscriminate pillaging of horses and supplies from both Union and Confederate sympathizers only lessened support for the Southern Cause west of the Allegheny Mountains. On the other hand, the raid did nothing to alter the momentum for statehood.[232]

As for damaging the railroad, the grand prize at Rowlesburg, while attainable, was never touched. Twenty-six other bridges were damaged or destroyed as well as miles of track, locomotives and rolling stock. That service was severely disrupted cannot be denied, but by this stage of the war, the B&O

had perfected the art of reconstruction and the damage on the main line was repaired before the raiders had returned to their starting points.

On a positive note from the Confederate point of view, Jones's commands killed, wounded or captured about 800 Union soldiers and home guardsmen. His greatest achievement was the destruction of the oil fields at Burning Springs. Because of the newness of the petroleum industry, the true value of its destruction was not appreciated until after the war.

CHAPTER FOURTEEN

BLOCKHOUSES

By the Spring of 1863 the Union Army knew it would never have enough men to guard every mile of track and every bridge and station on the B&O Railroad. On March 19, General Halleck issued orders to Colonel George Thom of the U.S. Army Corps of Engineers to survey the main line of the B&O from Baltimore to Wheeling and the Parkersburg Branch for suitable locations to erect blockhouses. He was to report his findings to General Schenck whose department would be responsible for the actual construction work. Thom was accompanied by Colonel William F. Raynolds who was the Chief Engineer of the Middle Department. Within a week's time, the two men had completed their mission and Colonel Thom submitted his highly detailed report to General Schenck on March 27, which gave both a description of the bridges to be guarded and the location where the blockhouses were to be built. It is reproduced almost in its entirety in order to give the reader a better understanding of the scope of the B&O's operations and the challenges faced by Kelley's Railroad Division in protecting it. Also, it should be noted that the damages reported occurred within the first two years of the war and predated the Jones-Imboden Raid.[233]

Colonel George Thom. He surveyed the main line and Parkersburg Branch for suitable locations to erect blockhouses. (L. C.)

"I have examined the Baltimore and Ohio Railroad and branches to the Ohio River, in which service I was accompanied by Col. W. F. Raynolds, A.D.C. The following are the positions selected by us for Block-Houses on that road to wit"

(1)   Monocacy River Bridge – 58 miles west of Baltimore. Iron bridge with three spans, each 108 feet, track 38 feet high. Destroyed and replaced by trestle work. Two large blockhouses – one near the N.E. angle and the other S.W. from bridge between turnpike and railroad bridges.

(2)   Catoctin River Bridge – 72 miles west of Baltimore. Two stone arches each 50 feet. One small blockhouse near S.W. angle, between the bridge and C&O Canal aqueduct.

(3)   Opequan River Bridge – 97 miles west of Baltimore. One span 48 feet, track 58 feet high. Has been burned three times. One small blockhouse on ridge 200 feet from N.E. angle.

(4)   Pillar Bridge at Martinsburg – 100 miles west of Baltimore. One span of 40 feet, track 20 feet high. Has been burned three times. One large blockhouse if not otherwise guarded by troops stationed in Martinsburg.

(5)   Back Creek Bridge – 10 miles west of Martinsburg. One stone arch of 80 feet destroyed and replaced with trestlework 141 feet long, tracks 67 feet high. One large blockhouse near N.W. angle.

(6)   Sleepy Creek Bridge – 18 miles west of Martinsburg. Two spans of 109 feet each. Burnt twice and replaced by trestlework, 225 feet long and 26 feet high. One large blockhouse near S.E. angle.

(7)   Great Cacapon River Bridge – 32 miles west of Martinsburg. Two spans of 132 feet each, track 30 feet high. Burnt three times and replaced with trestlework. One large blockhouse near N.W. angle.

(8)   Little Cacapon River Bridge – 57 miles west of Martinsburg. One span 131 feet long, track 27 feet high. Burnt three times and replaced with trestlework. One large blockhouse 200 feet N.E. of bridge.

(9)   South Branch of the Potomac River Bridge – 62 miles west of Martinsburg. Three spans Fink's suspension bridge, 121 feet each, track 40 feet high. One large blockhouse 120 feet S.W. from bridge.

(10) Patterson Creek Bridge – 8 miles east of Cumberland. Two spans of 72 feet each. Track 23 feet high. Burned twice and replaced with trestlework. One blockhouse at N.E. angle of bridge.

(11) North Branch of the Potomac – 6 miles east of Cumberland. Three spans Bollman's iron truss, each 135 feet and one span 131 feet across the C&O Canal. Track 45 feet high. One large blockhouse on knoll 150 feet S.W. of bridge between the river and the canal.

(12) Everett's Creek Bridge and C&O Canal aqueduct – 4 miles east of Cumberland. Deck bridge, one span 100 feet, track 35 feet high. One small blockhouse on embankment 40 feet west of bridge and south side of railroad.

(13) North Branch of Potomac Bridge (21st Bridge) – 20 miles west of Cumberland near New Creek Station. Wooden truss bridge, two spans of 156 feet each. Burnt and replaced with trestle work 38 feet high. One large blockhouse 120 feet east of north end of bridge.

(14) Savage Bridge – 29 miles west of Cumberland. Three stone arches, each 56 feet, track 60 feet high. One small blockhouse near N.E. angle.

(15) Youghiogheny River Bridge at Oakland – 54 miles west of Cumberland. One span Fink's suspension and wooden truss of 180 feet, track 30 feet high. One small blockhouse at S.E. angle.

(16) Cheat River bridge – 75 miles west of Cumberland. Two spans Fink's suspension covered bridge, one span 180 feet and the other 120 feet. One large blockhouse near S.E. angle and one small blockhouse at N.W. angle.

(17) Buckeye Viaduct – 76 miles west of Cumberland. Iron trestle work 340 feet long and 67 feet high resting on masonry. Two small blockhouses at N.W. angle of Viaduct.

(18) Tray Run Viaduct – 77 miles west of Cumberland. Iron trestle-work 440 feet long and 67 feet above masonry foundation. One large blockhouse at N.W. angle.

(19) Three Forks Run – 3 miles east of Grafton. Three spans of Fink's suspension deck bridge, two of 56 feet and one of 26 feet, 18 feet high. One small blockhouse 120 feet from north end of bridge.

(20) Monongahela River Bridge – 19 miles N.W. of Grafton on main line to Wheeling. Three spans of Fink's iron suspension bridge 205 feet long, track 60 feet high. One large blockhouse south of bridge.

(21) Valley River Bridge – at Grafton. Two spans iron bridge each 200 feet long, track 30 feet high. No blockhouse required as long as strong garrison remains in Grafton. If not garrisoned, one large blockhouse near N.E. angle of bridge.

(22) Trestlework – 6 miles west of Grafton on Northwestern Virginia Railroad. Wooden, 546 feet long and 40 feet high. One small blockhouse near N.W. angle.

(23) Simpson's Creek Bridge #1 – 16 miles west of Grafton, 100 feet long. Bridge # 2, 17 miles west of Grafton, 117 feet long. Bridge #3, 1/3 mile west of Bridge #2, 100 feet long. One large blockhouse on ridges between bridges # 2 and #3.

(24) Trestlework – 18 miles west of Grafton. Wooden, 320 feet long and 50 feet high. One small blockhouse 150 feet south of western abutment.

(25) West Fork of Monongahela RR Bridge – 23 miles west of Grafton. Iron and wood, one span 200 feet, tracks 65 feet high. One small blockhouse near S.E. angle.

(26) Ten Mile Creek bridge – 30 miles west of Grafton. Fink suspension bridge, one span 60 feet, tracks 70 feet high. One small blockhouse near S.E. angle and one small blockhouse near the N.E. angle to guard bridge and tunnel.

(27) Buckeye Fork Bridge (#3) – 46 miles west of Grafton. Two spans 62 feet each, track 30 feet high. One small blockhouse 100 feet from N.E. end of bridge.

(28) Buckeye Fork bridge (#4) – 48 miles west of Grafton. Fink's suspension deck bridge, Two spans 62 feet each and Middle Creek Bridge, one mile west, one span 150 feet long. One blockhouse midway between the two bridges.

(29) Hughes River Bridge – 58 miles west of Grafton. Fink's suspension deck bridge, one span 80 feet, track 42 feet high. One small blockhouse at N.E. angle of bridge.

(30) Bond's Creek Bridge and Tunnel #13 – 72 miles west of Grafton. One span 75 feet long. One small blockhouse near N.E. angle.

(31) Hughes River Bridge and Tunnels # 13 – 72 miles west of Grafton. Fink's suspension deck bridge, one span 100 feet, track 38 feet high. One small blockhouse near N.E. angle.

(32) Hughes River Bridge and Tunnel #17 – 74 miles west of Grafton. One span, Howe truss, 110 feet, 38 feet high. One small blockhouse near S.E. angle.

(33) Hughes River Bridge and Tunnel #18 – 74 miles west of Grafton. Wood and iron, one span 110 feet. One small blockhouse at S.W. angle.

(34) Hughes River Bridge – 75 miles West of Grafton at Cairo Station. One span 110 feet. One small blockhouse at S.W. angle.

(35) Goose Creek bridges number 1, 2, and 3 – 81 miles west of Grafton. Each bridge has one span of 75 feet. One small blockhouse on the ridge between bridges #1 and #2 can protect the three bridges and tunnel between #2 and #3.

(36) Goose Creek bridges number 4 and 5 – 82 miles west of Grafton. Each bridge has one span of 77 feet. One small blockhouse on rise between the two bridges and north of tracks.

(37) Goose Creek bridges #6, #7, and #8 – 83 miles west of Grafton. Each bridge has one span of 100 feet. One small blockhouse on the ridge between the two bridges and 50 feet north of tracks.

General Schenck readily agreed with the engineers' report. On March 31, he issued orders to Colonel Raynolds, now familiar with the designate locations, to take charge of the project. "Colonel Raynolds will give all instructions, direct the progress of the work and make requisitions on the Qr (sic) Master Dept. therefore as needed."[234]

The blockhouses built to protect the B&O Railroad were small two-story forts. Besides fighting positions, each first floor contained a storage room and facilities for feeding the men. The second floors were used for barracks and officers quarters. The corners of the second story were set at a 90-degree angle to the

Colonel William F. Raynolds. He was in charge of building blockhouses on the main line of the B&O Railroad. (L. C.)

Engineer's drawings of blockhouses to be built along the B&O Railroad. Exterior view. This and the following three illustrations are from the same report. (B&ORRM)

first. This allowed its defenders to fire in all directions. The blockhouse was in essence a force multiplier. A single company of infantry armed with long range muskets could hold off a regiment of cavalry for days if need be as long as they had a sufficient supply of ammunition and the attacking force did not have any artillery, which was usually the case. Various designs were later adopted

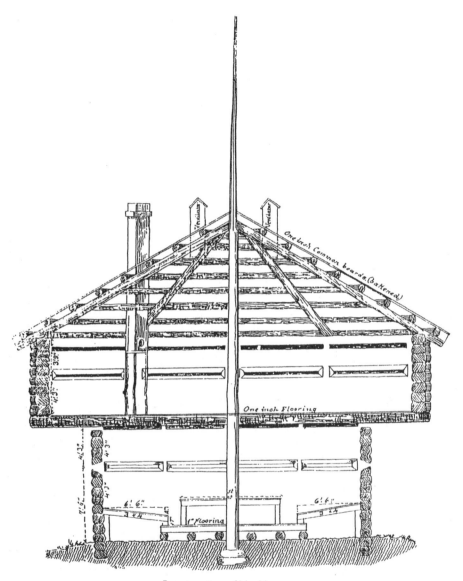

Interior view of blockhouse.

by other departments during the war, but the original concept as ordered by General Halleck was the first time in the evolution of warfare that a specific structure was designed to protect a railroad.[235]

While Colonel Raynolds worked to collect the necessary materials and manpower, Captain Sidney F. Shaw from Company G of the Fifteenth West

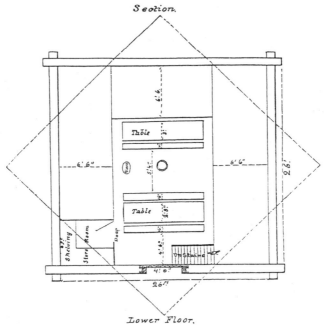

Lower floor plan.

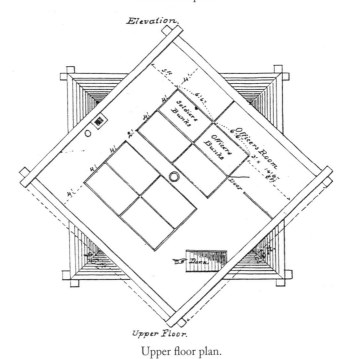

Upper floor plan.

166

Close up view of blockhouse at the Tray Run Viaduct. (B&ORRM)

Virginia Infantry was assigned to manage the actual construction work. In his postwar reminiscences published in the B&O's *Book of the Royal Blue* in 1898, he described how they were built.

"They were barns, constructed out of the largest and longest logs that could be obtained, each barn being from forty to fifty feet square and ten to twelve feet in height. They were timbered on the top to keep the shells out and were notched through the sides for the purpose of shooting through above the earthwork. In building them stone is first piled around the proposed foundation about four feet high, then a deep ditch, four or five feet wide, is dug around the stone pile, the earth from the ditch being thrown upon the stones to a height of six or seven feet to protect the inmates of the house from shot and shell. The whole is surrounded with an abatis; we had no barbed wire in those days and the entrance to the building was made in a zigzag fashion…"[236]

Rowlesburg was chosen as the site for the first blockhouse to be built. Before it could be completed, the Jones-Imboden Raid got under way and construction crews fled the area. As soon as the damage from the raid was repaired, a massive building campaign got underway. Many of the proposed sites were completed by the summer of 1863 and put to the test during the Gettysburg Campaign. By the end of the war, a total of forty-seven blockhouses had been built along the main line and Parkersburg Branch.[237]

Engine House of the Northern Central Railroad near Harrisburg. The Northern Central was a primary target of Lee's 1863 invasion of Pennsylvania. (Gill Barrett Collection)

CHAPTER FIFTEEN

GETTYSBURG

Following the debacle at Fredericksburg, General Burnside was relieved of command and Major General Joseph Hooker appointed the new commander of the Army of the Potomac on January 26, 1863. Hooker graduated from West Point in the class of 1837. He compiled an outstanding service record during the war with Mexico but left the Army in 1853. In 1862, he was commissioned a brigadier general and commanded a division under George McClellan. During the Peninsula Campaign in 1862, a typo in a newspaper story gave him the sobriquet "Fighting Joe Hooker." Promoted to major general, he commanded the First Corps at Antietam until wounded and forced to leave the field. Hooker did a credible job reorganizing the Army of the Potomac and improving morale. He devised a plan to pin Lee's army at Fredericksburg while he marched his army through the Wilderness to Lee's rear. Jackson's brilliant flank attack on May 2 caused Hooker to lose his nerve and order a retreat. Another stunning defeat for the Union, Lee's victory at the battle of Chancellorsville came at terrible price for the Confederacy. Stonewall Jackson was wounded by his own men and died eight days later.[238]

With back-to-back victories at Fredericksburg and Chancellorsville, Lee again looked to invade Pennsylvania. His primary targets were Harrisburg, the Northern Central Railroad, and the abundance of horses, cattle and crops in the southern part of the state. This time his army would be larger, and many believed that a decisive victory in Union territory would bring the war-weary North to the peace table.

Lee's invasion route would also be the same – crossing the Potomac River into Maryland, using the Blue Ridge Mountains to shield his right flank, and using the Cumberland Valley as his line of communication with the lower Shenandoah Valley. To protect his left flank he would again call on the Northwestern Brigade to attack the B&O Railroad west of Martinsburg. Barely two weeks after the conclusion of the Jones-Imboden Raid, Lee sent orders to General Imboden at his headquarters in Staunton, Virginia. "In view of operations in the Shenandoah Valley, I desire you to attract the enemy's attention in Hampshire County and proceed down to Romney, or such other point as you may consider best calculated for the purpose...In attracting their attention, and detaining whatever force they may have at New Creek, Cumberland, Cacapon, etc., you will of course do them all the injury in your power...It will be important, if you can accomplish it, to destroy some of the bridges so as to prevent communication and the transfer of reinforcements to Martinsburg." Two days later Imboden's independent brigade consisting of about 1,400 men and 6 pieces of artillery was on the move again. [239]

The vanguard of Lee's invasion force was Brigadier General Albert G, Jenkins's brigade of cavalry that crossed the Potomac River at Williamsport on June 15. It was followed two days later by White's Thirty-fifth Battalion of Virginia cavalry that crossed the river below Berlin. Lt. Colonel White's men attacked Point of Rocks and drove off a detachment of Means's Loudoun County Rangers (U.S.) capturing twenty men and their horses. He then seized B&O locomotive No. 108 and a train of seventeen cars, all of which were set on fire. Thus began the next great assault on the main line of the B&O that would disrupt service from Sykesville, only 32 miles from Baltimore in the east to the Rawlings Water Station, 160 miles to the west.[240]

The Army of Northern Virginia began to move north from its camps near Fredericksburg on June 3. Following the death of Stonewall Jackson, Lee reorganized his divisions into three army corps under Generals Longstreet, Ewell, and A. P. Hill. J.E.B. Stuart commanded the Cavalry Division. The Confederate Army crossed over the Blue Ridge Mountains and moved north through the lower Shenandoah Valley resulting in the Second Battle of Winchester on June 14. Major General Robert H. Milroy's forces were overwhelmed and he ordered a retreat shortly after midnight, losing 4,000 men and 23 pieces of artillery. General Robert E. Rodes's Division occupied Martinsburg the same day.

At the same time White's Battalion attacked Point of Rocks, a portion of Imboden's force commanded by his brother was approaching Cumberland. The news of Milroy's defeat at Winchester had already arrived and the two regiments garrisoning the town were transferred to New Creek. All rolling stock and removable railroad property was also sent out of harm's way. On the evening of June 17, two Confederate soldiers rode into town and presented Mayor Valentine Buckley with a written demand for the surrender of Cumberland. With no means of defense, Buckley quickly consented. Informed of the surrender, Colonel Imboden led his 350 men and two guns into the city. The Rebels stayed only long enough to destroy the telegraph lines and some railroad property. Then, gathering a number of horses and a few recruits from the area, they rode off two hours later. It was one of the shortest occupations of the war.[241]

General Kenly and his Maryland Brigade were now part of a division commanded by Major General William H. French. French, a fellow Marylander and Regular Army officer, had graduated from West Point in 1837. Having fought in every major battle of the Army of the Potomac from the Peninsula to Chancellorsville, he was given command of the Department of Harpers Ferry in June of 1863. The officials in Washington, DC, were not about to have a repeat of Miles's 1862 surrender. Kenly was ordered to abandon Harpers Ferry and transfer his men to Maryland Heights. Then the decision was made to evacuate Maryland Heights. Kenly spent June 28 and 29 removing the heavy guns from the Heights and loading them into canal boats for shipment to Georgetown. On June 30, French moved his division to Frederick City with orders to protect Meade's far left flank and keep open his line of communication with Washington.[242]

On the same day that Kenly moved to Maryland Heights, a courier arrived at Major General George G. Meade's headquarters in Frederick with the startling announcement that he been appointed the new commander of the Army of the Potomac! Meade immediately faced three challenges: first, find out where his army was; second, find out where Lee's army was; and third, devise a plan to protect Washington and defeat Lee if possible.[243]

While Meade pondered his options, Lee's army continued to move north on a broad front. To the west, Imboden divided his force before advancing on Cumberland. After leaving Cumberland, his men burned the trestling, engine house and water pumps at Patterson's Creek. At the same time, his other force destroyed the South Branch Bridge. This bridge consisted of three iron spans each 131 feet long. Lacking powder charges, an artillery piece was positioned at a right angle to the bridge. Solid shot was fired directly at the supports "…cutting the beams as if they had been pine." On the eleventh shot the bridge fell into the river. On June 20, General Lee wrote to President Davis outlining the damage wrought by Imboden's brigade within such a brief period of time. Besides the bridges already mentioned, he stated, "All the depots, water tanks and engines between Little Cacapon and Cumberland are also destroyed, with blockhouses at the mouth of the South Branch and Patterson's Creek." Considerable damage had also been done to the C&O Canal. McNeil's Rangers burned the Sleepy Creek and Back Creek bridges before crossing the Potomac River near Williamsport on June 18. The town was occupied with General Rodes's Division and they continued west on the National Road until they arrived in Hancock. The next day McNeil led his men west to Sir John's Run where they destroyed the water station, blacksmith shop, wood-house, sand-house, and supervisor's office. From there they continued on burning the water stations at Rockwell's and Willett's Run as well as the trestling on the Great

Cacapon Bridge. This was an immense amount of damage to be caused by a single company of no more than fifty men. Turning south, McNeil joined forces with Imboden's brigade at the Bloomery Iron Furnace on June 21. Imboden had received orders from General Lee the previous day to advance into Pennsylvania and continue to cover his left flank while gathering horse and cattle for the army. The next day he broke camp and headed north.[244]

Meanwhile, to the east J.E.B. Stuart with three brigades of cavalry was ordered to screen Lee's right flank. As the infantry formations moved north into Maryland, Stuart decided to cross the Potomac River near Seneca, Maryland, and ride around the Union Army to join Lee in Pennsylvania. What he did not realize was that the Army of the Potomac was also marching north and he was trying to circle a moving target. Entering Rockville on June 28, he captured a Union supply train consisting of 125 new wagons and 500 mules, along with about 400 Union soldiers that became prisoners. A valuable accomplishment in itself, it was a gigantic impediment for a fast moving cavalry operation. Rather than detach a force strong enough to escort the wagons and prisoners back to Virginia, Stuart chose to take them along. Moving through Montgomery and Howard counties, Stuart's brigades struck the main line of the B&O at Sykesville and Mount Airy, tearing up the tracks and cutting the telegraph lines. Confederate cavalry also burned the bridge at Piney Run on June 29. The bridge was rebuilt the next day in only thirty-five minutes.[245]

Pushing north on the afternoon of June 29, Stuart's main column was approaching Westminster on the Washington Road when it was attacked by Captain Charles Corbit with less than 100 men from Companies C and D of the First Delaware Cavalry. In the ensuing melee, two Confederate officers were killed and the Union formation shattered. Stuart decided to stay in the area that night and move into Pennsylvania the next day. Unknown to Stuart at the time, General Meade had planned to make Westminster his main supply base and form the Army of the Potomac in a defensive position along nearby Pipe Creek. The plan had to be abandoned when the two armies collided at Gettysburg on July 1. Also unknown to Stuart was the location of Lee's Army.[246]

While the two armies maneuvered north of the Potomac River, Herman Haupt, head of field operations for the United States Military Railroad, lobbied General Halleck for permission to join Meade at Frederick City, to plan the logistical support for the Army of the Potomac during the current campaign. Both Meade and Haupt were from Pennsylvania and had graduated from West Point in the class of 1835. Both men had resigned their commissions to become civil engineers. Meade, however, reentered the Army in 1842 and was assigned to the elite Corps of Topographical Engineers where he became well known for his design and construction of lighthouses. A Regular Army captain when the war began, he was promoted to brigadier general of volunteers in August of 1861 and major general in December of 1862 when he was given command of the Fifth Corps.[247]

Finally, on June 27, Haupt received the order from General Halleck he had been waiting for.

"Brig. Gen. H. Haupt, U.S. Volunteers, is hereby authorized and directed to do whatever he may deem expedient to facilitate the transportation of troops and supplies to aid the armies in the field in Virginia, Maryland, and Pennsylvania."[248]

With the rail and telegraph lines cut, Haupt was not able to reach Meade at Frederick. Instead, he went to Harrisburg to consult with Governor Curtin and Thomas A. Scott of the Pennsylvania Railroad, and returned to Baltimore via Philadelphia the next day. He knew the region well, having worked on the Western Maryland and the Pennsylvania railroads before the war. He had also lived in Gettysburg while teaching engineering at Pennsylvania College (now Gettysburg College). During the epic battle, a battery of Longstreet's artillery would be placed in the front yard of his home on Seminary Ridge. Haupt's primary mission was to find a way to resupply Meade's army.[249]

Lee had sent Ewell's Corps north on June 22 with orders to capture Harrisburg if possible. Ewell advanced north through Chambersburg with two divisions and sent a third commanded by Major General Jubal Early east toward York for the dual purpose of disrupting rail service between Harrisburg and Baltimore and covering his right flank. His ultimate objective was to capture the bridge over the Susquehanna River at Wrightsville. Meeting only token resistance from the local militia, Early's Division occupied Gettysburg on June 26. The next day he moved against York where the Northern Central had a major rail complex. At the same time, Confederate cavalry raided nearby Hanover Junction where the Hanover Branch Railroad met the Northern Central. From this point rail traffic moved west thirty miles to the town of Hanover where it could be interchanged with the Gettysburg Railroad. The raiders burned a covered bridge and turntable and cut the telegraph line temporarily halting communication between Harrisburg and Baltimore. Several rail cars were also set on fire. On June 29, Gordon's Brigade attacked Wrightsville. One of the longest covered bridges in the world connected Wrightsville with the town of Columbia on the east bank of the Susquehanna River. Once across the 5,629-foot long bridge, the Confederates could threaten Harrisburg, Philadelphia, or Wilmington, Delaware. Fearing his small force would be overrun, the Federal commander, Major Granville O. Haller, ordered the fourth span of the bridge, some 800 yards from the west bank of the river, prepared for demolition. Haller withdrew his forces from Wrightsville before the Rebels could capture the bridge and signaled for the charges to be ignited. When the smoke cleared, the bridge remained undamaged. Haller then ordered the span set on fire, which resulted in the entire structure and part of the town of Wrightsville being consumed in the flames.[250]

As the drama at Wrightsville was being played out, General Lee learned that the Army of the Potomac was nearby in Maryland. He canceled the advance on Harrisburg and ordered his far-flung division to reunite along the Blue Ridge Mountain Range in Pennsylvania. The Confederates marched away from Wrightsville on the last day of June. In their wake, they left downed telegraph lines, damaged track and burned out railroad equipment. They had also completely disabled the rail system in southern Pennsylvania by wrecking over thirty trestles and bridges on a number of different lines.

After his conference in Harrisburg, Haupt returned to Baltimore the next day and met with John Work Garrett and William Prescott Smith to determine a course of action. With the B&O severed in the west and the local lines in Pennsylvania damaged, their sole alternative was the Western Maryland Railroad. The Western Maryland was chartered in 1852 to build a line from the Relay House on the Northern Central Railroad seven miles north of Baltimore to Hagerstown, a distance of eighty miles. By agreement, the new railroad would enter Baltimore via the Northern Central's tracks and use its Calvert Street Station. Construction did not begin until 1858. The line was completed to Westminster on June 15, 1861 and Union Bridge in May of 1862. By 1863, the railroad owned only four locomotives; the "Green Spring," "Western Maryland," "Patapsco," and "Pipe Creek," and a small number of cars.[251]

The *Monocacy* was the fifth locomotive purchased by the Western Maryland Railroad. (B&ORRM)

On July 1, the same day the epic battle began at Gettysburg, Haupt made a personal inspection of the line. By the time he arrived in Westminster, it was clear that he was facing possibly the greatest challenge of his military career. The Western Maryland had only a single line track with almost no sidings and no turntable in Westminster. There were no water stations or telegraph service operated by the railroad. The average capacity for the line was four trains a day with a corresponding volume of fuel for the wood burning engines. By Haupt's computations, he would need to move thirty trains a day in both directions.

Herman Haupt's solution to this seemingly impossible challenge was so practical that it is almost impossible to believe it worked. Using the seldom invoked authority of the Railways and Telegraph Act of 1862, he took military control of the Western Maryland Railroad. He would then run trains of ten cars each in convoys of five trains at a time. Each train would carry supplies and ammunition out and return with wounded and prisoners of war. With no telegraph, the trains simply had to run on schedule. Additional tonnage would be moved by the B&O to Frederick to create a supply base under the protection of General French's Division. In order to amass the necessary number of locomotives and rail cars, Haupt called on the USMRR, as well as the B&O, Northern Central, Pennsylvania and Philadelphia & Trenton lines.

To ensure that the convoys ran on schedule, Haupt ordered his chief construction engineer, Adna Anderson, who was in Alexandria, to bring a train to Baltimore with 400 men equipped with an ample supply of buckets, lanterns and precut firewood for the locomotives. Crews would be dropped off between the Relay House on the Northern Central Railroad and Westminster with piles of wood to resupply the tenders. Lacking any water stations, other crews would be positioned near streams to provide bucket brigades to refill the water tanks on the engines. The lanterns would allow for twenty-four hour operations if needed.[252]

Once the operation was running as planned, Haupt turned it over to Anderson and set about repairing the damaged railroads in Pennsylvania. There were nineteen bridges out on the Northern Central alone. Haupt sent his construction crews to work from both ends of the line. At the same time, he personally supervised the repair work on the Hanover line with the Gettysburg railroad. By July 2, repairs had been made on the B&O's main line to Frederick and the Northern Central to Hanover Junction. Even after Meade's army moved out in pursuit of Lee, an immense amount of food and medical supplies were needed to care for the tens of thousands of wounded and the thousands of medical personal and support troops left in the area.

Starting on July 4, supply trains began returning to Baltimore and other cities with thousands of wounded and prisoners of war. Lt. Colonel Edward

P. Vollum, a surgeon and medical inspector for the U.S. Army, reported that by July 22, nearly 15,000 wounded were transferred from the field hospitals at Gettysburg to Baltimore, York, Harrisburg and Philadelphia. "Each car was supplied with a sufficient quantity of hay, and on longer routes, water-coolers, tin cups, bed-pans and urinals were placed in them." Several new U.S. Army General Hospitals were opened in Baltimore. So many POW's were sent to Fort McHenry as a result of the Gettysburg Campaign that an additional prison camp was established at Point Lookout in Southern Maryland. By the end of the war, it was the largest prison camp North or South.[253]

The United States Military Telegraph also made an appearance immediately after the battle. Because of Confederate raids in the area, the closest operating station was seventeen miles east of Gettysburg at Hanover. Telegraphers Edwards and Hall were sent there to open communications with the War Department via General Schenck's headquarters in Baltimore City. Edwards immediately started out with a crew to construct a temporary line from Hanover to Gettysburg. Not having any telegraph poles or insulators, they wrapped the wire around the necks of bottles and stuck them in the crooks of trees. At a stream where a section of wire was missing, they connected the two ends to an iron rail and propped it up on some empty bottles found in the stream to literally bridge the gap until permanent repairs could be made. Soon additional operators arrived at Meade's Headquarters and all the telegraph lines were repaired.[254]

That the B&O was deeply involved in the Gettysburg Campaign is reflected in a telegram John Work Garrett sent to General Halleck on July 9. "We are doing ever thing (sic) possible & our capacity is abundant for more than all you require if you can only have them (the Army) unload at destination & the military authorities will permit their early return. Our men are laboring most faithfully although many are greatly exhausted – The round trip should be made in 30 hours, whilst our engineers, firemen & conductors have been kept without sleep for 75 to 90 hours. Some rest must be had or sleep on duty & accidents will follow." This communication may have been the result of General French's actions at Frederick. French had twenty supply trains backup up around Monocacy Junction because he refused to allow them to be unloaded in Frederick. An additional fifteen trains headed west were stalled on the main line. When Haupt was informed of the problem, he hurried to Frederick and had the situation resolved by the night of July 8.[255]

The Gettysburg Campaign was the first time during the war that the B&O had an opportunity to fight back in its own defense. The idea came not from an experienced railroad man, but a newly commissioned second lieutenant. John Rogers Meigs was the son of Quartermaster General Montgomery C. Meigs.

He graduated from the U.S. Military Academy in the Class of 1863 and was assigned as an engineering officer to the Defenses of Baltimore just as Lee's invasion was getting underway. Meigs's uncle was Captain John Rogers of the United States Navy where he commanded several ironclad vessels. Lieutenant Meigs was fascinated with this new naval technology. He suggested to the department commander, General Schenck, that he be allowed to build a "fleet" of ironclad railcars to protect the B&O during the current invasion. Still smarting from the damage incurred by the Jones-Imboden Raid, Schenck readily agreed to the experiment. He sent a request to President Garrett to have five railroad "monitor cars" and five "rifle cars" constructed at once.

Garrett instructed his Master of Machinery Thatcher Perkins to commence the project immediately. Perkins summoned 300 workers to report without delay to the Mount Clare Shops. It was Sunday afternoon on June 28, and many of the Irish and German employees of the railroad were in church. Perkins organized the men into two shifts so that the work could go on around the clock. Realizing that standard field pieces would be too large to operate inside the confines of an armored car, Schenck ordered his post commanders to transfer a number of mountain howitzers and 6-pounder field pieces to Mount Clare with the required implements and ammunition.

The first cars constructed were for the artillery. Plates of Iron "T" rails were placed on a flatcar at a forty-five degree angle to form a protective casemate similar to that of a war ship. At each end of the car were openings that allowed the cannon to be fired in three different directions. Small loopholes ran along the length of the car so that infantrymen assigned to defend the gun crew could fire their weapons without exposing their bodies. Soldiers entered and exited the car through a trapdoor in the floor. Imbued with his family's naval tradition, Meigs named his railroad monitors after the Union victories *Port Royal, Antietam,* and the very recent *Gettysburg* and *Vicksburg.* Working at a phenomenal pace, all five cars were completed in just six days.

The second round of construction applied to the rifle cars. These were simply boxcars lined with rail or boilerplate to make them bulletproof. Again, loopholes would supply safe firing positions for the soldiers inside. Meigs planned to couple one rifle car to one cannon car in order to drive the marauding Confederates away from the tracks and protect the work crews as they repaired the damage. The forerunner of armored warfare, Patton and Rommel may have found the young lieutenant's thesis interesting reading.

Meigs would get an opportunity to put his theory into practice. As Lee retreated from Gettysburg, efforts were made to capture his army before it could cross the rain-swollen Potomac River. At Frederick on July 6, General Kenly was ordered to take three regiments of his Maryland Brigade and reoccupy

Maryland Heights. The next day he launched an attack against that well-fortified position. As Kenly's men ascended the Potomac side of the Heights, they were fired on by Rebel troops from the other side of the river. On this very same day, Lieutenant Meigs arrived at Frederick with his "armored column." With his cannon cars positioned in front of the locomotive and a number of flatcars laden with infantry attached to the rear, he proceeded to the base of Maryland Heights and bombarded the Confederates across the river. Kenly's attack was successful. Meigs and his armored train remained on the Maryland side of the river awaiting orders to rebuild the Harpers Ferry Bridge. On July 14, he received an order to turn over his command to General Lockwood, the new commander at Harpers Ferry, and return to Baltimore. Harpers Ferry became the "home port" for the armored railcars. Throughout the rest of the year, they were assigned singularly and in pairs to various construction trains in order to provide protection for the work crews. The following year, Lieutenant John R. Meigs saw extensive action in the Shenandoah Valley and received brevets to captain and major. He was killed at Harrisonburg on October 3, 1864.[256]

With the Confederate Army back in Virginia, the B&O set about the all-too-familiar task of fixing what had been broken. At Harpers Ferry, it was the Union cavalry, not the Rebels, that had burned the woodwork on the iron bridge there. At Martinsburg the Pillar Bridge was again burned. Eight miles of track were ripped up and the rails twisted after being heated on the burning ties. Repairs commenced eastward from Cumberland on July 14. Two days later work crews started on the Harpers Ferry Bridge and finished on July 20. Passenger and local freight trains began running as far east as Hancock on August 6. The entire line was in operation by August 10.[257]

CHAPTER SIXTEEN

CHICKAMAUGA & CHATTANOOGA

No two military operations during the war were more linked together by the railroad than the battles of Chickamauga, Georgia, and Chattanooga, Tennessee. Although successfully completed in both instances, a comparison of the two shows the diminished capacity of the Southern railroads and the unlimited potential of the Northern lines.

Following the Gettysburg Campaign, both armies returned to northern Virginia to lick their wounds and await the next move of their adversary. In the Western Theater, Union General William S. Rosecrans led his Army of the Cumberland against Confederate General Braxton Bragg's Army of Tennessee in a series of minor battles and brilliant maneuvers that forced Bragg to abandon the key city of Chattanooga on September 6 and retreat into northern Georgia. Should Rosecrans defeat Bragg in a stand up battle or maneuver around him, the way to Atlanta and the heartland of the Confederacy would be wide open. The Confederate high command determined to counter this threat by sending reinforcements from the Army of Northern Virginia. Major General James Longstreet was ordered to take two divisions of his First Corps by train and report to General Bragg. Bragg would then launch a counteroffensive with the additional manpower.

The original plan was for Longstreet's men to travel from Richmond on connecting lines to Lynchburg where they would take the Virginia & Tennessee Railroad the bulk of the way, passing through Bristol and Knoxville before arriving at Chattanooga on the East Tennessee & Georgia. The route would cover 540 miles and take four days to complete. Before any action could be taken, Union General Burnside, now in command of the Department of Ohio, occupied Knoxville and severed the proposed route.[258]

It fell to Captain Frederick W. Sims of Georgia, the recently appointed supervisor of railroad transportation for the Confederacy, to plan an alternate route. Sims's position was a watered down version of Colonel McCallum's as head of the United States Military Railroad. In fact, the Confederacy had no equivalent to the USMRR. By 1863, the collective ills of Southern railroading were combining to defeat "The Cause" as surely as any advancing Yankee army. From the very beginning of the war, the Southern lines were well behind their Northern rivals in the numbers of locomotives, railcars and miles of track. The paragon of States' Rights precluded any centralized management of resources or government support. As parts wore out there was no means within the Confederacy to manufacture replacements. One railroad superintendent summarized the situation for the entire South when he reported to his Board of Directors, "The locomotives are constantly used with loads to the extent of their capacity and cannot be spared (the time for) repairs; they run until they can run no longer." Finally, there was the lack of connecting lines and a standard track gauge. Truly, the railroads of the two warring factions were headed in different directions. The Northern lines had excellent repair facilities and a seemingly unlimited capacity to add new locomotives, cars and tracks to their systems while the USMRR rebuilt captured Southern railroads to standard gauge and used them against their former owners. It was against this array of challenges that Captain Sims set about to accomplish one of the most important rail marches of the war for the Southern Confederacy.[259]

The two divisions chosen to accompany General Longstreet were commanded by generals Hood and McLaws along with the corps artillery commanded by Colonel E. Porter Alexander, a total of about 15,000 men. Pickett's Division remained behind, still recovering from its third day charge at Gettysburg. Sims worked closely with his superior, Quartermaster General Alexander R. Lawton, to plan an alternative route and secure the equipment and cooperation of ten different railroads. Beginning on September 9, these troops were shuttled from their camps near Orange Courthouse via the Virginia Central Railroad to Richmond. Lacking any east-west connections, they began a circuitous route that would take them through North Carolina, South Carolina and the upper half of Georgia. Equipment was in both poor condition and limited supply. Longstreet's chief of staff, Lt. Colonel Moxley Sorrell, remarked, "Never before were so many troops moved over such worn-out railways." The trains were composed of boxcars, flatcars, coal cars and stock cars. Usually only the officers found accommodation in the few allotted passenger cars. Equipment was in such short supply that one company would be loaded into a boxcar and a second on top.

On September 15, the famed Texas brigade detrained near Ringgold, Georgia, and joined in the first day's fighting at Chickamauga. Other units completed their almost 900-mile rail march that day and the next, helping to defeat General Rosecrans's army and drive it back into the city of Chattanooga. Only half of Longstreet's men and none of his artillery arrived to participate in the battle, but their presence altered the balance of power in the west and threatened to destroy an entire Union army if the siege of Chattanooga was not lifted.[260]

It was the details of this gloomy turn of events that Assistant Secretary of War Charles Dana passed on to Secretary Stanton from the besieged city of Chattanooga, Tennessee. On the evening of September 23, Stanton called an emergency meeting with Lincoln, Halleck, Secretary of State William H. Seward, and Treasury Secretary Salmon P. Chase. After summarizing the reason for the meeting, Stanton startled the attendees with the announcement that he intended to transfer 30,000 men from the Army of the Potomac to regain the initiative in Tennessee. He quickly added in a not-too-subtle remark that Meade had done nothing with the Army of the Potomac since the Gettysburg Campaign and the men could be better used out west. Stanton concluded his presentation by stating that, "In five days 30,000 men could be sent to Rosecrans."

Lincoln responded first with a wager that the men could not be gotten from the Army of the Potomac to Washington City in five days. Halleck offered his usual negative opinion that the move would take a minimum of forty days if it could be done at all. Salmon Chase was the only one to side with Stanton.[261]

Stanton's closing argument was the result of some behind-the-scenes brainstorming. Major Thomas Eckert, the chief telegraph operator in the War Department, alerted Colonel Daniel McCallum, head of the USMRR and his assistant, W. H. Whiton, about the nature of the meeting and the likelihood that McCallum would be asked to supply a transit time to Halleck and Lincoln. The two men poured over timetables and maps until McCallum was summoned to the meeting. After a brief period of contemplation, the government's top railroad man flatly stated that the move could be done in seven days. After a few more questions, Lincoln told Stanton, "Mr. Secretary, you are the captain. Give the necessary orders and I will approve them."[262]

Stanton worked throughout the night. At 3:30 a.m., he sent a telegram to Dana informing him that help was on the way. The next day, some of the top railroad executives in the East convened at the War Department including the B&O's president, John W. Garrett, and his Master of Transportation, William Prescott Smith; Vice-president Thomas Scott of the Pennsylvania Railroad; Samuel Felton, president of the PW&BRR; and Colonel McCallum, head of the USMRR. They were, to steal the title from Doris Kearns Goodwin's book, a team of rivals whose collective knowledge and experience would result in the longest and most efficient rail movement of the war.[263]

In the meeting with Lincoln, Stanton did not reveal the source of his 30,000 men in five days computation but a likely source would have been Garrett. The two men had already forged an excellent working relationship by this point in the war. A subtle indication that Garrett had prior knowledge of the proposed troop movement is contained in his response to Stanton's generic telegram dated 11:15 p.m. on September 23.

"John W. Garrett, Esq., Baltimore.
Please come to Washington as quick as you can, and bring Smith with you.

Edwin M. Stanton"

Garrett replied the next day,

"I am on 8 o'clock train from Baltimore, and expect to be at Department at 10 o'clock with our master of transportation; **have arranged for full information regarding engines and cars**. (author's emphasis)"

One might ask how Garrett knew what information to bring.[264]

The troops selected for this long distance transfer were the Eleventh and Twelfth corps along with their associated artillery battalions, totaling some 20,000 men. Major General Joseph Hooker, one of the numerous ex-commanders of the Army of the Potomac, was to be the military commander of the expedition, but the railroad men were to have absolute authority over the trains. The final route was chosen to maximize the interchanging with standard gauge railroads and minimize the crossing of rivers during the low water season. The troops released from the Army of the Potomac would first travel by USMRR to Alexandria, Virginia, and then cross the Long Bridge to the B&O's passenger terminal in Washington. From there B&O locomotives would haul the trains along the Washington Branch to Relay where they would enter the main line and be carried all the way to Benwood on the Ohio River near Wheeling, West Virginia. At this point the men would detrain and be ferried across the river to Bellaire, Ohio. From there they would interchange with three different Ohio lines that would take them west to Indianapolis. From Indianapolis, they would travel south to Jeffersonville, Indiana, and cross back over the Ohio River to Louisville, Kentucky. Once south of the Ohio, they would board trains supplied by the Louisville & Nashville Railroad and proceed to Nashville where they would interchange with the Nashville & Chattanooga before completing the journey to Bridgeport, Alabama, from which they would march to the relief of Chattanooga. The entire trip would cover 1,200 miles and require the cooperation of eight different railroads.[265]

To ensure that everything stayed on schedule, each man at the meeting was given a particular area of responsibility. McCallum would be responsible for the positioning of the trains in Virginia and ensure their timely loading and transfer to Washington. Garrett would take over at the Washington Depot and manage the operation from there all the way to Jeffersonville, Indiana. Scott went to Louisville to supervise the final stage from there to Bridgeport. Felton was tasked with locating additional rolling stock and directing it where needed. Even Halleck was on board and sent instructions to General Meade at 2:30 a.m. on September 24 to have the Eleventh and Twelfth Corps sent to Washington by the morning of the twenty-fifth. At 9:45 a.m. he followed up with the emphatic statement, "…the Eleventh and Twelfth Corps are positively to be sent here with the least possible delay." Halleck then sent a telegram to General Benjamin F. Kelley in West Virginia advising him that troop trains would be passing through his Department and that he was to take every precaution against Rebel raiders. He was also ordered to close all the saloons in the major cities that the trains would pass through.[266]

Garrett was also leaving nothing to chance. He directed his Master of Machinery, Thatcher Perkins, to select the very best engines and crews for this vital operation. To the Master of Road J. L. Wilson he ordered all bridges and curves inspected to prevent the possibility of derailments. To his trusted Master of Transportation Smith he warned, "Let no engine be overheated. Moderate loads and regular running will accomplish the best results. Especially avoid fast speed at any point on the line." Garrett also assigned sections of the move under his responsibility to his subordinates for closer monitoring and immediate feedback if there was a problem. Alexander Diffey, the B&O's General Supervisor of Trains, was responsible for all activity between Washington and Piedmont, West Virginia. J. P. Willard was given the same task between Piedmont and Benwood. J. B. Ford, the freight agent at Wheeling, was to handle the transfer of troops across the Ohio River and their reloading at Bellaire. Ticket agent Louis M. Cole had the final responsibility from there to Jeffersonville, Indiana. All of these men were given captains' commissions from the War Department to facilitate their dealing with the military. William Prescott Smith had the dual responsibility of supplying McCallum with as many cars as he needed to transfer the troops to Washington and supervising the entire length of the operation controlled by the B&O Railroad. Garrett's relentless attention to detail paid off as soon as the movement got under way.

Garrett's responsibility went far beyond his own employees. He also had to communicate with the top management of the railroads in Ohio and Indiana to ensure that the proper number and types of cars were ready to meet the west bound trains at their designated interchange points. Sensing the urgency of the matter, their cooperation was forthcoming.[267]

With all of the planning and preparation, the moment of truth arrived on the morning of September 25, 1863, when soldiers in Union Blue began to climb aboard the trains in Virginia. It is no exaggeration to state that one of the largest and longest redeployment of troops during the Civil War, or any war at that time, was put into motion within forty-eight hours of its original proposal. It was a feat that may never have been exceeded.

The Eleventh Corps got off to a fast start. All but 1,700 men left on the first day and they were headed towards Washington by 6:00 a.m. on September 26. Colonel McCallum's first challenge came with the Twelfth Corps when he learned that it contained 2,000 more men than he had planned for. William Prescott Smith received an urgent request for 60 additional boxcars and 50 more stock cars. Smith responded with a promise of 200 cars by noon that day. This was followed by a request for additional cars bringing the total supplied by the B&O to over 600.

The trains that left Washington for Chattanooga bore little resemblance to those that had left Richmond a few weeks earlier. Most of the enlisted men were riding in boxcars forty to a car supplied with bench-like wooden seats. As to be expected, the officers enjoyed the comforts of a passenger car. A few unlucky soldiers ended up in stock cars but mostly these only carried the horses. Flatcars were provided for the artillery and additional boxcars for supplies and ammunition. Each train consisted of twenty to thirty cars and was pulled by a well maintained locomotive. By 5:00 p.m. of the first day, two trains totaling fifty-one troop cars and four flatcars of artillery were already on the Washington Branch. Trains continued to depart about every three hours until McCallum was finally able to report to Stanton that the last train had left Virginia shortly after noon on September 28.[268]

Master of Transportation Smith was at Relay when the first trains came through from Washington. He immediately took notice that they were averaging 28 cars. This was not a problem on the relatively flat Washington Branch but it would greatly slow down the average speed once they hit the mountains west of Harpers Ferry. He immediately sent a telegram to Colonel McCallum requesting that he reduce the maximum number of cars to twenty-two.[269]

By the third day of the operation, the B&O's main line and Washington Branch represented a giant conveyor belt carrying men, horses and cannons behind puffing locomotives. The cooperation between the military and civilian components was exemplary until Major General Carl Schurz decided to pull rank on a B&O employee. Schurz commanded a division in the Eleventh Corps. When he found out that he was traveling behind the lead elements of

Troop train crossing the Tray Run Viaduct. (F. L.)

his command, he sent an order to the station agent at Grafton to hold all the trains carrying the Third Division until its commanding officer arrived. All of the agents had been instructed by Smith to keep the trains moving unless they received orders directly from the War Department to the contrary. When Schurz arrived in Grafton, the trains were gone. He found it incredulous that a lowly railroad agent would defy a major general. He demanded that a special engine and car be dispatched so that he and his staff could catch up with their advanced units. This request was also denied and the general was forced to climb back on his train but not before he sent a similar order to the agent at Fairmont. This, too, was ignored. When William Prescott Smith learned of the incident in Grafton, he sent a telegram directly to the Secretary of War. "May I suggest that this kind of thing will cripple your entire movement?" Stanton concurred with the action taken by Smith's agents and sent a first class dressing down to General Schurz. "Major-General Hooker has the orders of this Department to relieve you from command and put under arrest any officer who undertakes to delay or interfere with the orders and regulations of railroad officers in charge of the transportation of troops." Schurz retained his command but the example was set and no further attempts were made to interfere with the railroad men.[270]

The troop trains continued in their original configuration until they arrived at Piedmont Station where they encountered the steep inclines of the Allegheny Mountains. Here, each train was divided into two or three sections with a powerful coal burning Winans Camel locomotive attached to its front and back to pull and push it over the mountains. The wood burning locomotives were sent back east for their next assignment.[271]

In the original planned move, the troops would detrain at Benwood near Wheeling and be ferried across the Ohio River on steamers. By the time the movement started, the water level had dropped to an insufficient level. Without hesitating, Garrett ordered a pontoon bridge of sorts built of scows and barges. By the time the first four troop trains arrived on September 27, the bridge was ready and the troops marched across to Bellaire, Ohio, where a new set of trains from the Central Ohio Railroad awaited them. Each trainload of troops made the crossing in about thirty minutes. Passing on through Columbus, the first train arrived in Indianapolis on the afternoon of September 28, and was at Jeffersonville by midnight. The water was deeper here and the men were soon being ferried over the Ohio River to Louisville where they were fed and boarded trains for Nashville. Nashville was the last interchange point. Most of the trains remained intact and were simply switched over to power provided by the Nashville & Chattanooga Railroad. The first four trains arrived in Bridgeport, Alabama, on the morning of September 30, just five days after they had departed Virginia. By October 5, the last infantry regiments were leaving Louisville and all of the artillery trains had crossed the Ohio at Benwood and were en route to Indianapolis.[272]

Most of the 20,000 men had made the 1,200-mile trip within nine days. Only elements of the Twelfth Corps were running behind and stretched the completion time to eleven and one half days. This, as Master of Transportation Smith explained to Stanton, was caused by nearly 20% more troops and over 50% more horses being tendered for shipment than had been planned for. Not only was the B&O Railroad responsible for managing 75% of the total track miles, it loaded 30 trains of 20 cars or more and in only five days transported them over 400 miles of its own system. It is appropriate to note that on the main line between Harpers Ferry and Grafton, many of the bridges and miles of track had been destroyed not once but twice within the six months preceding the transfer. Had the B&O not developed the remarkable ability to repair damage quickly, this route would not have been available to the Union Army.[273]

Before the railroad men could savor their collective accomplishment, a second phase of the operation had to be put into motion. Known to the military as impedimenta, it consisted of the wagons, ambulances, horses, and other heavy equipment necessary for two army corps to function in the field. This movement got under way on September 27, but was hampered by a lack of rail cars and the inefficiency of army personnel. When the USMRR requested more rolling stock, Smith had to admit that the well was nearly dry. Most of his empties were at Benwood waiting to make the return east. He managed to provide a few cars from other roads but pointed out that stock cars with a capacity of fifteen horses had been released with ten, and as few as four, animals in them. Apprised of the situation, Stanton wasted no time in summoning Garrett to Washington and asking him to take charge of this equally important movement.

Garrett responded with his normal degree of professionalism. Smith, Cole, Diffey, Ford, and Jewett were all informed of the second move that was expected to require an additional 550 cars. The division of labor along the route would remain the same, only the requirements for horses would be somewhat different, and platforms would need to be constructed for the offloading and loading of the wagons. Absolute control of the line from Benwood to Jeffersonville must be maintained. Locomotives and other rolling stock were to be seized if not voluntarily supplied by the connecting lines. The bridge over the Ohio River was still intact so that problem was already solved. Garrett also combed his system for available railcars and had the Mount Clare Shops convert a number of boxcars into temporary stock cars to accommodate the large number of horses and mules to be shipped.[274]

The second phase managed by the B&O began on October 4. The first train arrived in Washington at 5:00 p.m. Within three hours, 40 wagons and 300 mules had been transferred to B&O equipment and were headed towards Relay. The next day 100 wagons and 900 mules were transshipped at the Washington Depot. By October 7, the entire impedimenta of two army corps was headed west. All went well until these trains began to arrive in Nashville. From this point the Nashville and Chattanooga Railroad was the main supply line for Rosecrans's starving army in Chattanooga. With a shortage of locomotives, rations and forage was given priority over mules and wagons. At the same time, Hookers' two army corps were almost useless without their transportation. Thomas Scott was still in Louisville. To alleviate the traffic jam he suggested to Rosecrans's chief transportation officer, Colonel William P. Innes, that he run his trains straight through from Louisville to Bridgeport rather than transfer the freight and animals at Nashville, and promised to secure two additional locomotives to help make up additional trains. This arrangement allowed Innes to both feed the troops and supply Scott with empty trains at Louisville. On October 30, the siege of Chattanooga was broken but the Confederates remained a threat. On November 24 and 25, General Ulysses S. Grant, with the aid of the Eleventh and Twelfth corps under General Hooker, won the battles of Lookout Mountain and Missionary Ridge. General Bragg's Army was forced to retreat to Dalton, Georgia. The great objective of their transfer had been achieved.[275]

The B&O's participation in this historic rail movement did not come without a price. Alexander Differ, the Supervisor of Trains east of Piedmont, fell ill due to the excessive strain of the back-to-back moves and died before the end of the year. Differ was not the only casualty of the war. Throughout the conflict, B&O personal were killed, wounded, captured or injured in accidents while performing their railroad duties. In June of 1863, Garrett received a plea from several employees held as prisoners in Richmond to intercede in their release or exchange. They were T. D. Armstrong, John Coleman, William White, William Brown, P. M. Jeffreys, A. C. Gary, Ducket and Gathell, all bridgemen; Thomas Hill and Patrick, tunnelmen; Henry Parker and James Crone, trainmen; and John Roney, a trackman. Additional correspondence on this matter has not been found, but it may be assumed that Garrett would have contacted Secretary of War Stanton to aid in the release of these men.[276]

CHAPTER SEVENTEEN

THE QUIET
TIME

By the middle of October, the last horse and wagon had crossed the Ohio River at Benwood and the bridge of barges had been disassembled. The next order of business after the exhausted train crews were given a little rest was to return the large number of cars sent west back to Baltimore so that the railroad could resume its normal business. Fortunately for the B&O, enemy activity against the main line would be at a minimum for the next few months and the railroad could concentrate on internal improvements. Meanwhile the Winchester and Potomac was all but abandoned. Prior to the Gettysburg Campaign General Milroy, the Union commander at Winchester, had pleaded with General Schenck to repair the line in its entirety. "When it is remembered that the Valley is the key, not only to the Baltimore & Ohio Railroad, but all of West Virginia; that it is necessary to establish a permanent base at this place (Winchester) for supplies and operations...south to Staunton..." By June, the line was only operating as far as Halltown, a mere three miles from Harpers Ferry. When Herman Haupt arrived at Harpers Ferry in July to facilitate repairs to the B&O bridge there, he inspected the W&P line and reported to Washington, "The Winchester road cannot be relied upon for any transportation whatever. The rail is strap iron, the supports rotten, and the lightest engines run off the track continually."[277]

As a result of the tremendous number of Union casualties sustained during the battle of Gettysburg, a National Cemetery was established there. Because it was the largest Civil War battle fought north of the Mason-Dixon Line, its dedication ceremonies took on national significance. One of the leading orators of the day, the Honorable Edward Everett, was the guest speaker. President Lincoln was invited to attend and deliver "a few appropriate remarks." The date was set for November 19, 1863.

During the entire Civil War President Lincoln only left the confines of the Nation's Capital a total of nineteen times. Nearly every trip was related to a

President Abraham Lincoln traveled eight times on the B&O Railroad during the Civil War. (D. C. T.)

significant event during the war. Including his inauguration and funeral, Lincoln traveled eight times on the Baltimore & Ohio Railroad. The rest of his journeys were by steamer and usually to Virginia. When informed that the president would be traveling to Gettysburg, Master of Transportation Smith took personal responsibility for arranging the trip. He made arrangements with the officials of the Northern Central to deliver the president and his party on the B&O's private cars to their Bolton Station in Baltimore where the cars would be attached to a Northern Central locomotive. The route from there would be north to Hanover Junction and then west on the Hanover Branch to Gettysburg.[278]

At noon on November 18, the president's special train, decorated in flags and bunting, departed the B&O's passenger station on New Jersey Avenue. It consisted of four cars. The president and his aides Nicolay and Hay occupied one of the railroad's private cars. The other three were filled with cabinet members, diplomats, military personnel and the Marine Corps band. The train arrived in Baltimore at 1:10 p.m. Each car was uncoupled and drawn by horses through the city to the Northern Central's Bolton Station where General Schenck and his staff joined the entourage. A baggage car was added to the rear of the train to act as an improvised dining car. At 2:00 p.m., the five-car special departed for Hanover Junction where the cars were again switched to a train carrying Governor Curtin and a number of dignitaries from Harrisburg. Arriving at his destination near sundown, the President was greeted at the Gettysburg Station by an enthusiastic crowd.

Tens of thousands of people gathered at the dedication ceremonies the next day. Following a prayer by the Reverend Thomas H. Stockton, the chaplain for the House of Representatives, the Honorable Edward Everett delivered a two-hour speech that may in itself have invoked a few prayers. Then the President rose and in just two minutes gave his immortal Gettysburg Address.

When the ceremonies were over the President dined with Governor Curtin and a number of others before attending a patriotic gathering with John Burns, the senior citizen hero of the battle, as his guest. At 6:30 p.m., the Presidential train departed for Washington. Reversing its course, it arrived in Washington around midnight.[279]

On the same day the President began his journey to Gettysburg, an unusual attempt at sabotage took place near Paw Paw Station. As B&O Locomotive No. 232 passed west bound, an explosion occurred under the engine that shattered the head light and broke several windows in the passenger cars. L. C. Boehm, the telegraph operator in Cumberland, wired details of the incident to William Prescott Smith, "We find dents in the drive wheel, the brass binding on foot board is broken in two, the shield over the driving wheel has a piece broken out and bent. The rack is not injured…." Upon further inspection, a piece of artillery shell was found sticking in the boiler casing. The Civil War version of IED's, an innovative attempt at sabotage was made by placing three shells with contact fuses on the track. Two were found unexploded.[280]

In Baltimore, work at the important Mount Clare Shops went on unabated. Four new locomotives were received from the manufacturer Ross Winans and put into service during the first three months of the year. The Winans Camels were numbered 188, 199, 204 and 235. Four additional first class passenger engines were also manufactured on the premises and numbered 13, 14, 35 and 36. All eight engines were given the numbers of engines that had been previously in service. By October 525 railcars had been constructed and plans were under way to build 200 additional coal cars. A reporter for the *American Railroad Journal* noted, "Among the curiosities of Mount Clare Depot are debris of rails, locomotives, etc., which were destroyed by the rebels. There are successive piles of twisted rails, sections and rods of bridges, bolts, screens, car wheels and boilers of excellent locomotives, fragments of coal-cars, axles and demolished tenders. …There are millions of pounds of damaged iron… that is placed into the melting furnaces and again wrought into such parts of engines and cars as required." By the end of the year, a new foundry was under construction to expand this process as well as a new wheelhouse.[281]

At long last the laying of a second track on the Washington Branch was begun in October. Several times materials stockpiled for the project had been shipped west for emergency repairs of the main line. The first section ran from Elk Ridge on the south side of the Patapsco River to Annapolis Junction and was completed on January 25, of the following year. A month later, the tracks had been laid across the Thomas Viaduct to connect with the main line. Also in January the east and west spans of the iron bridge over the Monocacy River were installed.[282]

During the winter months, the two great armies in the east remained in their camps. There were also changes in the U.S. Military Telegraph and Signal Corps detachments assigned to the Department of West Virginia. Due to illness, Captain Thomas B. A. David resigned his position as the USMT's superintendent of the department on January 20. Prior to the war David had been manager of the telegraph office in Wheeling. He was replaced by Captain Stafford G. Lynch. Captain Lynch had joined the USMT in 1861. His first assignment was at New Creek. When General Kelley occupied Romney, he installed a telegraph line to his headquarters. After that, he was assigned to the War Department's telegraph office where one of his duties was to censor stories filed by reporters.

When Lynch returned to West Virginia, he was made responsible for the operation and maintenance of lines that followed the B&O Railroad and those installed in the Kanawha Valley. With a force that averaged only forty men, he maintained communications over 372 miles of wire. In one twelve month period, his staff processed 120,000 telegrams.[283]

The men of the Signal Corps assigned to the department were no less diligent. At the beginning of the year, they consisted of four officers and forty-five enlisted men. In March, Captain F. E. Town assumed command of the Signal detachment. Throughout the year a number of men were transferred to the department until Town's unit numbered 13 officers and 161 enlisted men. Unfortunately, many of the men lacked the necessary training or equipment to operate in the field. Captain Town established a camp of instruction at his headquarters in Cumberland.[284]

While the major armies remained idle in their winter camps, the irregular commands of Mosby, McNeil and Gilmor began to stir. In addition, General Jubal A. Early sent Brigadier General Thomas L. Rosser with his famed Laurel Brigade to capture a large wagon train moving between New Creek and Petersburg. After capturing the wagon train, he moved against Patterson Creek eight miles east of Cumberland where he captured the bridge guard consisting of forty men. After burning the bridge, water station, and engine house and cutting the telegraph, he followed the tracks north and burned the North Branch Bridge on February 2, before returning to his camp in the Shenandoah Valley.[285]

The next attack came on the night of February 11. Major Harry Gilmor with twenty-eight men from his Second Maryland Battalion penetrated the Union lines near Charles Town and proceeded up the main line of the B&O to a place called Brown's Crossing about eight miles east of Martinsburg. Here he had his men erect a barricade near a stretch of tracks known as Quincy's Siding. Then, cognizant of the fact that many civilians, women, and children would be on board, he had his men place fence rails in advance of the blockage hoping that they would cause the engineer to reduce his speed and avert a deadly derailment.

At 8:30 p.m., the evening express train departed Camden Station for the 379 mile run to Wheeling, West Virginia, where it was due to arrive at 4:40 p.m. the next day. The train consisted of five passenger cars and one each freight, baggage and sleeping cars. As the train approached the obstructions the engineer managed to reduce his speed to such a degree that when the train derailed some of the passengers slept through the event. The Rebel raiders quickly climbed onto the cars and with a few pistol shots announced their presence. By now, no one was sleeping and pandemonium broke out among the passengers. The first car Gilmor entered was filled with Union officers. After he demanded their surrender, one of the officers attacked him with a sword. Gilmor pistol-whipped the man and threw him off the train. By the time he made his way to the freight car, the Adams Express agent had escaped with the key to the company's safe. As a consolation prize, Gilmor ripped open a number of mailbags and made off with $900 in Greenbacks as the U.S. paper currency of the day was called. Meanwhile, his men were systematically robbing the passengers of their money, watches and jewelry. Then they broke into the baggage car and helped themselves to an excellent assortment of clothing and personal items.

Gilmor had posted a lookout in each direction to warn him of oncoming trains. When one of these men reported what he thought was the approach of an eastbound train, Gilmor ordered his men to saddle up and rode off without setting fire to the captured express. It was a false alarm and saved the train from being destroyed. The train crew with the help of some of the passengers worked for three hours and eventually got the engine back on the tracks and continued on westward. The total take by the raiders was estimated at $20,000 to $30,000. A large figure then, it equals over ten times that amount today.[286]

On March 12, Major General Lew Wallace replaced General Schenck as the commander of the Middle Military Department and the Eighth Army Corps. A native of Indiana, he served as a lieutenant in the Indiana Infantry during the Mexican War. When he returned home, he practiced law and was elected to the state senate. At the outbreak of the Civil War, he was commissioned colonel of the Eleventh Indiana Regiment and occupied Cumberland in May of 1861. A division commander under Grant at the fall of Fort Donelson, he was promoted to major general in 1862. After the battle of Shiloh, Wallace fell out of favor with Halleck and Grant and lost his field command. His new assignment was fortuitous for both the citizens of Baltimore and President Lincoln. More flexible than the old Regular Army officer General Wool, and less occupied with politics than Schenck, he proved to be an able administrator and a competent field general when faced with an emergency. After the war, he served on the commission that tried the Lincoln conspirators. His greatest fame would come in 1880 when he authored the biblical novel Ben Hur. Lew Wallace would not be responsible for protecting the entire main line of the B&O Railroad. By the time he assumed command, the western boundary of the Middle Department was the Monocacy River, about fifty miles from Baltimore and just east of Frederick City.[287]

While Confederate operations were at a minimum, the railroad bridge at Harpers Ferry once again sustained weather related damage. On April 10, the Potomac River was again flooding. Loaded ore cars were placed on the trestle spans to help hold them in place. Near midnight the wide span, including the Winchester track was swept away taking twelve cars with it. The main line had been in service for some time and a large number of freight and passenger trains were on it including troops heading east to Washington, DC. With the water raging, it was impossible to lay a pontoon bridge. A special train from Baltimore brought out cables and within two days, a suspension bridge had been installed. On April 14, work commenced on replacing the trestling and was completed four days later. In the process, the railroad lost another valuable employee. John McLaughlin, foreman of carpenters, fell from the bridge and was drowned.[288]

In April President Lincoln made a brief visit to Baltimore City to attend the Maryland State Fair for U.S. Soldiers Relief. The occasion was a collaboration between two benevolent organizations, the United States Sanitary Commission and the United States Christian Commission. Commonly referred to as the Baltimore Sanitary Fair, its purpose was to raise money through donated items to be used to supply the personal needs of Union soldiers, sailors and marines. Fairs like this were held throughout the loyal states, but Baltimore's legacy of the Pratt Street Riot made it important to show a strong support for the Union in Maryland. To that end, President Lincoln was invited to attend the opening ceremonies on April 18, and spend the night at the home of Mr. William J. Albert, co-chairman of the event and a prominent Unionist. Always mindful of his precarious relationship with the State of Maryland, Lincoln agreed to attend. At 6:00 p.m., the President's train arrived at Camden Station and he and Mrs. Lincoln were taken by carriage to the Maryland Institute where the event was held. In a brief speech that evening, Lincoln alluded to the coincidence of the date. Three years ago to the day, the Pennsylvania Volunteers had arrived by train from Harrisburg and were attacked as they passed through the city en route to defend the capital. Prior to the President's arrival, Union regiments, both white and black, had paraded the streets to the cheers of the bystanders. The next day Lincoln returned to Washington. Mrs. Lincoln remained in town for a few days. On April 20, she attended the fair again accompanied by the B&O's president, John Work Garrett.[289]

Following the surrender of Vicksburg, Mississippi, and the defeat of Bragg at Chattanooga, Tennessee, Ulysses S. Grant was promoted to Lieutenant General and given command of all the Union armies. Meade remained in command of the Army of the Potomac; Halleck functioned as Chief of Staff in Washington; and Grant coordinated all military operations throughout the South while making his headquarters with the Army of the Potomac. On May 5, he initiated his Overland Campaign which began with the fighting in The Wilderness and ended with the siege of Petersburg. To support what was hoped to be the final campaign, Governor John Brough of Ohio offered President Lincoln 30,000 men from his newly reorganized Ohio National Guard to serve for 100 days. The Buckeye regiments would be used to garrison forts and guard railroads and bridges in order to release a like number of three-year men for active field service. Lincoln accepted the offer and requested the other Union states to do the same. Many of the 42 regiments (130th to 172nd) sent from Ohio were stationed in the fortifications of Baltimore and Washington and distributed along the main line of the B&O Railroad. While it was not intended for these units to seek active combat, many of them had the war come to them during the Summer of 1864.[290]

On May 5, McNeill's Rangers, now commanded by Captain Hanse McNeill after the death of his father, attacked the stations at Bloomington and Piedmont. After capturing the stone arched bridge at Bloomington, a mail train consisting of B&O locomotive No. 206 and its tender, a baggage car, a mail car and four passenger cars were captured and burned. Two additional freight trains with a total of eighteen loaded cars met the same fate near the bridge. A detachment was sent into Piedmont to destroy the B&O's property at the station. The machine shop, paint shop, sand house, and oil house were all set on fire. The engine house was partially burned along with twenty-two additional cars found in the yard. Approximately 2,000 feet of track were also destroyed. A repair crew arrived as soon as the Rebels left. By midnight the next day, the fires were out and the tracks replaced as far as the damaged bridge.[291]

The same day McNeill's Rangers struck at Piedmont, Union Major General Franz Sigel assumed command of the Department of West Virginia. Sigel fled Germany after the failed revolt of 1848 and was living in New York when the war began. Anxious to mobilize the German population behind the Union cause, Lincoln appointed him a brigadier general on August 7, 1861. Several field commands followed and the rank of major general in 1862. Sigel's appointment may again have been political with an eye to the fall elections, but no one was going to gamble with the security of the B&O Railroad. On May 9, General Kelley was given command of all the troops assigned to guard the railroad from Monocacy Junction to the Ohio River. Titled the Railroad District of West Virginia, he would have an independent command and report directly to the War Department. This arrangement would remain in effect until the end of the war.[292]

Sigel made his headquarters at New Creek. On May 7, he notified President Garrett, "I am advised that several regiments of Ohio militia are on the way to Cumberland and Harpers Ferry. When they arrive they will be used to protect the road." The arrival of the 100-day regiments coincided with an upturn in activity against the railroad. The 152nd Ohio Infantry left Camp Dennison near Cincinnati on May 12. Their train stopped at Piedmont Station where Corporal Clifton M. Nichols, after surveying the recent damage caused by McNeil's raid wrote, "The sight of these ruins aided us to appreciate the fact that we were in an enemy country." The regiment arrived at New Creek on May 16 without incident. Their companion regiments destined for Baltimore and Washington were not so lucky. The same day Corporal Nichols detrained at New Creek, another flood washed out the pontoon bridge and most of the railroad bridge at Harpers Ferry. Several 100-day regiments waited two days for the water to subside before they could be brought across the Potomac River in boats. On May 19, sufficient repairs had been completed to allow rail traffic to resume.[293]

CHAPTER EIGHTEEN

MONOCACY

Grant began what became known as the Overland Campaign on May 4, 1864. A string of bloody battles were fought in the Wilderness, Spotsylvania Court House, and Cold Harbor, that led to the siege of Petersburg. Located twenty miles south of Richmond, Petersburg was the vital rail center for supplying the Confederate Capital and the Army of Northern Virginia. Here the South Side connected with Lynchburg, a large supply and hospital center in the Shenandoah Valley. The Petersburg Railroad ran south to Weldon, North Carolina, where it connected with the Wilmington & Weldon, Lee's lifeline to the Carolinas and the Port of Wilmington, the last refuge for blockade-runners on the East Coast. All of these fed into the Richmond & Petersburg for freight going to Richmond.

Grant's forces missed a golden opportunity to capture Petersburg on June 15. After that, both armies entered into a protracted siege. Miles of trenches and concentrated artillery bombardments were a precursor to the World War I battlefield. Only the barbed wire and machine guns were missing. Grant had failed to take Petersburg with a cheap victory but his threat to Lee's supply lines robbed Lee of his mobility for the rest of the war.

To put added pressure on the Richmond–Petersburg defenses, Grant ordered Major General David Hunter with a force of 8,000 men to march up the Shenandoah Valley and destroy its capacity to feed the Confederate Army in the coming winter. Once he arrived at Lynchburg, he was to turn eastward and move against Richmond destroying the Virginia Central Railroad and the James River and Kanawha Canal. Hunter named his new command the Army of the Shenandoah and set out from his headquarters near Strasburg on June 22, to lay waste to the Valley. Following a successful defense of the valley in May, Lee had transferred all available units east to help in the defense of Petersburg. All that remained was "Grumble" Jones's brigade and a few scattered troops totaling about 5,000 men. Jones attempted to stop Hunter before he could reach Staunton and on June 5, the battle at Piedmont was fought. Jones was killed and his forces routed. Hunter occupied Staunton the next day where he paused to await reinforcements. Grant wanted to deliver a knockout blow to the Shenandoah Valley and sent General George Crook's infantry and General William W. Averell's cavalry divisions to raise Hunter's total strength to 15,000 men.[294]

As Hunter moved up the Valley, not only were legitimate military targets burned, but also barns, houses and anything else that got in his way. At Lexington, he burned the Virginia Military Institute and the home of Virginia's Governor, John Letcher. Then he set out for Lynchburg on June 14. Lee could no longer ignore the threat to this vital supply base and transferred Major General John Breckenridge's division to defend Lynchburg. Breckenridge soon advised Lee that his two small brigades were no match for the Army of the Shenandoah. Lee was forced to thin his lines yet again and ordered the newly promoted Lieutenant General Jubal A. Early to take the remnants of Jackson's old Second Corps to the Valley and defeat Hunter. A West Point graduate and veteran of the Mexican War, Early had been a disciple of Stonewall Jackson during the famed Valley Campaign of 1862. Arriving by train on the morning of June 17, he managed to stave off Hunter's attack. The next day Hunter attacked again. The daylong battle ended with a Union withdrawal that night. Early pursued the beaten Yankees for two days. Then, rather than retreat down the Valley the way he had advanced, Hunter chose to move into the southern part of West Virginia. This virtually took him out of the war for several weeks

as he strove to reach the Union supply base at Parkersburg on the Ohio River.[295]

The situation for the Confederacy in July of 1864 was critical. Since the twin losses of Gettysburg and Vicksburg the previous summer, it had been losing ground rapidly. Lee was tied to the defenses of Petersburg and Sherman was marching on Atlanta. At the same time, Lincoln was not the martyred President we think of today. He was the chief executive of a war that had lasted too long. Grant's casualties had brought death and despair to thousands of families in the North. With his popularity slipping, Lincoln faced reelection in November. His opponent was Gen-

Lt. General Jubal A. Early. (USAMHI)

eral George B. McClellan. A War Democrat, McClellan accepted the nomination despite his opposition to the party's peace platform. Unable to win on the battlefield, the South's last best hope was to secure a negotiated peace. To do this it would need to tie the staggering losses accumulated during the Overland Campaign with some sort of spectacular military achievement in order to win the election for McClellan. Jubal Early was about to be given that opportunity.

Once Early had neutralized the threat from Hunter's army, Lee had given him the option to either return to the siege lines at Petersburg or move north down the Valley, cross into Maryland and, if possible, lay siege to the Union capital. All of this was made possible by two factors. First, the Shenandoah Valley was void of Union troops all the way to Winchester and second, although Washington was the most heavily fortified city in the world at the time, it had been stripped of most of its defense forces to feed Grant's war of attrition in Northern Virginia. These units were replaced for the most part with walking wounded and the 100-day men from Ohio. Early's small force could never hope to hold the Union capital for any great length of time, but even a day or two could possibly be the spectacular military achievement that would win the election for McClellan. A near miss would also have its rewards. Once Early crossed into Maryland, Grant would be forced to transfer large numbers of troops from the Army of the Potomac to protect Washington. Of course, the B&O Railroad would also be a target of opportunity. After resting and refitting his army at Staunton, he marched north on June 28.[296]

One of the remarkable things about Early's move down the Valley was that Grant did not believe he had ever left Petersburg and took no immediate action to guard against the blow that was coming. In the lower Valley General Franz Sigel held Martinsburg with a force of about 5,000 men. Brigadier General Max Weber commanded the garrison at Harpers Ferry. When Early arrived at Winchester he had under his command four divisions of infantry, four brigades of cavalry, and about fifty pieces of artillery with a total of not more than 15,000 men. He dispatched General John McCausland's cavalry to move west to North Mountain and cut the B&O line to prevent reinforcements from being sent east from Cumberland. Newly promoted to command "Grumble" Jones's old brigade, Brigadier General Bradley T. Johnson was to cross the main line east of Martinsburg and join forces with McCausland in order to cut off Sigel's retreat to the Potomac. Faced with the approach of Confederate infantry from the south, Sigel removed as much government property as possible by rail and wagon train and then made good his escape before the trap could be closed. Rebel troops under the command of General Breckinridge occupied Martinsburg on July 3.[297]

The 135th Ohio, one of the 100-day regiments left their induction camp on May 11, en route for Wheeling where they boarded a train that took them to Martinsburg. There Colonel Legg was ordered to send companies B and F under the command of Captain Ulysses Westbrook to occupy the blockhouse at North Mountain Depot. The remaining seven companies of his regiment were stationed at Martinsburg. On July 2, Captain Westbrook learned that a previously rumored Rebel advance was indeed real, and in the middle of the night ordered his 162 men into the blockhouse and surrounding trench. The next day McCausland's brigade attacked with 1,300 men and a battery of horse artillery. The blockhouse showed its worth, absorbing the cavalrymen's pistol and carbine bullets while the untested Ohioans held off the Rebels for two hours with their long-range rifles. Then McCausland was able to get his artillery into position and blasted the Yankees out of their little fort. In a cruel twist of fate, the 100-day men were marched off to prison and ninety of the enlisted men died at the infamous Andersonville prison camp. McCausland burned the blockhouse and the nearby Back Creek Bridge and then rode on.[298]

On the Fourth of July, Confederate cavalry struck the B&O bridges at Patterson's Creek and South Branch. The defenses at South Branch were a showcase for the technologies developed to protect the B&O railroad during the Civil War. A blockhouse had been constructed on the west bank of the river to protect the bridge. One of the armored cars built at Mount Clare the year before stood on the tracks not far from the blockhouse. It contained a 12-lb. gun and a crew of seven from Company K of the Second Maryland Potomac Home Brigade. The "Railroad Monitor" had a six-inch porthole at either end to minimize exposure to the crew when the cannon was fired and a metal hatch cover operated with a lever to seal the hole when not firing. The crew entered through a trapdoor in the floor. The blockhouse was manned by one company from the 153rd Ohio National Guard.

Imboden's Brigade attacked with a force of about 1,500 men and 3 pieces of artillery. Despite a severe shelling, the troops in the blockhouse managed to hold out. Unable to reach a position from which he could shell the bridge, Imboden had his gunners concentrate their fire on the ironclad railcar. The first shot missed. The second shot struck the roof and bounced off. The third shot unbelievably passed through the six-inch porthole and at the same time struck the lever in such a way as to slam the hatch cover shut. The shell bounced around inside the car. The burning fuse filling the car with acrid smoke as its occupants frantically attempted to exit through the trap door in the floor. In an act worthy of the Medal of Honor, Corporal John W. Croston tried to pick up the sputtering projectile and heave it out of the car but the heat from the shell burned his hands and face. The brave soldier just managed to dive through the escape hatch as the shell exploded which gave him severe powder burns on his face, hands and neck. The interior of the car caught on fire and soon the battery's magazine erupted in a series of secondary explosions. Croston was sent to the U.S. Army Hospital in nearby Clarysville, Maryland. His attending physician noted that he had originally been treated with a mixture of olive oil and chimney soot and "presented a hideous aspect." Remarkably, Corporal Croston made a full recovery and returned to duty on July 22.

With the railroad battery out of action, Imboden's men were able to set fire to the east end of the bridge but were driven off by the approach of more armored cars from the west. A secondary force led by Captain McNeill attacked Patterson Creek and set it on fire before being driven off by a relief force from North Branch. General Kelley reported that the damage could be repaired in forty-eight hours.[299]

Also on the Fourth of July, Early, with the left wing of his army, moved against Harpers Ferry in a reenactment of the 1862 siege. General Weber removed as much material as possible and retreated to the safety of Maryland Heights that night. Sigel arrived a few hours later and joined forces with Weber on the Heights. The pontoon bridge was taken up and the woodwork on the iron railroad bridge burned. At this point, the B&O was on its own. On this same day, Mosby, with a force of 250 men, crossed the Potomac River and attempted to capture the eastbound mail train as it approached Point of Rocks. The fireman was seriously wounded but the engineer quickly put his locomotive in reverse and ran safely back to Sandy Hook. The raiders also drove off the guard detachment at Point of Rocks and captured one officer and several enlisted men. Mr. W. W. Shock, the telegraph operator described what happened next. "They cut the telegraph lines in several places...I saved all my instruments, but at great risk to my life. They took our agent, Mr. Means, prisoner after taking all of his moveable property. I will have to go to the mountains again...and will stay here until they starve me out. They left here about 6 P.M."[300]

Unable to learn any details from the army, four employees of the B&O including J. P. Williams, Supervisor of the road, and the telegraph operator, Mr. Ludwig, took the yard engine No. 31 and left Sandy Hook at 8:00 a.m. the next day to inspect the tracks between there and Monocacy Junction. When they arrived at Point of Rocks, they were fired on from across the river by Mosby's men with rifles and one piece of artillery. The tracks were undamaged and No. 31 returned to Sandy Hook to act as a pilot for the mail train and four freight trains from Harpers Ferry filled with government supplies. All four trains made it safely to Monocacy Junction.[301]

As the presence of enemy forces near the Potomac River became evident, plans were made to remove the sick and wounded soldiers from the hospitals in Frederick and as much of the government stores as possible. At 4:30 in the morning of July 4 B&O Locomotive No. 72 left with twenty-eight cars of convalescent soldiers. At 11:00 p.m. on July 7, an additional seven loads of wounded soldiers arrived at Annapolis Junction behind B&O Locomotive No. 172 without notice and were forced to lay over until morning in the cars. About 1,000 men were transferred to the hospitals in Annapolis.[302]

On July 5, Early's infantry began to cross the Potomac River at fords above Harpers Ferry. After probing the base of Maryland Heights, he soon determined that the Union position was too strong to assault and ordered it by-passed. Crossing the river at Shepherdstown and Boteler's Ford, his main force moved east through South Mountain using the same passes that had been so valiantly defended while Stonewall Jackson besieged Harpers Ferry in 1862. His next objective was Frederick. One of the largest cities in Maryland, it was a major supply base for the Federal Army. A single-track spur line connected the heart of the city with main line of the B&O as it crossed the Monocacy River and swung south towards Harpers Ferry. Thus the name Monocacy Junction. Here Early found a collection of valuable targets. In the city were warehouses stuffed to the rafters with war materials. The iron railroad bridge and associated B&O property were at the junction. Last, but not least, the city was surrounded by large farms with an abundance of horses, cows and grain for the taking.[303]

Grant's denial that an invasion was possible persisted until July 5. Garrett had warned Stanton on July 3 that his train crews and telegraph agents were reporting considerable Confederate activity in the lower Shenandoah Valley; and that Early, Breckinridge, and Imboden had passed through Winchester with 15,000 to 30,000 men, and that Martinsburg and Harpers Ferry had been abandoned. None of this resulted in any action until Confederate troops were actually tramping on Maryland soil. Grant ordered General Meade to send "one good division" to Baltimore by steamers but held off sending an entire corps until more information was available. Meade selected Ricketts's Third Division of the Sixth Corps, but the movement would take time. It would be up to John Work Garrett and Major General Lew Wallace to fight the battle that would save the Capital and maybe Lincoln's re-election.[304]

Lew Wallace faced a number of challenges in planning a course of action. He had received no instructions from Sigel at Maryland Heights or Halleck in Washington. His first responsibility was to defend Baltimore City, which, like Washington, had been stripped of its heavy artillery regiments to replace Grant's mounting casualties incurred during the Overland Campaign to Petersburg. Finally, the western boundary of his department was the east bank of the Monocacy River. Frederick City and the advancing enemy were on the west side. On thin ice with Halleck and Grant, he knew that if he crossed the river and failed it would mean the end of his military career. Wallace could have played it safe and advanced no farther than Relay and the Thomas Viaduct in order to protect the Washington Branch. To his credit, rather than give up fifty miles of the B&O Railroad and leave the door open to Early for a rapid advance on Washington, he chose to engage the enemy where he found him and hope that reinforcements arrived in time. Wallace culled through the remaining units in and around Baltimore City. He ordered Brigadier General Erastus B. Tyler to move his Third Separate Brigade from Relay to Monocacy Junction and take charge of all available troops in the area.

Major General Lew Wallace. (D. C. T.)

On the night of July 4, Wallace sent Garrett a request for a locomotive to take him to the Junction as quickly as the tracks could be cleared. He and a single staff officer climbed into the cab of an engine and departed Camden Station shortly after midnight. Wallace spent the night in the blockhouse at Monocacy Junction, which temporarily served as his headquarters. The next day he surveyed the surrounding terrain features and ordered the last of the troops that could be spared from the defenses of Baltimore to join him.

At about 6:00 p.m. on July 5, Wallace requested trains to take the Eleventh Maryland Infantry from Relay and Alexander's Battery of Light Artillery from Baltimore to reinforce Tyler. The Eleventh Maryland was one of the state's two 100-day regiments. Alexander's Battery was a veteran organization and its six guns would be the only field artillery Wallace would have in the battle. B&O Locomotive No. 70 with twenty-five troop cars and one stock car left Relay at 11:00 p.m. The artillery departed from Camden Station the same night.[305]

On the morning of July 6, Wallace was still in the dark as to the size of the army he was about to confront. His own force at this time consisted of 2,500 men and the 6 guns of Alexander's Battery plus 2 additional pieces of artillery at the blockhouse. Sigel's Reserve Division remained camped out on Maryland Heights and the first of Hunter's men were just beginning to leave Parkersburg 326 miles away. The damaged track east of Cumberland made their availability uncertain. The tension of the moment may have been reflected in the telegraph

Wallace snapped off to William Prescott Smith, "Your telegraph operator at Monrovia has deserted his post. Please send him back or supply his place with another man."[306]

On the morning of July 7, Wallace ordered Colonel David R. Clendenin with 230 men of the Eighth Illinois Cavalry supported by two guns from the Maryland battery commanded by Lieutenant Peter Leary to move west along the National Road in an attempt to determine the strength and direction of Early's army. A few miles east of Middletown, Clendenin's force collided with Johnson's Brigade of cavalry screening Early's advancing infantry divisions. Bradley T. Johnson was not only Maryland's newest Confederate general, he was a native of Frederick City. Clendenin fought a running battle all the way to the suburbs of Johnson's hometown.

Earlier in the day, Garrett had sent some welcome news to Lew Wallace, "A large force of veterans have arrived by water, and will be sent immediately. Our arrangements are made to forward them immediately. As Genl. Sigel's forces remain on Maryland Heights, you are doubtless aware of the great importance of preserving Monocacy bridge. If it be damaged or destroyed, great delays will result in getting forward reinforcements to Genl. Sigel." Fearing he may have to abandon Frederick, Wallace informed Garrett at 4:55 p.m.," My troops are engaging the enemy to the west... I will hold the bridge at all hazards. Send on troops as rapidly as possible."

Clendenin was forced to fall back to the outskirts of Frederick City where Captain Alexander joined him with a third gun and some much needed infantry support. The fighting lasted until after 6:00 p.m. when, to Johnson's displeasure, his division commander General Robert Ransom ordered a withdraw. When apprised of the turn of events Wallace wrote to his adjutant-general, Lt. Colonel Samuel B. Lawrence in Baltimore, "I have had the best little battle of the war." Ironically, he would forty-eight hours later.[307]

The long awaited arrival of reinforcements from the Army of the Potomac demonstrated yet another outstanding example of the B&O's logistical support for the Union Army. Perhaps never before had an inter-modal move of this magnitude taken place. An entire infantry division was transported hundreds of miles from City Point, Virginia, first by boat and then by train and delivered directly to the battlefield. As can be imagined, this movement did not take place without its challenges. The following list of telegrams and train movements illustrates the ferocity in which Garrett and his employees attacked these problems. The time sequence begins on July 7, 1864.

6:05 P.M. Garrett to Wallace, "Our most effective officers are doing all that is possible to urge the loading and prompt forwarding of the troops now arriving."

7:15 P.M. Garrett to Stanton, "I regret to cite that no troops are yet disembarked. Unfortunately, orders were given by the Commanding General (Ricketts) that none should be landed till he arrived. Would not a dispatch from your department to the officers in command, insure more rapid disembarkation?" In this same telegram, Garrett brought up the boundary issue. "Our agent at Monocacy states some difficulty with…General Wallace and Tyler in commanding the troops in action west of the Monocacy, in view of their Departmental limits. Can you not issue such orders as will relieve this difficulty?"

Time/date not stated, Garrett to Wallace, "I telegraphed the secretary of War regarding your position in connection with Departmental lines. To relieve you from any delicacy on this subject, he advises me you have been ordered to operate without reference to departmental lines."

Stanton sent orders through Garrett to the officer on the boat to disembark immediately. The first steamer docked at Locust Point in the Baltimore harbor near Fort McHenry and began unloading about 11:00 p.m. The second one tied up around thirty minutes later. At 3:30 in the morning of July 8, B&O Locomotive No. 178 with twenty-six carloads of soldiers from the Sixth Corps departed for the battlefield. Five more steamers arrived by 4:00 a.m. Between 7:45 a.m. and 7:45 p.m. four troop trains totaling over ninety cars departed the Locust Point terminal. All passenger service on the main line was halted to let these trains through. By 11:00 a.m., five more steamers arrived. One of these carried the division commander General Ricketts. He immediately sent Smith a request for a special train to take him to the front. Obviously, he had not heard what happened to General Schurz on his way to Chattanooga in 1863. Smith saw to it that the general's car was attached to a troop train that left that afternoon. The last troop transport ship arrived at Locust Point early on the morning of July 9 and the men were transferred to trains by 7:00 a.m.[308]

Wallace put General Tyler in charge of holding Frederick and sent the first trainload of reinforcements to arrive on July 8 to help strengthen his grip on the city. Things remained static along the lines as Confederate infantry marched east along dusty roads while their Union counterparts rode west in the relative luxury of freight cars. Two important highways emanated from Frederick and represented an inverted "V." Turned upside down, the apex of the "V" was Frederick. Its right side was formed by the Baltimore & Frederick-Town Turnpike, an extension of the National Road, that crossed the Monocacy River on a stone bridge and ran east through Ellicott's Mills to Baltimore City. The left side of the "V" was formed by the Georgetown Pike that crossed the river on a covered wooden bridge and ran south to Washington. Just north of the covered bridge was Monocacy Junction and the B&O's iron bridge protected by

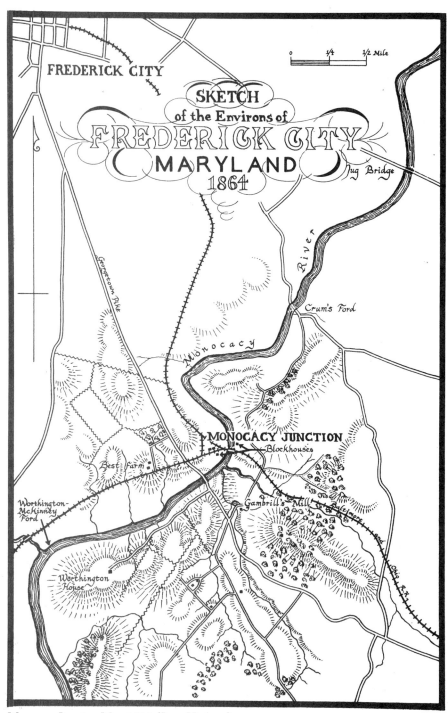

Monocacy Junction Map, 1864. (Jerry Harlowe)

two blockhouses. Near 6:00 p.m., Wallace received word that a strong enemy formation was observed moving towards his left flank that indicated the probable direction of Early's army was Washington. With Baltimore or the capital at stake, Frederick became expendable. Wallace ordered the city evacuated that night. During the withdrawal B&O Locomotive No. 47 derailed between the city and the junction. Agent Mantz wired Smith, "I have ordered all force that can be got to go to the assistance of getting engine on. This blocks the train of sick and wounded."[309]

On the morning of July 9, Wallace's main line of defense ran along the east bank of the Monocacy River with small detachments on the east side opposite the bridges. He placed Ricketts's veteran regiments to cover his left flank and put General Tyler in charge on the right. His total force, including three regiments still en route from Locust Point, did not exceed 6,000. Knowing the vulnerability of both Baltimore and Washington, he put his miniature army in a position to block the most direct routes to both cities. He would not measure his success in ground gained or lost but in the number of hours he delayed Early's advance.

There have been many fine books and articles written about the details of the battle of Monocacy. It would not add to that body of knowledge to recount those details here, nor fulfill the objective of this work. The purpose of briefly describing the combat action around Frederick City was to dramatize the pending doom that Wallace faced while awaiting the arrival of Ricketts' Division. It is the author's belief that Monocacy was not only the battle that saved the capital, but that is was the B&O's battle as well. With the exception of a few hundred cavalrymen, almost every Union soldier was transported to the battlefield by train.

One aspect of the battle that does pertain to our story is the action around the blockhouse and railroad bridge. It will be remembered that in the report issued by Colonel Thom in March of 1863, he recommended that two large blockhouses be constructed to protect the Monocacy River Bridge. One would be on the northeast side and one on the southwest side. When General Lew Wallace took command of the Middle Department, he made a point of inspecting his key areas of responsibility. In April of 1864, he and his chief engineer officer, Captain William P. Craighill, took a train to Monocacy Junction to survey the bridge and its defenses. Craighill recommended a piece of artillery be placed in one of the blockhouses to cover the nearby wooden bridge. Wallace ordered General Tyler at Relay to send up a gun and crew. Tyler's First Separate Brigade took the place of the old Railroad Brigade and was responsible for the main line of the B&O between Monocacy Junction and Baltimore City. He sent a 24-pounder howitzer that was positioned on the high ground near the east bank blockhouse. This gave it a wide field of fire along both the

B&O tracks and the Georgetown Pike. For some reason during the battle, the gun was not manned. This was a sizable piece of artillery and could aid significantly in defense of the bridge. During the battle the blockhouses were manned by two companies of the First Potomac Home Brigade.

Captain William H. Wiegel was serving on the staff of General Tyler. When he noticed that the gun was sitting idle he rode up to General Wallace, saluted and asked permission to put it into action. Wallace readily agreed and with an *ad hoc* crew began dropping rounds on the Confederate artillery advancing along the Georgetown Pike. Eventually Wiegel was wounded and one of the inexperienced gunners loaded the shell before the powder charge rendering the gun inoperable. When the retreat was ordered, Captain Alexander took special pains to make sure none of his guns were captured. As he moved them off the field, he noticed the abandoned howitzer and a smaller piece inside the nearby blockhouse. He had his men load the smaller piece into a wagon and abandoned another to provide horses for the howitzer.[310]

By the end of the day, Early's superior numbers were the deciding factor. After a valiant effort, Wallace's men were driven from the field. Their escape route ran east along the turnpike to Ellicott's Mills. The B&O's performance was not perfect. At the height of the battle, the telegraph operator at Monocacy ordered the train that Wallace was holding nearby for the evacuation of his wounded back to a safer location and left with his key and receiver. This left Wallace without any means of communicating with Garrett or Halleck.[311]

During the retreat that night, Wallace stopped at the B&O's telegraph office at Plane No. 1, eight miles east of Sykesville and sent the following message to President Garrett, "I did as I promised. Held the bridge to the last. They overwhelmed with numbers. My troops fought splendidly. Losses fearful. Send me cars enough to Ellicott's Mills to take up my retreating columns. Don't fail me."[312]

The next day Early put his army in motion on the Georgetown Pike. Before leaving, he collected a $200,000 ransom from the Mayor of Frederick. Upon entering the city on the night of July 8, he had demanded the money and threatened to burn the city in retaliation for Hunter's actions in the Shenandoah Valley if not paid. The City Council and mayor worked with the local banks to arrange the payment. Not until a month later did the citizens of Frederick appreciate the wisdom of their actions.

Early had won a battle that he did not want to fight and suffered casualties he could not replace. More importantly, he had lost a day on the march to Washington. On the morning of July 10, he moved south. Left behind was a detachment with orders to burn the B&O's buildings at Monocacy Junction and the blockhouses. A gun crew also stayed and fired solid shot at the iron bridge in an attempt to destroy it. As Early's men marched along the Georgetown Pike, the remaining two divisions of the Sixth Corps under Major General Horatio G. Wright were sailing north from City Point, Virginia, directly to Washington, DC. The Confederates arrived in front of Fort Stevens on the outskirts of Washington on July 11. Just as Early was about to launch an attack on the lightly held fortification, the lead elements of the Sixth Corps arrived and he was forced to cancel the assault. Early had lost the race to the capital by a matter of hours – hours he had lost along the banks of the Monocacy River.[313]

Brig. General Bradley T. Johnson. (USAMHI)

A sub-plot to Early's march on Washington was the Johnson-Gilmor Raid. A little known operation, if it had been successful it would have been the most spectacular cavalry operation of the war. The commander of the operation was General Bradley T. Johnson, a native of Frederick City and direct descendent of Thomas Johnson, the first governor of Maryland after the Revolution. Before the war, he had been one of the militia officers that went to Harpers Ferry to subdue John Brown. When Johnson assumed command of "Grumble" Jones's command, he brought with him the First Maryland Cavalry Battalion and two guns of the Baltimore Light Artillery. At Winchester he was joined by Gilmor's Second Maryland Battalion.

Johnson's Brigade did not take part in the battle of Monocacy. It remained near Frederick and once a Confederate victory was assured, he headed northeast toward Westminster. His mission was to ride around Baltimore City and cut rail and telegraph lines in order to delay any reinforcements that might be sent in pursuit of Early's army as it advanced on Washington. He was then to reverse his route and travel south all the way to the prisoner of war camp at Point Lookout where on July 12, eight hundred Confederate marines would launch an amphibious attack from two converted blockade runners. Johnson would attack from the land side. At stake were ten to fifteen thousand Confederate POWs. Once the guards had been overrun, the newly released prisoners would be formed into a division and march to join Early in the siege of Wash-

Major Harry Gilmor. (USAMHI)

ington. This was no hare-brained scheme. The naval expedition was commanded by Jefferson Davis's nephew, Commander John Taylor Wood. The land operation was to be commanded by General George Washington Custis Lee, Robert E. Lee's oldest son. In the course of the raid, nearly every railroad in the state of Maryland would be damaged in some way.[314]

Major Harry Gilmor and a small group of Marylanders took the lead. On the first day, they burned the bridge and station on the Western Maryland Railroad at New Windsor and took out the telegraph office at Westminster. On July 10, Johnson's men destroyed two bridges north of Baltimore City on the Northern Central Railroad at Cockeysville.

Then Johnson reversed his route and began the long march to Point Lookout. He had no way of knowing that the naval expedition had been canceled that same day. The details of the ultra secret operation had been printed in a Richmond newspaper and President Jefferson Davis ordered the ships not to sail.

Johnson traveled through Howard and Montgomery counties. Behind schedule, he struck the Washington Branch at Beltsville on July 12 where he captured a construction crew and work train consisting of seven cars. The train was burned along with thirteen additional cars found on a siding. Eight telegraph poles were cut down disrupting communication between Baltimore and the Capital. The wood work on the iron bridge over Paint Branch was also burned. This was the only time during the war that the Washington Branch came under attack by Confederate forces. William Prescott Smith was prophetic when he wired the commander of the Defenses of Washington, Major General Christopher C. Augar, on the night of July 7, "I presume no apology is necessary for my repeating to you the substance of my first warning of last night about the inadequacy of the guard upon important bridges of our railroad between Annapolis Junction and Washington…" Just as Johnson had put his column in motion southward, a courier arrived from Early advising him that the expedition had been canceled and he was retreating into Virginia. The next day Union cavalry from the Defenses of Washington made a sweep of the area. A handcar then traveled from Bladensburg all the way to Relay, checking the condition of the tracks. It was followed later that day by B&O Locomotive No. 19 from Washington with the first news that the Confederate army was retreating. Operation of the Washington Branch was fully restored on July 14.[315]

Early's near miss at capturing Washington not only caused Grant to transfer the Sixth Corps from the Army of the Potomac but the Nineteenth Corps was rerouted in transit from New Orleans as well. The original plan was for the corps to reinforce Butler's Army of James. With Early threatening the Nation's Capital, the transports were redirected to Washington and the port of Baltimore. The first ship landed at the wharves in Washington on July 11 and the troops on board were sent to garrison Fort Saratoga, one of the many forts that surrounded Washington City. Other ships made their way up the Chesapeake Bay and landed at Locust Point beginning on July 14. The corps commander, Major General E. O. C. Ord, was born in Cumberland and raised in Washington, DC. He made a request directly to President Garrett for enough trains to move 4,000 infantry, a battery of artillery and 3 general officers and their staffs to Washington. Garrett replied that the required transportation would be arranged by Master of Transportation Smith.[316]

When Johnson left Cockeysville, he detached Harry Gilmor with 135 Marylanders to continue around Baltimore City and disrupt the Philadelphia, Wilmington & Baltimore Railroad. Gilmor struck the PW&B the next day at Magnolia Station, nineteen miles from Baltimore. Here he captured and burned two trains, the station, and the draw bridge over the Gunpowder River.

Gilmor's detachment burned two trains and the Magnolia Station on the PH&B Railroad. (D. C. T.)

On one of the trains were a number of Union officers including Major General William B. Franklin. After burning the bridge, Gilmor headed south to rejoin the main column. Along the way, his guards fell asleep and all of his prisoners escaped. The Johnson-Gilmor Raid failed in its ultimate mission to free the prisoners at Point Lookout but collectively the two commands destroyed three trains, three bridges, two stations, and miles of telegraph lines while suffering the loss of only one man. They kept the Union forces in Baltimore on the defensive until after Early had safely crossed the Potomac River back into Virginia.[317]

Throughout the night of July 9 and all the next day, Wallace's men ran, walked and limped down the National Road. Their immediate destination was Ellicott's Mills where thirty-car trains were being sent out from Mount Clare to pick them up. The veterans of Ricketts' Division and the guns of Alexander's Battery formed a defensive shield in case the Confederate forces unexpectedly attacked. B&O Locomotive No. 47 was sent out with a single passenger car to pickup General Wallace and returned to Baltimore on the night of July 10.

On July 18, Lew Wallace sent the following letter to John Work Garrett.

"Hon. John Garrett
Pres. B&O Railroad Co.

Dear Sir:

I avail myself of the first leisure moments to express to you and Mr. W. P. Smith my most sincere acknowledgements for the very great services rendered to me and my little army before and after the battle of Monocacy.

To sum it all up in a few words, I say frankly, that without your road, under your energetic and zealous management, it would have been impossible for me to maintain my position five minutes in presence of the force that attacked me on that occasion. Therefore, please accept my thanks and believe me.

Most truly and faithfully
Your friend & SVA (servant)
Lew Wallace
Maj. Gen Comd. 8th AC
& Mid Dept"[318]

CHAPTER NINETEEN

CHAMBERSBURG

At the same time the survivors of Monocacy were making their way back to Baltimore, Union General David Hunter's men were traveling by boat from Charleston, West Virginia, via the Kanawha River to the Ohio and north to Parkersburg where low water on the river continued to delay their arrival. As fast as possible, B&O agents arranged trains for their eastward movement. By the middle of July, Hunter and the vanguard of his fugitives arrived at Martinsburg. It was not until July 22, that all of his troops had arrived at Harpers Ferry. Again, the rapid repairs to the damage on the main line made this troop movement possible. Repair crews moved east and had the tracks open to Martinsburg by July 14. Nine spans of the Pillar Bridge in Martinsburg were replaced and work began on the Opequon Bridge on the eighteenth. On July 15, a construction train arrived at Monocacy Junction from Baltimore. They found the agent's house, station, and telegraph office burned. It was necessary to trestle under the iron bridge because three of the towers and seventeen suspension rods had been shot away by cannon fire. The train crossed the bridge two days later and repair crews began working at Harpers Ferry on July 18. Twenty-seven culverts and miles of telegraph line had been destroyed between Harpers Ferry and Martinsburg. Through service was restored on the main line by July 25, just in time for the next Confederate offensive.

Jubal Early had retreated into Virginia, but unlike Hunter and Wallace, he had not been defeated. After resting his men and sorting out his plunder, he turned on Hunter's pursuit force commanded by Brigadier General George Crook at Kernstown on July 24 and sent it racing back towards the Potomac River. This uncovered the main line of the B&O and Martinsburg fell into Confederate hands once again on July 25. All engines and rolling stock were sent off before their arrival. During the next two days, Early's men burned the Back Creek Bridge and tore up fifteen miles of new track between there and Harpers Ferry.[319]

Upon Hunter's return from West Virginia, he began a new round of atrocities in both Maryland and the lower Shenandoah Valley. Money was extorted from citizens accused of being Southern sympathizers and their homes were burned. Early ordered a retaliatory raid into Pennsylvania to show the people in the North the type of warfare being waged against Southern civilians. The target was Chambersburg. It was both the center of operations for the Cumberland Valley Railroad and headquarters of the Department of the Susquehanna commanded by General Darius N. Couch. Confederate cavalry had raided the city in both 1862 and 1863, but only burned legitimate military targets. This time it would be different.

Early sent Brigadier General John McCausland with his and Johnson's cavalry brigades into southern Pennsylvania with orders to ransom Chambersburg for $100,000 in gold or $500,000 in paper currency in retribution for what Hunter had done in Virginia. If the demand was not met, the city was to be burned to the ground. From there he was to go to Cumberland and deliver the same set of demands. Whether he received the money or not, he was to destroy the B&O facilities there and the C&O tunnel at Paw Paw before crossing the Potomac River at New Creek and burning the bridges there. Couch had less than 500 men to defend the city, McCausland; had over 2,500.[320]

The Confederate cavalry led by Harry Gilmor and the two Maryland battalions crossed the Potomac River at McCoy's Ferry on the morning of July 29. They arrived at Mercersburg around 5:00 p.m. McCausland allowed his men to rest until 10:00 p.m. before continuing the march. Since crossing the river, their advance had been slowed by a number of ambushes led by Lieutenant Hancock T. McLean and forty-four men of the Sixth U.S. Cavalry. This gave General Couch time to remove his quartermaster supplies and headquarters by train to Harrisburg.

Shortly after 5:00 a.m. on July 30, McCausland's artillery fired a salvo over the sleeping city to announce his arrival. He then sent dismounted cavalry in to secure the town before riding in with his staff to present their demands. Unlike the citizens of Frederick, the residents of Chambersburg failed to take the threat seriously.

Brig. General John McCausland. (WVDC&H)

The burning of Chambersburg by General McCausland. (D. C. T.)

McCausland wasted little time in implementing his final option and ordered the city burned. By noon, the Confederate column was headed west. Left behind was a giant pall of black smoke that marked the destruction of over 550 buildings. In pursuit was a Union cavalry division under the command of General William W. Averell.[321]

McCausland's command spent the night at McConnellsburg. Upon their arrival, they wrecked the telegraph office to prevent any knowledge of their movements from being transmitted to Union commanders. The next day they rode off towards Hancock, Maryland. When Averell arrived, he found that the fifteen-year-old telegraph operator, Thomas F. Sloan, had hidden a second set of instruments and was already in contact with General Kelley's headquarters in Cumberland. The two Union generals were able to coordinate their efforts to intercept the Rebels at Hancock.[322]

When McCausland's lead units arrived at Hancock, they found Alpine Station on the other side of the river guarded by Company I, of the 153rd Ohio National Guard. By coincidence, a portion of Company H, Twelfth West Virginia and some other stragglers under the command of First Lieutenant David Powell had arrived that morning. They were part of Crook's force that had been defeated at Kernstown on July 24. Throughout the morning, more Confederate troops arrived in Hancock and two pieces of artillery were put into position to fire across the Potomac River. Thanks to Tommy Sloan's hidden telegraph instrument, an armored train arrived from Cumberland around 10:00 o'clock in the morning. Captain Peter B. Petrie and a detachment from Company K, Second Maryland Potomac Home Brigade manned the artillery car and Captain Charles J. Harrison with men from Company I, of the Sixth West Virginia Infantry occupied the rifle cars. The "Monitor car" fired two rounds without effect. Then the Confederates' guns opened up. The first round pierced the locomotive's firebox. The second round struck the smokestack. Captain Petrie ordered the engineer to back out of range of the enemy's guns. The Confederate artillery then began to shell Alpine Station. When their cavalry threatened to cross the river, Lieutenant Powell's men held them off with long distance musket fire until ordered to disengage. Then he marched his men up the tracks about a mile and climbed aboard the armored train. The Ohio company did the same thing and together they rode up to Sir John's Run. Seeing the Alpine Station abandoned, some of the Rebel cavalry crossed the river and burned it.[323]

About 5:00 p.m., Averell's Division struck McCausland's picket line outside of Hancock. McCausland ordered Johnson to form a rear guard and headed west on the National Road. General Kelley received orders from Halleck to do everything in his power to protect the major rail center at Cumberland and supply base at New Creek. Kelley used his armored train to gather up other detachments and deposit them at Green Spring Station across the river from Old Town. Here Colonel Israel Stough of the 153rd Ohio National Guard had a mixed force of 450 men to block McCausland if he tried to cross the Potomac River at Old Town.

On August 1, McCausland's force was reported to be twelve miles east of Cumberland. Kelley sent out the 156th Ohio National Guard regiment under Colonel Cassius C. Marker and four companies of the Eleventh West Virginia Infantry commanded by Major James L. Simpson supported by four guns from Battery L, First Illinois Light Artillery to a concealed position about three miles outside of town overlooking Flock's Mill. The rest of his forces remained in the forts around the city. McCausland's lead companies crossed Evitt's Creek Bridge around 3 p.m. and the artillery opened fire. The startled Confederates took shelter in the buildings around Flock's Mill. McCausland deployed his entire brigade and put his four guns into action. Johnson's Brigade arrived later in the day but did not take part in the battle. The two generals conferred and both agreed that with strong fortifications in front and Averell advancing on their rear, their best course of action was to disengage and return to Virginia.[324]

Unfamiliar with the region, Harry Gilmor was ordered to find a way to the Potomac River. Gilmor grabbed the first civilian he saw, put him on a horse and at gunpoint forced him to lead them through the night to a river crossing. Johnson's Brigade took the advance and McCausland's covered the rear. As dawn broke they approached Old Town, a small village located on the north side of the Potomac River opposite Green Spring Station. The C&O Canal ran through the town. Between the canal and the river was a wooded ridge known as Alum Hill. Colonel Stough brought six companies of his 100-day Ohio men across the river to oppose any crossing from the Maryland side and placed them on the ridge. He also had the flooring from the nearby canal bridge removed to further impede the enemy's advance. Behind the ridge was a ford that led to Green Spring Station. Covering both the ford and the station was one of Colonel Raynolds' two story blockhouses manned by Company D of the 153 Ohio National Guard. General Kelley had also sent an armored train to block the ford. The train was state-of-the-art in mechanized warfare. The locomotive and tender were located in the center. Two ironclad rifle cars were positioned in front of the engine and two behind. At either end of the train were cannon cars with artillery pieces mounted at both ends. Company K of the Second Maryland Potomac Home Brigade supplied the gun crews. The rifle cars were manned by Company I of the Sixth West Virginia Regiment. [325]

Gilmor's advance party drew fire from the Yankees on the ridge and pulled back until Johnson arrived with the rest of the brigade. Stough's men resisted several attacks until Johnson's artillery began to drop shells on Alum Hill. He then retreated across the river and took up a new position behind the railroad embankment at Green Spring Station. The armored artillery units still made crossing the ford impossible for the Confederate cavalry. Because of the tree line on the ridge, Johnson's gunners could not see to aim at the train. Finally, Lieutenant John R. McNulty led his two guns of the Baltimore Light Artillery across the hastily repaired bridge and went into battery on Alum Hill. Corporal George W. McElwee, a gunner on one of the pieces, then took aim at the armored train. His first round struck the locomotive and exploded the boiler. Unbelievably, for the second time in less than thirty days, his next shot passed through a porthole on one of the "railroad monitors" and dismounted a cannon. A third round exploded in the rail bed showering the Union infantry with debris. The soldiers on the immobilized armored train jumped off and fled, as did most of the Ohio regiment. Stough and a handful of his men bravely joined Company D, in the blockhouse. The fugitives climbed aboard the troop train that had brought them, and Captain Cross of Company F assumed everyone was on the train and ordered it off to North Branch.

Despite Corporal McElwee's fancy shooting, the Union soldiers in the blockhouse were still able to cover the ford with deadly musket fire and the tree line still prevented the Marylanders from sighting their guns on the blockhouse. The gunners fired about fifty rounds blindly over the treetops. Their attempt at indirect fire control proved ineffective. It was now 11:00 a.m. and the fighting had been going on for six hours. McCausland was worried that either Averell would strike his rear or Kelley would send trainloads of reinforcements from Cumberland to seal the crossing. Just before launching a bloody frontal assault, someone suggested that they simply ask the soldiers in the blockhouse to surrender. Abandoned by their friends and cut off from any communication with Kelley's headquarters, they had no way of knowing how desperate the Confederates were to cross the river. Bradley Johnson sent his adjutant, Captain George W. Booth, under a flag of truce to the blockhouse to present its commanding officer with a written demand for its immediate surrender. Colonel Stough read the document and stepped back into the blockhouse to confer with his officers. They had no communication with Cumberland; they had been abandoned by the men on the train and most of their own regiment; his 82 men were vastly outnumbered and running low on ammunition. Finally, their 100-day enlistments would expire in about two weeks. It was time to surrender but with his back to the wall, the gutsy colonel issued his own terms before doing so. He and his men would immediately be paroled. The men would be allowed to retain their haversacks, canteens, blankets and rations. Stough would be supplied with a handcar with which to transport his wounded to Cumberland. To save time and casualties, the Confederates readily agreed.

McCausland then set about destroying the armored train and B&O property in the area. Crossties were jammed under the armored cars and set on fire. The blockhouse, water station and engine house at Green Spring were also burned. A detachment was sent two miles down the tracks to burn the woodwork on the South Branch Bridge. Then the Confederates made good their escape. McCausland camped along the South Branch of the Potomac after crossing and destroying the wire suspension bridge near Springfield. He then joined McNeil at Romney where he laid his plans to attack New Creek.[326]

New Creek was a small railroad town located twenty-two miles southwest of Cumberland on the North Branch of the Potomac River. By this point in the war, it had become a major supply base for the Union Army. The post was commanded by Lt. Colonel John F. Hoy of the ubiquitous Sixth West Virginia Infantry. It was defended by an earthwork named Fort Fuller that contained four pieces of artillery and a lesser work named Fort Piano. Total troop strength was about one thousand men and eight guns, all under the command of Colonel Robert Stevenson of the 154th Ohio National Guard. The terrain was rugged and favorable to defensive operations. McCausland launched an attack August 4. As soon as the firing broke out, Colonel Stevenson notified Kelley that New Creek was under attack. Kelley, in turn, told Stevenson to hold to the last man as reinforcements were on the way. By 4:00 p.m., Fort Piano had been overrun and the Confederates were closing in on Fort Fuller when a train arrived from Cumberland with a battalion of infantry and Battery L of the First Illinois Artillery. As the train neared the town, it was fired on by the Rebels and the conductor was wounded in the leg. Stevenson ordered the newly-arrived troops to counterattack and drive the Confederates out of Fort Piano.[327]

McCausland retreated along the Northwestern Turnpike. The next day he made camp along the South Branch about three miles from Moorefield. McCausland crossed the river with his brigade and ordered Bradley T. Johnson to remain on the north bank. The horses were unsaddled and allowed to graze for the first time in a month. The men looked forward to an extended stay. They would not get one. General Averell had been in dogged pursuit of McCausland and Johnson since the burning of Chambersburg on July 30. Now he was closing in for the kill. Using a special unit of Union soldiers wearing Rebel uniforms known as Jessie's Scouts, he was able to capture a number of Johnson's pickets. At dawn on the foggy morning of August 7, Averell's men charged into the sleeping camp and utterly destroyed Johnson's Brigade. Then they crossed the river and smashed into McCausland's Brigade. A number of Confederate soldiers were captured and later escaped but lost their horses and equipment. Both Southern generals managed to evade capture, but Johnson lost his headquarters flag. In Averell's after action report, he listed three additional flags captured and a total of four pieces of artillery, 420 prisoners, and over 400 horses. As a result of these losses, Early would never again have a sufficient cavalry force with which to defend the Shenandoah Valley.[328]

Prior to the burning of Chambersburg, Grant had remained focused on the siege lines at Petersburg. He trusted Sigel and Hunter to regain control of the lower Valley or perhaps hoped that he could defeat Lee before things got any worse. After Chambersburg, political and military considerations combined to force his personal intervention. On August 4, Grant boarded a steamer and, in one of his rare departures from the Virginia battlefield, sailed to Washington. After a brief meeting with Lincoln, Stanton, Halleck and Sheridan, he took the 3:00 p.m. train to Monocacy Junction. Here he found that the recent battlefield had been turned into a giant rest camp for the Union Army. The Sixth Corps, Hunter's Army of West Virginia, a portion of the Nineteenth Corps, and various other commands were recovering from their summer battles with Jubal Early. Not wishing to see a repeat of McClellan's days along the Antietam, he called a meeting of his senior officers at "Araby," the Thomas farmhouse directly on the battlefield, where he ordered an immediate advance of the units assembled to Halltown, a few miles south of Harpers Ferry. On August 6, Sherman met with Grant at Monocacy Junction before continuing on to Harpers Ferry. Then, with the approval of Lincoln, Grant issued the following orders through the Secretary of War.

"General Orders No. 240   Washington, August 7, 1864

1. The Middle Department and the Departments of Washington, of the Susquehanna, and West Virginia will constitute the Middle Military Division.

2. Maj. Gen. P. H. Sheridan is assigned by the President to the temporary command of the Middle Military Division"[329]

The same day he wrote to Sheridan, "Do not hesitate to give commands to officers in whom you repose confidence. Without regard to claims of others on account of rank. What we want is prompt and active movements after the enemy…" Upon accepting his new command, Sheridan designated Harpers Ferry as headquarters for the Middle Military Department. General Max Weber was made the post commander there, which now carried the elaborate title Military District of Harpers Ferry. The sweeping changes made by Grant altered the course of the war in the Valley and sounded the death knell for Early's Army of the Valley District. It will be noted that no mention was made of any changes to the Railroad Division. Sheridan would clear out the valley and leave guarding the B&O to General B. F. Kelley. Later this same month, President Lincoln acknowledged Kelley's performance in the defense of Cumberland and his efficient service throughout the war with the rank of Brevet Major General.[330]

An immediate problem looming for the defense of the railroad was the completion of service by the 100–day men from Ohio. General Hunter informed Sheridan on August 8, "…there are at present within this department eleven regiments of Ohio National Guard whose term of service will expire in six or eight days. Sending these troops home to be mustered out…will leave the Baltimore and Ohio Railroad and the Kanawha Valley in an almost defenseless condition." On the same day, President Garrett wrote to Stanton, "Pickets have only been sent as far as two miles west of Harpers Ferry and General Weber states that the time of his entire force, excepting eighty men, namely, three regiments of 100-days men will expire on Monday next, and that he, therefore will have no power to protect or assist in reopening the road." Governor John Brough could be proud of his Ohio Volunteers who had been the first of the 100-day men to serve and protect the B&O Railroad during some of the heaviest fighting of the war that occurred on the main line between Frederick and Cumberland.[331]

Sheridan wasted no time going after Early. On August 7, he began moving his army by train from its camps along the Monocacy River to Halltown. Early responded to this threat by abandoning Martinsburg and falling back

Troop train on the Winchester and Potomac Railroad. Sheridan moved his army by train from its camps along the Monocacy River to Halltown in August of 1864. (HFNHP)

to Bunker Hill. Thus, the main line of the B&O was once again released from his grip. Early later retreated to Winchester where, on August 19, Sheridan, having been reinforced with two divisions of cavalry from the Army of the Potomac and a second division of the Nineteenth Army Corps, shattered Early's army at the Third Battle of Winchester. However, Sheridan's dominance in the Valley did not guarantee complete security for the B&O Railroad.[332]

On the night of October 14, John Singleton Mosby, the "Gray Ghost," perpetrated what may well have been the most financially rewarding military operation of the war for the men involved. Earlier that evening the Express Train to Wheeling had left Baltimore with a mixture of soldiers and civilians including a passenger car full of German immigrants westward bound to homestead on federal lands. The railroads established special one-way rates and sometimes provided entire "immigrant trains" to foreigners arriving in the eastern port cities en route to settle on the western frontier. Two passengers Mosby did not count on were Majors David C. Ruggle and Edward Moore, paymasters from Sheridan's army.

At 9:15 p.m., B&O Locomotive No. 127 pulled out of Camden Station with Elijah Collins at the throttle. His son William was the fireman and A. P. Shutt the conductor. Other official personnel were Ticket Agent Louis Cole and Adams Express agent William De La Rouche. The train consisted of five passenger cars, a sleeper car, a baggage car, and a freight car. La Rouche rode in the freight car with a strongbox containing $20,000 consigned to a bank in Cumberland.

Col. John S. Mosby, the "Gray Ghost." (D. C. T.)

The train passed Brown's Crossing about ten miles east of Martinsburg at 2:30 the next morning and entered a deep cut that ran west of Quincy's Siding. By this point of the war, Mosby had perfected the art, if not science, of wrecking trains. He instructed his men to loosen one of outside rails and elevate it with crossties so that there would be no sign of an obstruction. The engineer would have no chance to slow down before the locomotive went up and off the track crashing into the embankment. The derailment brought an abrupt halt to the train, throwing many of the sleeping passengers from their seats. When the locomotive derailed, its boiler exploded, badly scalding the engineer and his son. As a result of his injuries, Elijah Collins died on November 5. His son William recovered and returned to work on the railroad.

Shots were fired and Rebel raiders poured into the passenger cars with revolvers at the ready. Private Charles Dear captured some Union officers standing around a stove and ushered them off the train. As he turned to leave, he noticed a satchel on the floor and picked it up hoping to find some useful clothing in it. To his surprise, he found it was filled with Greenbacks. Another Ranger named West Aldridge found a strongbox hidden under a rubber blanket. The two soldiers dutifully reported their findings to Colonel Mosby. Mosby immediately summoned Lieutenant Charles Grogan and ordered him to take the money back to their camp in Loudoun County, Virginia. He detailed Aldridge, Dear and another man named Wiltshire as escorts.

While Mosby issued instructions to Lieutenant Grogan, his Rangers had ushered most of the passengers off the train and were systematically robbing them, just as Gilmor's men had done nearby the previous February. Mosby gave the order to burn the train but the German immigrants refused to leave their seats. When his men began to ignite the interior of their passenger car they got the idea that it was time to go. With train ablaze and the loot secured, the Union prisoners were mounted on previously-captured horses and the Rebel raiders rode off to the security of "Mosby's Confederacy." When they returned to their camp, the captured money was found to total $173,000, a figure that would amount to about $2,000,000 today. Taking nothing for himself, Mosby saw to it that each man received $2,000 and the source of their new found wealth was forever known as the "Greenback Raid."

Mosby's men rode off leaving the passengers stranded in the cold night air. The burning train provided an elongated bonfire and they huddled along its length to keep warm. It also provided an unexpected repast. In the burning freight car cans of oysters began to explode from the heat. Some of the men pulled them out and with bits of other salvaged food; an enjoyable meal was had by all. Unfortunately, the $20,000 in the Adams Express strongbox did not survive the flames. A train arrived after daylight and took the survivors on to Martinsburg. Repair crews had the track cleared by 3:00 p.m. the same day. [333]

In November, Thomas L. Rosser was promoted to major general and given command of the remnants of Early's cavalry in the Valley. On the twenty-eighth, he attacked New Creek and Piedmont in the new state of West Virginia. Colonel George R. Latham of the Fifth West Virginia Cavalry commanded New Creek with a force of 300 men. An advance force of about 100 of Rosser's men dressed in captured Union uniforms marched through the picket line without being challenged and entered the fort. The main force then

Train burned by Mosby's Rangers during the "Greenback Raid." Wreckage like this was taken to the Mount Clare Shops where it was either salvaged or melted down and recast into new parts. (B&ORRM)

charged in and captured nearly the entire garrison. Latham and a handful of soldiers escaped into the mountains. The Confederates set fire to all the government warehouses and spiked the guns in the fort but did not damage the bridges in the area.

While at New Creek, Rosser sent a detachment of 300 men to attack Piedmont. Captain John Fisher of the Sixth West Virginia Infantry with only sixty men fought them off after a three-hour engagement. Fisher sustained no casualties and captured about a dozen of the enemy. The Confederates did manage to burn the B&O's front roundhouse, carpentry shop and a large quantity of lumber. Four cars and two tenders in the repair shop were also destroyed.

Kelley sent Captain P. B. Petrie with an armored railcar to cover the Twenty-First Bridge. He also sent a telegraph operator with Petrie to keep him informed of any advance on Cumberland. At the same time, Sheridan sent reinforcements from Martinsburg by train to Kelley, who in turn pushed them on to New Creek with the following order.

Cumberland, November 29, 1864
"Commanding Officer Advance Troop Train:
Sir: You will move at once with your train to New Creek, disembark, occupy the fortifications, and assume command of the post, and report upon arrival by telegraph. The train conductor will move upon being shown this order."

These troops arrived at New Creek at 11:00 a.m. on November 29. The New Creek Bridge had not been damaged and the B&O resumed rail service the same day. Also on November 29, Kelley issued General Orders No. 50. Item IV stating, "Col. George R. Latham, Fifth West Virginia Cavalry, for permitting the garrison at New Creek, W.Va., to be surprised by the enemy on the 28th ultimo, is placed in arrest, and will proceed to Grafton, W. Va., and there await further orders."[334]

General Sheridan was furious with Kelley and his West Virginia troops. To Kelley on the day of the attack he wrote, "In your telegram to Major-General Crook …you state, 'that you intend to fight Rosser to the last if he attacks you.' I give you no credit for this remark, as I expect you to do so." Kelley had virtually taken one of the first bullets for the Union long before Sheridan had ever been heard of and was not about to be derided by the pugnacious little cavalry officer. After explaining that he was merely informing his commanding officer of his intention to defend Cumberland despite the small force at his disposal he shot back, "This I deem proper and respectful, and I exceedingly regret you do not so regard it."

The next day Sheridan piled it on. To Kelley he wrote, "The accumulation of any large amount of stores and wagons at New Creek was stupidity on the part of the officer who is responsible. The capture of New Creek can only be attributed to the cowardice of the officers in charge." On December 1, 1864, he wrote to General Halleck, "I have not had a report from New Creek. It appears to have been a disgraceful affair. I very much fear that, until all the troops of Western Virginia are sent to points remote from their homes, there will be a recurrence of discreditable conduct." Three days later, he finally calmed down and wrote to General Crook, "Say to General Kelley not to take my dispatches to him too much to heart. I was very much chagrined about the New Creek affair when they were written." Rosser's raid on New Creek and Piedmont was the last full scale attack on the B&O Railroad. For the duration of the war, enemy action against the B&O would be limited to quick strikes and train wrecks lead by Mosby, McNeill and Gilmor.[335]

A month after Sheridan's victory at the Third Battle of Winchester, Early launched a surprise attack at Cedar Creek. Initially successful, Sheridan arrived from Winchester in time to launch a counterattack that drove Early's army from the field with the loss of most of his artillery. In late November, General Grant determined that the balance of power had shifted to such a degree in the Shenandoah Valley that he would return the Sixth Corps to the Army of the Potomac. On November 29, Sheridan contacted President Garrett to orchestrate another one of the B&O's troop redeployments by rail.

During the war, the Winchester & Potomac Railroad had been severely damaged and for most of 1864 was only operational between Harpers Ferry and Halltown. In October of 1864, Stanton ordered the W&P repaired but service was only extended to Stephenson's Depot until after the war. Garrett informed Sheridan that, "We can furnish the transportation, but our engines are too heavy for the trestling and bridges upon the Winchester road." He suggested that since the United States Military Railroad was operating the W&P, they use their lighter engines to shuttle empty cars from Harpers Ferry to Stephenson's Depot where the troops could be loaded and run back to the Ferry. From there, the B&O would carry them on to Washington. He also offered to send Mr. Mantz, the B&O's Supervisor of Trains, to coordinate the move with the officials of the W&PRR.[336]

The next day Sheridan sent an order to J. G. Beggs, the Superintendent of the Winchester & Potomac Railroad, "The Baltimore and Ohio Railroad will furnish sufficient cars for the transportation of 4,000 men to you at Harpers Ferry. I want you to have that transportation at Stephenson's Depot at 10 a.m. tomorrow using your own engines." He also advised General Halleck that the First Division of the Sixth Corps would depart on December 1, and that the other division would leave at 24-hour intervals. The move was further simplified by the fact that Grant had no need for the corps' artillery and only the horses associated with the officers and their staffs would need to be transported.[337]

During this same week, the Confederates hit the main line of the B&O for the last time in the calendar year of 1864. On December 5, the track only three miles from Harpers Ferry was torn up and a passing engine, tender, and several baggage cars were derailed. The fireman was also slightly injured. In order to minimize the damage to trains and injury to passengers, a line of "silent watchmen" was established along the most frequently attacked sections of the main line. The idea was not to stop the Rebels from damaging the rails but to alert the next train through to avoid a train wreck and expedite the repairs.[338]

After repairing the damage to the main line caused by the Confederacy's third and final invasion north of the Potomac River, the track crews returned to the Washington Branch on October 7. Working from Beltsville south, the double tracking of the Washington Branch was finally completed on December 12, 1864.[339]

CHAPTER TWENTY

THE UNION
PRESERVED

During the Civil War, much of Washington, DC, was illuminated with gaslights. In mid-December of 1864, the winter weather set in and the C&O Canal Company was forced to cease operations until spring. This greatly reduced the amount of coal being shipped to the Nation's Capital. On January 10, 1865, President Lincoln sent a personal letter to John Work Garrett. "It is said we shall soon all be in the dark here unless you can bring coal to make gas." Lincoln truly trusted Garrett in time of need, and the lights stayed on.[340]

During the winter of 1864 Grant maintained a stranglehold on the Richmond-Petersburg lines, and Sherman concluded his march to the sea by celebrating Christmas in Savannah. With military operations diminished in the Western Theater, Grant ordered the Twenty-Third Army Corps sent east. It would be a reversal of the 1863 troop movement that lifted the siege of Chattanooga. In similar fashion, the movement commenced within five days of conception. The one great difference being that this time it would take place during the dead of winter when ice and snow made even normal railroad activities difficult. Garrett and Smith would be front and center in coordinating the movement from the Ohio River to Washington, DC.

Colonel Lewis B. Parsons, Chief of Rail and River Transportation for the U.S. Army, was directly in charge of the operation. He left Washington City on February 2, 1865. En route, he met with railroad executives from the lines he would need to support the move. The original plan was for the troops to move by steamboats up the Ohio River to Parkersburg and then by rail to Washington. Just as the first boats were departing, severe weather set in, bringing a combination of fog, ice floes and a drop in the water level on the river. Adjusting to the situation, Parsons redirected the troop transports to Cincinnati for an extended rail route across the state of Ohio.

In mid-January 1865, troops began to board steamers at Clifton, Tennessee, and traveled up river to Cincinnati where the first contingent arrived on January 21. They then marched from the levee to the station of the Little Miami Railroad where troop trains waited to take them north to the state capital in Columbus. The Ohio Central Railroad received the trains at Columbus and took them east to Bellaire where the troops crossed the Ohio River to Benwood, West Virginia.

The intense cold played havoc with equipment of the Ohio lines. On January 28, Thomas Lough, superintendent of the Steubenville and Indiana Railroad, explained a twelve-hour delay to Colonel Parsons was "…caused by breaking of driver on engine on one train, which set the tender and twelve cars off the rail; another broken rail set two cars off the bridge and broke the cross-ties in bridge for about thirty feet." The weather caused numerous other minor derailments.

As the troop movements progressed, Colonel Parsons transferred his headquarters to Bellaire and supervised the operation from there until all of the men and equipment had crossed the pontoon bridge to Benwood. This occurred on the last day of January. Throughout the move, he continuously bombarded the railroad men with directives concerning the comfort of the soldiers.

To Captain J. B. Ford, the B&O agent at Wheeling, "I must again call attention of your company to furnishing stoves in cars moving troops. I am not willing to allow the movement of troops without further protection from this cold weather on the mountains."

To Captain Gus. Artsman, Assistant Quartermaster, "You will please deliver to Capt. J. B. Ford,…as many good Sibley tent stoves as he may require for warming cars transporting troops east."

At Benwood, just south of Wheeling, the B&O had trains waiting to take 20,000 men, 800 animals and the corps artillery to Washington City. As before, the 1,400-mile transfer by land and water was accomplished within eleven days. It required the services of five different railroads and over forty transport vessels. In a report to Colonel Parsons, William Prescott Smith listed some of the difficulties incurred by the Baltimore & Ohio Railroad during the successful completion of what was the most difficult troop movement of the war.

"Two thirds of the entire movement now in Washington, and remainder moving successfully over line. Many of our train men and others have been frost-bitten(sic), and several killed by accident and exhaustion, but no soldier frozen, and only one killed by breakage of a United States car, thirty miles from Baltimore, that threw three cars off the track. We have had great trouble in many ways with government cars. They are not adapted to our curves and grades."

In his report to the Quartermaster General after the move had been completed, Colonel Parsons stated, "The circumstances, I think, render it not invidious that I should especially refer to the management of the Baltimore and Ohio Railroad, where indomitable will, energy and superior ability have been so often and conspicuously manifested and where valuable service has been rendered to the government…it has moved this large force in the shortest possible time, with almost the exactness and regularity of ordinary passenger trains and with a freedom from accident that I think has seldom, if ever been paralleled."[341]

On the night of January 19, a detachment of Mosby's men under the command of Captain Thomas Richardson struck the B&O about four miles west of Harpers Ferry near Duffield's Station. Acting on information that a Federal paymaster would be on board, they hoped for another successful Greenback Raid. By taking up a rail, they caused a freight train to run off the tracks but were unsuccessful in attempting to set it on fire. Instead of money, the freight car contained cases of luxury items consigned to Union officers stationed up the line. Mosby's Rangers made off with wine, cakes, oysters and coffee – all items in short supply in the blockaded South. One of the newly appointed "silent watchmen" was also captured. The Rangers dubbed the event the "Coffee Raid."[342]

This minor event caused a flurry of activity within Sheridan's department. Brigadier General John D. Stevenson, the current commander at Harpers Ferry, ordered Colonel M. A. Reno of the Twelfth Pennsylvania Cavalry to send out a 100-man patrol to hunt down the Rebels. He also ordered the colonel to begin patrolling the main line of the B&O between Harpers Ferry and Kearneysville on a regular basis. Sheridan issued General Orders No. 18 the next day, which, in part, ordered Major F. C. Newhall to make an inspection of all points on the W&P between Stephenson's Depot and Harpers Ferry and on the B&O from Harpers Ferry as far west as Martinsburg "…for the purpose of investigating the circumstances attending the late raid…" In General Stephenson's report to Sheridan's Chief of Staff dated the same day, he stated that Reno's patrol failed to make contact with the Rebels because no one from the railroad had notified him until 10 o'clock. Sheridan immediately demanded to know "…the name of the person or persons responsible for not reporting the raid (sooner)." Considering the vast amount of damage incurred by the railroad during the war and the indifference initially shown towards the B&O by the War Department, this level of reaction seems almost humorous.[343]

In February, President Lincoln left Washington on a highly secret mission. The South was on its knees and wanted to talk peace. Lincoln had to walk a fine line. To publicly meet with the representatives from Richmond would be an acknowledgement of the Confederate government's right to exist, something he had carefully avoided doing throughout the war. Jefferson Davis had sent his Vice President Alexander Stephens and two additional "Peace Commissioners" to Grant's headquarters at City Point. Grant passed them along to Fortress Monroe where they waited in company with U.S. Secretary of State William Seward. Lincoln was not eager to meet with the commissioners. The war would surely be won as soon as Grant launched his spring offensive. On the other hand, that victory could be months away and the war was costing 2.5 million dollars plus hundreds if not thousands of lives a day. He would have to go but with the least amount of publicity.

Complicating Lincoln's movements was the fact that the country was experiencing a severe winter and the Potomac River was full of ice. George S. Koontz, the B&O's Washington agent, arranged for a special train consisting of B&O Locomotive No. 18 and a single passenger car to depart the Washington station at 11:15 a.m. on February 2. Traveling with the President were his bodyguard Andrew Smith, Charles Forbes his valet and agent Koontz. The train traveled north on the Washington Branch to Annapolis Junction where it entered the Annapolis & Elk Ridge Railroad for the twenty-mile run to the state capital in Annapolis. Lincoln's party arrived at the Annapolis terminal just after 1:00 p.m. They were met by Captain Gardner S. Blodgett of the Quartermaster Department who escorted them to the Naval Academy dock where the steamer *Thomas Collyer* was waiting to take the President to Fortress Monroe.

The Hampton Roads Peace Conference took place on the *River Queen* the next day. Lincoln was unshakable on the issue of a single United States. The Confederate commissioners were unwilling or unable to agree to the concept and the meeting ended in failure. Lincoln and Seward remained on the *River Queen* and immediately set sail for Annapolis. They arrived at the Naval Academy dock around 7:00 a.m. on February 4. Secretary Stanton had arranged with Garrett to have a second special train waiting at the Annapolis station to

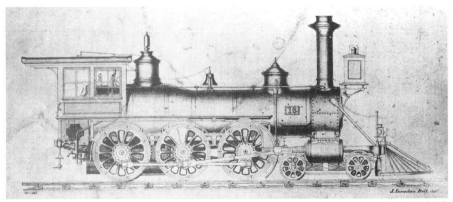

B&O Locomotive #18 took President Lincoln to Annapolis in February of 1865. (B&ORRM)

take the President's party back to the Capital. It departed at 7:30 a.m. and arrived at the Washington terminal two hours later. It was the last ride President Lincoln would take on the Baltimore & Ohio Railroad while alive.[344]

Back on the main line, incidents of sabotage and small raids continued to occur. On February 3, rails were placed in a culvert near the 84th mile marker. B&O Locomotive No. 119, its tender and two freight cars were derailed but not seriously damaged. The track was back in service by dawn the next day. A week later one of the watchmen was captured only three miles west of Harpers Ferry.[345]

In the dead of winter, military operations in the mountainous regions of Maryland and West Virginia came almost to a standstill. Brevet Major General B. F. Kelley had spent the entire war protecting the B&O Railroad. For most of this time, he had made his headquarters in Cumberland. Through his extended stay in the area, he became acquainted with and eventually married Miss Mary Clara Bruce who sang at the local theater. General Kelley kept an apartment at the Barnum Hotel. Major General George Crook also resided in Cumberland during the winter of 1864-65 and had a long-standing relationship with West Virginia and the B&O Railroad. In 1861, he served under McClellan as colonel of the Thirty-Sixth Ohio Infantry. As a brigadier general, he fought at South Mountain and Antietam. Following the inglorious return of General Hunter from Lynchburg, he was given command of the Department of West Virginia. After serving as corps commander under General Sheridan, he was again assigned to command the Department of West Virginia in February of 1865. Crook made his headquarters at the Revere House in Cumberland. After the war, he would marry the proprietor's daughter Miss Mary Dailey.[346]

Both generals slept comfortably on the night of February 20, knowing that the "Queen City" with its important rail center and Army supply base was surrounded by at least 7,000 Union soldiers. That same day, Lieutenant Jesse McNeill led sixty-three men from their camp near Moorefield, West Virginia, across the Potomac River and through the deep snow to the outskirts of Cumberland. His father, John Hanson McNeill, had been killed the previous year and his son become the partisans' leader. Their mission was to capture Generals Crook and Kelley. Jesse had sent John B. Fay and Charles R. Hallar into the city to confirm the locations of the targeted generals. Fay was a native of Cumberland and made contact with George Stanton, an employee of the B&O Railroad and, despite his Irish heritage, an ardent secessionist. After capturing a picket post and securing the password, the Rangers pushed on and entered the city shortly before sunrise on February 21. Riding boldly down the middle of the streets and whistling Yankee tunes, they gave the impression of a cavalry patrol returning from a hard night's scout. The column stopped on Baltimore

Captain Jesse McNeill. (D. C. T.)

Street where the two hotels were 100 yards apart.[347]

The two squads dismounted and quietly captured the sentinels in front of their assigned hotels. Sergeant Joseph W. Kuyendall of the Seventh Virginia Cavalry led the way into the Barnum Hotel. He had been a prisoner of General Kelley and could identify him if any confusion prevailed. On the second floor, the first room they entered was occupied by Kelley's adjutant, Major Thayer Melvin, who unknowingly directed them into the general's room before both men were captured.

George V. Vandiver was in charge of the detail to capture General Crook. With him were Sergeant James Dailey, Crook's future brother-in-law, and Private Jacob Gassman who had been a clerk at the hotel before the war and had an intimate knowledge of the building's interior. Knocking on the door, they entered room number 46 and announced to General Crook that he was their prisoner. Half-asleep, Crook replied, "What authority do you have for this." Sergeant Vandiver replied, "...Fitzhugh Lee's division of Cavalry" and added, "I am General Rosser. We have surprised and captured the town." Crook then dressed for the long cold ride south.[348]

While the generals were being taken from their beds, other men wrecked the nearby telegraph office and took several headquarters flags as trophies. The prisoners were then mounted double behind their captors and the column proceeded to the government stable where several horses were taken including General Kelley's favorite mount "Philippi." Then they began to make their way out of town. When halted at a picket post, one quick thinking Rebel responded that they were General Crook's bodyguard and passed on. McNeill and his prisoners crossed the Potomac River at Wiley's Ford just as the sun was coming up. While not burning a bridge or wrecking a train, they had successfully captured two major generals closely associated with defending the B&O Railroad. Not until much later was it known that two future Presidents of the United States, Brigadier General Rutherford B. Hayes and Major William McKinley, were sleeping in the same hotels that night.[349]

The opposing armies may have been in winter camps, but the repair crews of the B&O still had to battle the forces of nature. During the last week of

February, the intense cold weather caused unusually thick ice to form on the rivers. When this ice broke loose, it slammed into the bridges causing considerable damage. On the twenty-fourth, four trestles from the Great Cacapon Bridge and one from the Little Cacapon were carried away. Two days later the Little Cacapon was again damaged, as was the bridge at Sleepy Creek. Loaded cars were parked on the Harpers Ferry Bridge until February 28 when passenger trains were again allowed to cross. Complete service to the main line was restored on March 1.[350]

During the month of February, Grant held tight to the lines at Petersburg while Sherman burned his way through the Carolinas with the ultimate aim of joining Grant in Virginia. On March 2, Sheridan delivered the knockout blow to Early in the Shenandoah Valley and headed east to join the Army of the Potomac. On March 4, Lincoln delivered his second inaugural address on the steps of the Capitol. With an eye towards reuniting the country and not punishing the South, he spoke the immortal words, "With malice towards none; with charity for all…let us finish the work we are in; to bind up the nation's wounds…" In Richmond, the Confederate Congress approved a revision of the design for the national flag of the Confederacy. Peace would not come easily.[351]

On March 25, Lee launched his last offensive of the war. Major General John B. Gordon led a surprise attack on the far right of Grant's siege lines against Fort Stedman. In the initial success, he captured the fort. Then the Union forces counterattacked in overwhelming numbers and drove the Confederates back to their lines with the loss of 4,000 men that Lee could not replace. On April 1, Sheridan struck a significant blow at Five Forks, Virginia, and threatened to cut the South Side Railroad. That night Lee advised Jefferson Davis to leave Richmond. The next day his lines were broken and Lee began a retreat that ended with his surrender at Appomattox on April 9, 1865. The other Confederate field armies soon followed suit and the Union was finally preserved.

Lincoln's Funeral Train

The victory celebrations in the North were cut short when on the night of April 14, John Wilkes Booth assassinated President Abraham Lincoln as he attended a performance at Ford's Theater. The entire nation was in shock. The South feared immediate retribution and the North a renewal of hostilities. As the greatest manhunt in American history took place, arrangements were being made to return the body of President Lincoln to Springfield, Illinois, for its final burial. In February of 1861, Lincoln had traveled by train to his inauguration in a circuitous route through seven states in order to introduce himself to the American people. It was decided that his funeral train would make a similar journey back to Springfield so that the American people could say good-bye to their martyred President. After considerable negotiations, Chicago was added to the original schedule and the cities of Cincinnati and Pittsburgh deleted.

Secretary of War Edwin Stanton was the ultimate authority when it came to organizing the funeral train. Stanton called on Governor John Brough, the man who had mobilized the Ohio National Guard during the summer of 1864, and his trusted friend John Work Garrett of the B&O Railroad to head the planning committee that would finalize every detail of the mournful journey.[352]

Assistant Secretary of the Treasury George A. Harrington was given the difficult task of arranging Lincoln's funeral in Washington. Lincoln's casket was placed in the East Room of the White House on the night of April 17. The next day the room was opened for public viewing. Lincoln's official funeral was held on Wednesday April 19. This was four years to the day that the Sixth Massachusetts Regiment was attacked on Pratt Street as it passed through Baltimore en route to Washington. After the funeral, the coffin was taken out and placed on a specially constructed wagon to allow maximum visibility during the procession from the White House to the Capitol's Rotunda. An estimated 60,000 people watched the funeral procession from every possible vantage point. The next day the President's body was again open to viewing for the public.

A special detachment composed of four officers and twenty-five first sergeants from the Veteran Reserve Corps under the command of Captain James M. McCamly were assigned to act as pallbearers and honor guard. The Veteran Reserve Corps was composed of men who had seen active duty and through wounds or illness were no longer fit for field service. Rather than take discharges, they volunteered to serve in rear echelon positions in order to free up able-bodied men for front line duty. The Veteran Reserve Guard Escort accompanied Lincoln's coffin at all times until the final services were concluded in Springfield, Illinois. They were the only ones to carry it on and off the train at the designated points of public viewing.[353]

On Friday morning, April 21, a short prayer service was held in the Rotunda and then the coffin was closed. It was taken to the nearby B&O station on New Jersey Avenue where newly-sworn-in President Andrew Johnson said a final farewell. Waiting at the station was Lincoln's first funeral train. It consisted of a locomotive and tender, seven passenger cars, the funeral car, and a baggage car. The B&O provided two brand new locomotives, the baggage car, and six passenger cars. The funeral car was provided by the United States Military Railroad. The Philadelphia, Wilmington & Baltimore Railroad loaned its Directors' Car for the use of general officers and the immediate family.

Lincoln's funeral car was to have been his private presidential car – an 1865 version of Air Force 1. Named the "United States," the car had been constructed in the USMRR's Car Shops in Alexandria, Virginia. Construction had begun in 1863, but the demand for wartime repairs delayed its completion until February of 1865. The interior of the car consisted of a dining room and a parlor separated by a stateroom in the center. In the stateroom were two lounges of extra length to accommodate the President's great height and could be opened for beds at night. The exterior of the car was painted a dark brown with "UNITED STATES" painted on each side and an oval plaque containing a full color representation of the nation's coat of arms. The car was mounted on four trucks of four wheels each to give it the smoothest possible ride. The wheels had extra wide flanges to allow it to travel on tracks from the standard gauge of 4' 8 ½" to 5'. Before the "United States" left the Car Shops, alterations to the interior were made to accommodate the President's coffin and that of his son Willie, who had died three years earlier. The platform railing on one end was removed and rollers installed to facilitate the off and on loading of Lincoln's coffin at points of public viewing. Finally, black bunting was hung above and below the windows running the full length of the car on both sides.[354]

At 7:50 a.m., B&O Locomotive No. 239 with William Galloway, engineer, and James Brown, fireman, departed the Washington station pulling a single car containing soldiers and railroad employees. The purpose of the pilot engine was to make sure the tracks were perfectly clear all the way to Baltimore. At 8:00 a.m., Engineer Thomas Beckitt pushed the throttle forward on No. 238 and put Lincoln's funeral train into motion. Behind the engine and tender was a baggage car followed by six passenger cars, the "United States" and the PW&B's Directors' car. Only the last two cars would make the entire trip to Springfield. En route, connecting lines would supply their own locomotives and cars. On the front of the locomotive were two U.S. flags and a framed portrait of Abraham Lincoln. Black material was hung from various parts of the locomotive and tender. The same arrangements were made on the pilot engine. Aboard the funeral train were approximately 150 official mourners including the B&O's President Garrett.

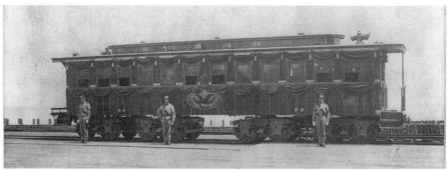

Lincoln's private car – an 1865 version of Air Force 1. (L. C.)

The train proceeded along the Washington Branch at an average speed of twenty miles an hour. It made two stops before reaching Baltimore City. The first was at Annapolis Junction where the Governor of Maryland, Augustus W. Bradford, and the delegation from Baltimore boarded the train. The second stop was at Relay where a group of ladies were allowed to place flowers on Lincoln's coffin. Mrs. Lincoln was so distraught that she did not attend either the funeral in Washington or trip to Springfield.[355]

The train arrived at Camden Station just before 10:00 a.m. Lincoln's final visit to the city would only last about five hours. The station and yard were draped in mourning, befitting for the occasion, as was nearly the entire city of Baltimore. A detail of the Veteran Reserve Corps sergeants removed the coffin and placed it in a rosewood hearse pulled by four horses with black plumes on their heads. Moving to the measured beat of the "Death March," the funeral procession passed along the city streets lined with thousands of people despite the pouring rain. At the Merchant's Exchange, the coffin was opened for a single hour and an estimated 10,000 people viewed Lincoln's body.[356]

Brigadier General John R. Kenly, who had once been the post commander at Harpers Ferry in 1862, gave a rare first person account of Lincoln's funeral in Baltimore.

"On the 21st of April I accompanied Major General Lew Wallace U.S. Vol., commanding the Middle Department 8th Army Corps to Camden Station of the Baltimore and Ohio Railroad on Camden Street, City of Baltimore where at 10 o'clock all remains of the President were received and I participated in the funeral pageant which proceeded through the streets of the city to the Rotunda of the Exchange Building. Here the remains lay in state to let the people look upon all that was mortal of Abraham Lincoln. I had the distinguished honor to be assigned a position at the head of the coffin whilst the citizens of Baltimore passed to view the dead and those hours of silent contemplation were filled with many and varied images of the past, the present, and the future of my country."[357]

At 2:00 p.m., the casket was closed and returned to the hearse, which took it to the Northern Central Railroad station on Calvert Street where the two designated cars had been transferred by horse power from Camden Station. A locomotive with seven additional cars from that line waited to pull the funeral train to Harrisburg where the sad drama would be repeated. At the state line, Governor Curtin boarded the train for the duration of its travels through the state of Pennsylvania. From Harrisburg, the funeral train would pass through Philadelphia, New York, Albany, Buffalo, Columbus, Indianapolis and Chicago before arriving in Springfield on May 3 – a distance of 1,600 miles traveled on 25 different railroads.[358]

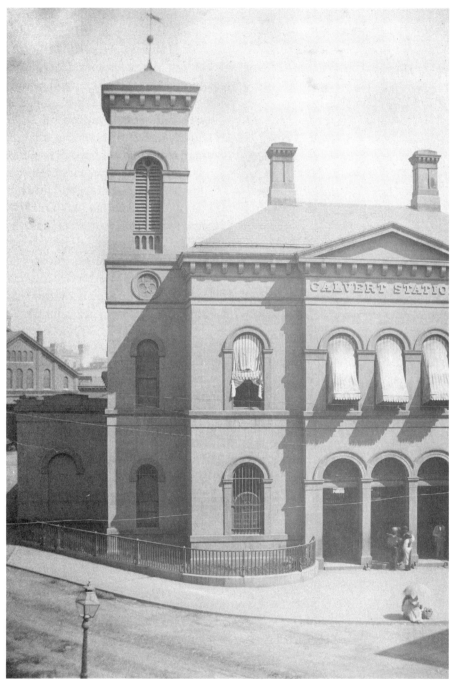

Calvert Street Station of the Northern Central Railroad in Baltimore. From here, Lincoln's funeral train left for Harrisburg. (Gil Barrett Collection)

Brigadier General John R. Kenly. (D. C. T.)

When the USMRR began to sell off its rolling stock, Lincoln's private car was purchased by Thomas Durant, the Vice President of the Union Pacific Railroad and a major player in the construction of the Transcontinental Railroad. In 1866, Durant included the car in a lavish excursion train to show off the progress of his railroad to newspapermen and potential investors. Durant later sold it to a man named Franklyn Snow who attempted to exhibit the "United States" as a commercial venture. When this failed, Snow sold the car to railroad executive Thomas Lowry. Lowry restored the car and exhibited it around the country. In 1911, a brush fire swept through the suburbs of Minneapolis, Minnesota, and destroyed the storage building where the car was kept. The Lincoln funeral car was a total loss.[359]

Demobilization

When the Civil War began in April of 1861, the United States Army numbered 16,367 officers and enlisted men. When Lee surrendered to Grant on April 9, 1865, that number had grown to over 1,000,000. This does not include an additional one million men who had died of wounds or disease, or had been discharged between 1861 and 1865. Nor was Lee's the only surrender. A series of Confederate capitulations large and small followed until June 23, when Brigadier General Stand Watie surrendered his combined Indian forces in present day Oklahoma. The men in Blue at the end of the war could not simply be discharged in place. They were serving all over the South – some a thousand miles from home. Disbanding the Army would be the last great logistical challenge of the war.[360]

The ultimate responsibility for returning the soldiers home fell to Secretary of War Stanton. Stanton did not wait for the last shots of the war to be fired. Before the end of April, he held a meeting with Colonel Thomas M. Vincent who was the Assistant Adjutant General in charge of Volunteer Forces. Stanton wanted a plan to demobilize the Army that would be quick, efficient and as fair to the soldiers as possible. Vincent presented his recommendation to Stanton on May 1.

Vincent's plan called for a two-step process. First, the forces in the field would maintain their current organization at the corps and division levels. These units would be moved to Field Rendezvous Points where rail or water transportation was available. The Field Rendezvous Points for Sheridan's Army were the Defenses of Washington, Harpers Ferry and Cumberland. For the Middle Department, it was Baltimore City. Other points throughout the South included Charleston, Mobile and Vicksburg. It will be remembered that corps, divisions, and even brigades were composed of regiments and batteries from different states. These units had to be sorted by common destination before transportation arrangements could be made.[361]

The second phase of Vincent's plan was to have State Rendezvous Points established. These were usually the same locations where the troops had been inducted into service during the war years; an example being Camp Carroll next to the B&O's Mount Clare Shops. In Maryland the cities of Frederick and Baltimore were designated, and Wheeling in West Virginia. In all there were nearly fifty cities designated in twenty-two different states ranging from Wilmington, Delaware to Fort Snelling, Minnesota. Here the soldiers' out-processing began. Muster Rolls containing a man's vital statistics and service record were updated. Missing equipment had to be accounted for. The men could purchase their weapons at a rate established by the War Department: Muskets with accoutrements, $6.00, Spencer Carbines, $10.00, sabers and swords, $3.00. They could keep their knapsacks, haversacks and canteens at no charge. This was a practical decision as the men would need these items during their final journey home and their storage was a dead expense for the government. Here also, the final discharge papers were issued and the paymasters dispersed their long awaited funds.[362]

Camp Carroll in Baltimore. From here Maryland Union regiments left for the war in 1861 and returned to be discharged in 1865. (B&ORRM)

Before phase two could go into effect, a victory parade was held in Washington, DC. It was the grandest military spectacle held in the United States until the end of World War I. Both Sherman's Army of the West and Meade's Army of the Potomac marched north and camped along the banks of the Potomac River. Combined they represented nearly 20 percent of the Union Army at that time. The ceremonies opened on May 23, when the Army of the Potomac marched down Pennsylvania Avenue. A reviewing stand had been erected in front of the White House for President Andrew Johnson, General Grant and his staff, and a number of dignitaries. Marching sixty men abreast, the Army of the Potomac took six hours to pass in review, the next day the Army of the South took seven hours. It would forever be known as "The Grand Review." As each soldier passed the reviewing stand, he headed in a new direction – home.[363]

For one last time the federal government turned to the B&O Railroad to manage a large-scale troop movement. President Garrett and Master of Transportation Smith would not let them down. During the next few days, the regiments would leave their old divisions and brigades forever and move in a new formation based on geography. On May 29, the first troop trains departed the Capital and traveled along the Washington Branch of the B&O to Relay. There the trains were directed east to Baltimore for connections with the Northern Central and Philadelphia, Wilmington & Baltimore railroads that would take them north to Pennsylvania, New York, and the New England states. Others went west along the main line to Wheeling or Parkersburg. At Wheeling, steamers took the men across the river to connect with the Central Ohio Railroad for the trip westward. At Parkersburg, 92 steamboats laden with men and equipment sailed down the Ohio River to Cincinnati, St. Louis and Louisville in less than thirty days. During the next two months, the B&O moved over its Washington Branch 233,300 soldiers, 12,838 horses and 4,300,850 pounds of freight. Most of the soldiers had gone to war by train and now the railroads were taking them home.[364]

That the trains were ready to take the troops home is a testimony to the endurance of the B&O Railroad and its employees. Despite extensive losses to its infrastructure and rolling stock by enemy action, the B&O not only remained in operation, but also posted a net profit that increased during each of the calendar years of the war with the exception of 1865 when hostilities ended. That the railroad was able to show a profit is even more remarkable when one considers the fact that there is not a single reference in any of the annual reports for the fiscal years 1861 through 1865 that shows an application for or payment by the federal government as compensation for damages incurred as the result of military action by either the Union or Confederate armies.

CHAPTER TWENTY-ONE

LOST AND FOUND

During the Civil War, no Union railroad suffered more damage by enemy activity than the Baltimore & Ohio. These events have been chronicled in the previous chapters. Besides outright destruction by both Northern and Southern forces, a tremendous amount of the B&O's property was captured and transported south for use by the railroads of the Confederacy. In his post war correspondence, Captain Thomas Sharp stated that during the occupation of Harpers Ferry and Martinsburg in 1861, he supervised the removal of 14 locomotives, 160 rail cars, 36 miles of track and 102 miles of telegraph line. These figures do not account for the subsequent attacks in 1862, 1863 and 1864 when considerably more damage was done and more supplies and machinery were taken. The pursuit of these lost locomotives, cars, and their repair equipment began before Lee surrendered at Appomattox and continued into 1866. The driving force behind this massive recover project was a man named Edward Keith. The reports he filed during this time period reveal not only the massive amount of material confiscated by the Confederate Army during the war but how it was distributed and used by the Southern railroads.

This recovery effort began with the fall of Richmond on April 3, 1865. Major General Godfrey Weitzel commanded the troops that marched into the Confederate capital that day. On April 8, an article appeared in a local paper, the "Baltimore Clipper," that read in part, "General Weitzel telegraphs from Richmond that of the railroad stock he found there 28 locomotives, 44 passenger and baggage cars, and 106 freight cars." Master of Machinery for the B&O at this time was Thatcher Perkins. Being responsible for the maintenance of all locomotives and rail cars as well as the fixed machinery of the company, he took a professional interest in the article and passed it on to President Garrett with the comment, "In all probability some portion at least of the stock belongs to our Co. and I would propose that a reliable man, acquainted with our machinery be sent to Richmond as soon as possible to try to identify Rolling Stock as may be there."[365]

Garrett wasted no time in initiating the search. He secured the services of Edward Keith at the rate of $3.75 per day plus expenses. He also showed a

Roundhouse at Alexandria, Virginia. This was the operational center of the United States Military Railroad during the war and the point where all captured property was returned to the B&O Railroad. (N. A.)

tremendous ability to focus on what was best for the B&O despite the highly emotional events that were surrounding him. With the hunt for John Wilkes Booth still underway and plans being made to disband the Army, he wrote to General Daniel C. McCallum, General Superintendent of the USMRR on April 19, the day of Lincoln's funeral in Washington, requesting a pass for Keith that would allow him to travel throughout Virginia and North Carolina in search of company property.

Undoubtedly in acknowledgement of both the B&O's and Garrett's personal services during the war, McCallum readily responded with a pass and a letter of introduction that ordered any officer on the USMRR, which was controlling nearly all of the railroads in the South at this time, to "offer every facility for identifying the property of the B&ORR Co. and when so identified, take all reasonable and proper means to cause it to be delivered (back to them)."[366]

Armed with this valuable document, Keith still faced an array of challenges. Much of the railroad network in Virginia and North Carolina had been destroyed in the final days of the war. A significant portion of the B&O

property he located would be isolated until the USMRR completed repairs and then military trains would have first priority on their use. Added to this was the fact that the government required all recovered railroad property to be cleared through Alexandria, Virginia. This precluded shipping anything from North Carolina by water directly to Baltimore. Finally, the managers of the Southern railroads that had benefitted from the use of the captured B&O equipment would be reluctant to cooperate in its return, especially when faced with rebuilding their lines with limited resources for the foreseeable future.

Keith's first finds came at Petersburg. Locomotive No. 8, the "Holden Rhodes" was being operated by the USMRR out of City Point. City Point was located on the James River and had become the major supply base for the Army of the Potomac during the siege of Petersburg. It had been run out of Richmond during the evacuation and then recaptured by the Union Army. In the Weldon Railroad shop at Petersburg, he found Locomotive No. 208. It was up on jacks but all of its wheels and connecting rods were present. He also found 2 iron and 13 wooden house cars (boxcars were called house cars at this time), 4 gondolas and 4 pairs of trucks. He hired labor to put trucks under the 208 so it could be moved to City Point for transshipment to Alexandria.[367]

On April 26, Keith wrote to President Garrett, "I found a boiler, center bearing and cylinders of an engine that was taken early in the war. I also found two house cars but the wood work is rotten and will not pay to move." On the first day of May, he wrote from Petersburg, "There are many bodies of cars that are not worth moving. I thought it best to load the trucks into the cars that were and have them hauled to City Point and shipped." He also found one of the lathes probably taken from Martinsburg at the Richmond & Danville shop in Richmond. The USMRR official must have been cooperating because he also told Garrett in the same report, "Nos. 225 & 226 are on the Piedmont Road. No. 83 in Raleigh. No. 188 North Carolina Rd."

A familiar name surfaced in the next paragraph. "The big lathe taken from Martinsburg I am told is in Burns Shop at Danville. Most of the others I am informed were taken to Raleigh by a man named Sharp who had charge of the Confederate Government shop and took them to that place." Captain Thomas Sharp was the officer in charge of transferring the locomotives and shop equipment from Martinsburg by horse power up the Valley Turnpike in 1862. He concluded his report by saying that trucks had been placed under No. 208 and "I hope to have her and the Holden Rhodes home next week."

Keith's reports begin to give some idea of the variety of equipment taken south. When one considers the fact that not a single locomotive was constructed in the Confederacy during the war, the acquisition of spare parts and repair machinery becomes all that more valuable.

On May 5, Keith informed Garrett, "Since my last letter to you I have found a lathe and planer belonging to the Company at the Fredericksburg shop in good running order. I have been told that a man by the name of Sharp was the Master Mechanic of the Confederate Govt. shops disposed of this machinery to different companies, and shops but I have confidence to believe I shall trace it all out." He also began to feel the effects of demobilization. Referring to the locomotives he had prepared for shipment, "But since the Army is ordered home, the Govt. has had a great deal of ordnance to ship so that Mr. Moore told me it might be ten or twelve days before he could ship our engines and cars home."[368]

Keith returned to Baltimore on May 15, for a conference with President Garrett. While there, he submitted a report giving the location and condition of 14 locomotives, 19 rail cars and various pieces of repair shop machinery. Five days later, he was in New Bern, North Carolina, where he presented his credentials to Major General Jacob D. Cox and received his full cooperation. He found Locomotive No. 225 in serviceable condition and had it run up to the North Carolina Railroad yard at Greensboro. This would allow him to shift cars and load shop equipment found there. He also reported finding 4 more gondolas and 2 house cars.[369]

In closing his May 20 report, Keith suggested to Garrett that the property found there be shipped by water from New Bern. Three days later, he received explicit instructions to first, move all equipment found south of Danville, Virginia, to that point; second, inventory and place in safe storage all disabled equipment that cannot be moved to Danville; and third, he was advised that the movement of damaged equipment was not a priority. "Your chief aim should be to trace and examine all the property of the Company, making full reports as to its location, character and condition."[370]

On May 25, Keith reported finding at Wilmington Locomotive No. 126 and that it had been christened the "Stonewall Jackson." Another house car was also there. Keith incorrectly reported that the boiler from Locomotive No. 34 had been put in the gunboat *Flora McDonald*. He was mistaken. It was the ironclad *CSS Neuse*. On March 10, 1865, the ship was blown up to avoid capture. The wreckage was recovered from the Neuse River in 1961. The engine and boiler mounts were that of a locomotive identical to the No. #34.[371]

In a report dated May 31, Keith stated that he had just returned from Weldon, North Carolina, where he found one set of trucks that belonged to the company from a group of cars that had been burned and one good car. At the North Carolina Railroad shop, he discovered one pair of drive wheels and a large number of car springs. Movement to Greensboro was slow due to the heavy flow of government trains. He added that he was moving everything he could to Greensboro before the USMRR returned control of the lines to their original owners. When this happened, the B&O would lose the advantage of moving freight at government expense. As soon as he got the "Stonewall Jackson" to Greensboro, he would send everything there behind the one operational B&O locomotive to Danville.[372]

Throughout the summer months, Keith crisscrossed the states of North Carolina and Virginia. From Danville on June 4, he reported finding in Raleigh 52 car springs and a pair of engine truck wheels taken from Locomotive No. 208 that he planned to put under the No. 204 to facilitate its movement. He added that from Danville, "I am ready to ship eleven engines and twenty-three car loads of machinery (to Richmond)."[373]

Keith was having an amazing success rate. On June 9, he reported finding a large quantity of engine and car parts. "…in fact I cannot enumerate to you all as it lies in piles in such a manner that I cannot tell you how much of each until I load it up." He added that, "My train at the NCRR Shops consisted of 4 engines and 7 cars. I have brought engines 225 & 199 & 6 car loads of machinery to Danville. Got big lathe on the train and I have found another since I last wrote."[374]

On June 16 Andrew Anderson, Garrett's secretary wrote to Keith in Richmond, "The President has received your com'n of the 5th, 9th and 11th inst, and is pleased with your actions as therein reported." And then added, "The President is desirous that you press the Gov't. authorities to get our machinery shipped to Alexandria at the earliest practicable moment."[375]

On July 18, Keith was back at Danville. "I have got all of the stock away from here but five engines and 9 B&O cars loaded and hope by the last of this week to have all away." The rails had been full of troop trains taking the soldiers home and he was having a difficult time making shipments. "I watch every train and if I think there is the least possible chance to put on a car or engine I get it on."[376]

As Keith's shipments began to arrive at the Mount Clare Shops, John C. Davis, the Assistant Master of Machinery reported to President Garrett on the condition of the equipment recovered.

MASTER OF MACHINERY OFFICE
Baltimore and Ohio Railroad Company
Baltimore, July 25th, 1865
John W. Garrett, Esq.,
President, Camden
Dear Sir:
The Engines 235-231 & 208 received from the south a short time

since will be ready for service in about the following time viz; 235 in 5 weeks – 231 in 6 weeks & 208 in 8 weeks.

Those received Sunday night and yesterday are in very bad condition and we could not name a date for the completion of the repairs they need. They will cost from $4 to $5,000 each.

Their original numbers were 226 now the "General Lee," the 83 now the "Raleigh" and the 199 now bearing the name "Dixie."

A number of car loads of machinery and car wheels have also arrived and some 5 or 6 tenders. They are all extremely dilapidated and bear the marks of bad usage and little care.

Very Respectfully
J. C. Davis
Asst. M of M[377]

From Richmond on August 5, Keith informed Garrett of his progress. "We have 6 engines and tenders – 13 B&O cars loaded with wheels & machinery, also 15 tires for drive wheels – 4 pair wheels on axles and 36 wheels without axles that are laying on the dock. I loaded two lathes and one planer yesterday into an Orange & Alexandria car but the trucks under the car are B&O trucks. I shall ship it today over the Va Central. The car is No. 40."[378]

On August 11, Keith reported from Petersburg, "On the 9th I shipped one B&O car from Fredericksburg Depot found on Richmond and Petersburg RR. On the 10th shipped two B&O cars over Va Central RR. One of these cars was loaded with four pair car wheels. I found two pair car trucks at Fredericksburg Shop and shall put them under the boiler at Va. Central Depot." Still in Richmond on the 14th, he wrote, "I got all the stock I can find & identify on this line at City Point and the barges will load today for the last time. It or they will take Engine 33, three B&O cars loaded with engine and coal hopper springs – 4 pair driving wheels – 2 cylinders belonging to Engine 34 – 3 pair car trucks – 12 pair car wheels – 1 punch, also head lamp – pilot tools & co belonging to (the locomotive) Calvin Graves." Informed that the bridge over the Roanoke River would not be completed until January, Keith inventoried what he was not able to ship from North Carolina and made arrangements to return to Baltimore.

Keith also relayed to Mr. Garrett the fact that Captain Thomas Sharp was currently residing in Middletown, Delaware, and that if contacted by him, Sharp would supply additional information on the location of company property. His August 16 report contained a somewhat humorous development. Keith found a B&O car stuck somewhere along the Richmond & Petersburg line and asked one of the managers if he would stop an engine and pull it out for him to inspect. He responded that they were too busy and held that they had never used any of the B&O's cars during the war until Keith pointed out that he had four B&O cars with their name on them. He went on to say, "They also had the Holden Rhodes and Powhatan in use at one time during the war and the President, Mr. Ellis, told me he had thought of sending a bill to you for repairs on those two engines."[379]

From City Point on August 21 Keith advised Garrett that the government was discontinuing the steamer between there and Alexandria and that the Army's property would tie up the barges for a month or more. Fearing a change in the weather by then he cautioned, "…one of the engines here is one of the best that was down here. I mean the Calvin Graves a passenger engine." Keith's constant traveling throughout the heat of the summer was taking its toll. He closed his report to Garrett on a personal note. "I am nearly worn out with the dysentery caused by drinking so many kinds of water."[380]

Keith remained in Virginia throughout the month of September. On September 21, he advised the shipment of one camp car. His last known telegram came through on October 10. "Shipped this morning at 5:30 over Virginia Central and Orange & Alexandria two flats loaded with boiler of Engine 50, also two trucks." As a result of his efforts, the B&O was able to reclaim twelve of the fourteen locomotives taken in 1861 and the remaining parts of Engine No. 50. Only No. 34 was a total loss due to its association with the Confederate States Navy. Keith probably recovered less than half of all the rail cars taken. The large number of wheels and trucks shipped back tells the tale. Destroyed either by military action or excessive use, the cars had become casualties of the war. On the other hand, the immense amount of machinery and spare parts found could immediately be put to use and help offset the initial losses from the war.[381]

After Keith returned to Baltimore he presumably took a well-earned break. Then he traveled to Middletown, Delaware, to personally meet with Captain Sharp who had established a business there – the Peninsular Machine Works. Sharp was very cooperative, and upon his return he reported to Garrett what Sharp had said. A few of his remarks are quoted here. They indicate just how important the property taken from the B&O Railroad was to the Confederate war effort and how foolish the officials in Washington were in not protecting the main line of the B&O during the first year of the war. "The large wheel press taken from Martinsburg was left at Newtown. Copy press was left at Raleigh, N.C., at Quarter Master's Department, Maj. W. W. Pierce." The safe was left at Charlotte, N.C. Sent some machinery to Salisbury, N.C. Unloaded a lot of machinery at Millbrook, 6 miles out of Raleigh…" "Mr. Brown was Chief of Ordnance for Confederate Government. I delivered the boiler taken from the

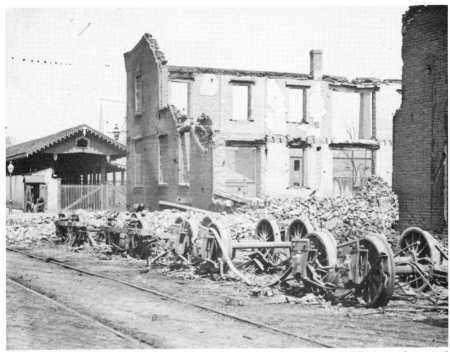

This photograph of destroyed buildings and rail cars after the capture of Richmond in 1865 explains why so few rail cars were returned to the B&O Railroad. (N. A.)

shop at Martinsburg to him. I took 90 tons of iron from Duffields, and it was rolled into plates for gunboats." This included the CSS *Virginia*. As a result of this information and other correspondence between Garrett and Sharp, Keith returned to Virginia to ferret out even more B&O property that extended his employment until July of 1866.[382]

Long after the recovery project was concluded, Thomas Sharp remained on the mind of John Work Garrett. William Prescott Smith, the brilliant Master of Transportation who had so often been Garrett's man on the ground during the war years, died on September 15, 1872. In need of a replacement, Garrett summoned Captain Sharp to his office in Baltimore where he told the former Confederate officer, "A man who can steal a section of railroad, not to mention several million dollars worth of rolling stock, move the plunder across country on a dirt road and place it on another fellow's line ought to be pretty well up in the transportation business. We have a vacancy in that department and I have sent for you to offer you the position of master of transportation, not doubting your ability to fill it after the demonstration you gave at Martinsburg." Sharp accepted the offer and served as Master of Transportation for the B&O Railroad until 1877.[383]

CHAPTER TWENTY-TWO

THE LAST
TROOP TRAIN

The object of this chapter is not to tell the post war history of the B&O Railroad but present its condition and direction for the following decades. With the end of hostilities, Garrett turned his attention to two main objectives – repairs and expansion. The bridge over the Potomac River at Harpers Ferry had been destroyed and rebuilt nine times during the war. Only four sections of Bollman trusses that had been installed in 1862 remained in place. The rest of the bridge in each case was supported by temporary trestling. By 1868 additional spans of Bollman trusses had been installed. Work was also commenced to complete the missing sections of double track between Harpers Ferry and Relay. This, too, was completed in 1868.[384]

When the war ended, the Winchester & Potomac Railroad was still only operating between Harpers Ferry and Stephenson's Depot. General Sheridan had chosen that point over Winchester as the major supply base for his operations in the Shenandoah Valley. On December 15, 1865, General McCallum ordered James J. Moore, Chief Engineer and General Superintendent of the USMRR in Virginia, to return the control of the W&P to its pre-war owners and offer them the opportunity to purchase the locomotives and rail cars then in use by the government. The management declined to make any purchases having arranged for the B&O to take over the operation of their line. Possibly, because of repair work on the main line, the laying of the last four miles of track did not begin until February of 1866. On May 3, service was again restored between Harpers Ferry and Winchester. Locomotive engineer Joseph H. Toomey, Sr. was given the honor of bringing the first train through to Winchester. This was an important economic event in the life of this Valley city. When the train stopped at the depot, a committee of ladies decorated Toomey and his locomotive with flowers.[385]

A minor expansion project was the construction of a branch line to the city of Hagerstown. Known as the Washington County Railroad, the B&O

The Potomac River bridge at Harpers Ferry was destroyed and rebuilt nine times during the war. By 1868, all the sections had been replaced with Bollman trusses using the original masonry piers erected in 1836. (L. C.)

supplied three-quarters of the initial capital investment. It then leased the line and operated it as its own. Work began on the line in 1866 and was completed on November 21, 1867.[386]

Garrett also had bigger plans in mind when it came to expansion. In the sell off of government property after the war, the B&O purchased four first class steamers in July of 1865. Their military names were changed to *Allegany, Carroll, Somerset and Worcester*, all counties within the state of Maryland. Their purpose was to inaugurate service between the port cities of Baltimore and Liverpool. Combined with the bridging of the Ohio River at Parkersburg and the eventual extended service to Chicago, Garrett envisioned a through rate intermodal service almost a century before the railroads and steamship lines established a similar system after the advent of containerization.[387]

USMRR Locomotive *Genl. Haupt* was purchased by the B&O Railroad after the war. (N. A.)

To support his expansion plans Garrett needed more rolling stock. He acquired it in several different ways. First, was through the rehabilitation of the recently recovered equipment. Although originally B&O property, it had been missing for four years and had the same effect as a new addition.

Second, was through the purchase of locomotives previously operated by the United States Military Railroad. Most of these engines had been purchased new from their Northern manufacturers in late 1862 and throughout 1863 in order to meet its rapidly expanding role in supporting the Union armies in the field. In fact, by the end of the war, the USMRR could have been considered a first class railroad. Its engines were reasonably well maintained thanks to the rail complex established by Herman Haupt in Alexandria, Virginia. The B&O purchased fifteen locomotives and tenders in 1865 including the originally titled "General Haupt." It was purchased from the William Mason locomotive works on January 13, 1863. After Haupt left the service, it was renamed the "General J. C. Robinson." By coincidence, Robinson commanded the Railroad Brigade in Maryland in 1861. In 1864, he commanded a division in the Army of the Potomac that included the Maryland Brigade. He was severely wounded and lost a leg while leading a charge at the battle of Laurel Hill for which he was awarded the Medal of Honor.

Garrett's third means of expanding his locomotive capacity was through direct purchases from the factories. In 1865, five first-class locomotives were acquired from the Lowell Machine Shops and nine from the New Jersey Locomotive works. An additional thirty-five passenger and four baggage cars were purchased in the same year.

The company also had the ability to produce its own rolling stock. In the Annual Report for the fiscal year ending September 30, 1865, John C. Davis, Master of Machinery, stated that 7 first class locomotives, 163 freight cars and 5 passenger cars "...with the requisite conveniences desirable to travelers" had been built in the Mount Clare Shops. In all, the B&O Railroad faced its peacetime pursuits with 243 locomotives and 3,713 passenger, freight, and special purpose rail cars. In the fall of 1865, John Work Garrett was elected to his seventh term as president of the Baltimore in Ohio Railroad, a position he held until his death in 1884.[388]

As the nation expanded behind the ever-increasing power of the locomotive, the Transcontinental Railroad was completed in 1869 and several territories became states. Well into the twentieth century, railroads were the dominant form of transportation. Despite their constant leaning towards the future, they maintained one important connection with the past – the Civil War veterans.

The Civil War was the largest conflict ever to take place on the North American Continent. When it was over, those who survived sought to main-

Route guide and train schedule for the G. A. R. National Encampment
in 1902. (D. C. T.)

tain some form of contact with those they had served with, or at the very least with others who had shared the same experiences. Founded in 1866, the largest of all veterans' organizations was the Grand Army of the Republic. Its counterpart was the United Confederate Veterans. Both organizations maintained national commanders and their staffs. Each state also had a commander and staff. Finally, there were the individual Posts for the GAR and Camps for the UCV. In each case, they were named for either local or national heroes of the war. Besides these two primary organizations, there were literally thousands of others ranging from the Society of the Army of the Potomac to associations composed of members of a single company or battery. The "Veterans' Period" lasted for roughly seventy-five years after the war. For most of that time, these groups were collectively a powerful economic and political force and always a centerpiece of American society.[389]

Each year the Grand Army of the Republic held a national encampment in a major city. These meetings were not limited to the original Union states. They ranged from Philadelphia, Pennsylvania, to San Francisco, California, and from Portland, Maine, to Salt Lake City, Utah. Five national encampments were held in Washington, DC, and only one in Baltimore City, in 1882. These were major economic and social events with tens of thousands of veterans and their families attending. The only way to move large numbers of people over long distances was by train and the B&O Railroad had considerable experience in that department.

When an encampment city was identified, one or more trains would be chartered by the state departments attending. At the same time, the railroads would publish special rates for smaller groups and individuals. When the 36th National Encampment was held in Washington, DC, the B&O published a pamphlet to solicit business for the main event and additional revenue through tourism. Touting "THE GREAT BATTLEFIELD ROUTE," this pamphlet contained a route map with a rate schedule. "Tickets will be sold from all points on the line of the Baltimore & Ohio Railroad to Washington at GREATLY REDUCED RATES," it informed the potential traveler. It also contained a photograph and description of the Civil War related sites in the area. "SPECIAL RATES FOR SIDE TRIPS TO BATTLEFIELDS AND PROMINENT POINTS" were also listed under the heading "STOP-OVERS."[390]

Not all of the railroad's involvement with the veterans was on as grand a scale. When General Benjamin F. Kelley died in 1891, the B&O did not forget his wartime service as commander of the Railroad Division. After his funeral services were completed at St. Matthew's Episcopal Church in Oakland, Maryland, on July 19, the B&O provided a special train to carry his coffin to Washington, DC, for internment at Arlington National Cemetery. The funeral

COMMANDER IN CHIEF AND DEPARTMENT OF MARYLAND

G. A. R.

SPECIAL TRAIN TO DENVER, COL.

Thirty-Ninth National Encampment, September 4-7, 1905.

BALTIMORE & OHIO R. R.

Schedule for Commander in Chief's special train to Denver for G. A. R. Encampment in 1905. Note touching reference to wounded veterans in its cover design. (D. C. T.)

Veterans arriving by train for the fiftieth anniversary of the Battle of Gettysburg in 1913. (Official reunion report, State of Pennsylvania)

party consisted of his widow, her mother, and the mayor of Cumberland. They were escorted by five members of the Grand Army of the Republic post in Oakland.[391]

The 39th National Encampment was held in Denver, Colorado, in September of 1905. This reunion held a special meaning for the Union veterans in Maryland because one of their own, John R. King, was the National Commander of the GAR at that time. A special Commander in Chief's train was arranged to leave Baltimore on September 1. A combination program and time schedule was printed by the B&O. This, as well as the Washington, DC, pamphlet contained beautiful cover art relating to the wounded warriors of that war.[392]

The railroads' involvement was not limited to national encampments. They also ran special trains or rates for the monument dedications and battlefield commemorations. In 1903, the State of Maryland dedicated a unique monument on the Chattanooga Battlefield. At the base of the monument were two bronze figures, one depicting a Union Soldier and one a Confederate. The monument contained inscriptions of equal respect to the Third Maryland Infantry USA and the Third Maryland Artillery CSA. The men of the Third Infantry had traveled by train as part of the epic troop movement of 1863 to confront their fellow Marylanders at the siege of Chattanooga.[393]

Major reunion events took place on the fiftieth anniversary of significant battles like Antietam and Gettysburg. In 1913, all living veterans of the war, Union and Confederate, were invited to attend a reunion on the fiftieth anniversary of the Battle of Gettysburg. Transportation from any point in the United States by rail would be provided free of charge as well as housing in a tent city, food, medical care and admission to all events held during the re-

Brochure for B&O exhibit in Hagerstown, 1937. (D. C. T.)

The first special train arrives in Gettysburg for the last reunion of the Blue and Gray. (P. L. R.)

union. The reunion was co-sponsored by the State of Pennsylvania and the federal government.

The two railroads serving the town of Gettysburg were the Western Maryland and the Reading. Each line upgraded its station at their own expense to accommodate the projected 100,000 spectators and participants soon to converge on the now-famous battlefield. When the ceremonies opened on July 1, there were over 50,000 veterans in attendance and a like number of visitors. Forty-seven different railroads participated in their cross-country movement. The average cost of a round trip ticket for the veterans was $7.35, whether from Maryland or Montana. By July 2, it was determined that 171 of the old men in Blue and Gray had lost their return tickets home. When informed of the situation, the Governor of Pennsylvania told the railroad companies to let them board and send him the bill.[394]

In 1937, a two-week long ceremony was held to commemorate the seventy-fifth anniversary of the Battle of Antietam and the one hundred and seventy-fifth anniversary of the founding of Hagerstown. As before, the railroads provided a significant amount of the transportation. The B&O Railroad also put on an elaborate exhibit and program of its own, taking parts of what had been designed for its "The Fair of the Iron Horse" in 1927, "A Century of Progress" held in Chicago in 1933, and the "Great Lakes Exposition" held in Cleveland in 1936. From the accompanying brochure, the visitors were informed, "The choicest of the B&O exhibits shown at all three of these expositions, are now in Hagerstown…"[395]

Ceremony at the Eternal Light Peace Memorial July 3, 1938. (P. L. R.)

When the Fiftieth Reunion at Gettysburg came to an end, Governor John K. Tener of Pennsylvania issued an invitation for all surviving veterans of the Civil War to attend a seventy-fifth and final reunion of the Blue & Gray in 1938. Remarkably, this promise was kept. The event was again co-hosted by the State of Pennsylvania and the federal government. Every living veteran of the Civil War was sent an invitation and upon acceptance given free transportation from their home to and from Gettysburg. Even with the advent of the automobile and air travel, the dominant form of long-distance travel was still the railroad. About 2,000 of the veterans accepted the invitation but many died before they could attend the event. In the end, 1,845 ancient warriors traveled from as far away as California and Florida. Their average age by now was in the high 90's with some going over the century mark. Each veteran was required to travel with an attendant whose expenses were also paid for in full.

The highlight of the reunion was the lighting of the Eternal Peace Light Memorial by President Franklin D. Roosevelt on July 3. A special rail siding was installed to accommodate the President's train. It was estimated that 450,000 people were in attendance that day. Even if that figure was to be discounted by one half, it shows a tremendous respect and affection by the American people for their Civil War veterans.

Then it was over. One old soldier died on the last day of the reunion. Six more did not survive the trip home. The last troop train had left the station.[396]

APPENDIX A

B&O LOCOMOTIVES CITED IN TEXT

No.	Type	Builder	Date	Name	Comment
18	"One-Armed-Billy" 4-2-0	W. Norris	1838	Jos. W. Patterson	
22	"One-Armed-Billy" 4-2-0	W. Norris	1839		
25	4-4-0	Mason	1856	Now named the William Mason, it is the only operating Civil War locomotive in the world and is on exhibit at the B&ORR Museum.	
30	4-4-0	Eastwick & Harrison	1842	Minerva	
31	4-4-0	W. Norris	1843	Stag	
33	Mud Digger 0-8-0	Winans	1844	Hercules	Captured 1861
34	Mud Digger 0-8-0	Winans	1844	Gladiator	Captured 1861
47	4-4-0	New Castle	1846	New Castle	
50	Flexible-Beam Truck 0-6-0	Baldwin	1847	Wisconsin	Captured 1861
70	Camel 0-8-0	Winans	1851		
72	Camel 0-8-0	Mt. Clare	1851		Captured 1861
76	Camel 0-8-0	Mt. Clare	1851	CSA Raleigh	Captured 1861
83	Camel 0-8-0	Mt. Clare	1851	CSA Gen. Price	Captured 1861
108	Camel 0-8-0	Winans	1852		
119	Camel 0-8-0	Winans	1852		
126	"Dutch Wagon" 4-4-0	R. Norris	1853	CSA Stonewall Jackson	Captured 1861
127	"Dutch Wagon" 4-4-0	R. Norris	1853		
165	Hayes 4-6-0	Denmead	1853		
166	Hayes 4-6-0	Denmead	1853		

No.	Type	Builder	Date	Name	Comment
172	Camel 0-8-0	Winans	1853		
178	Camel 0-8-0	Winans	1853		
188	4-4-0	Mason	1858	CSA Calvin Gray	Captured 1861
199	Hayes 4-6-0	Denmead	1853	CSA Dixie	Captured 1861
201	"Dutch Wagon" 4-4-0	R. Norris	1854		
204	Hayes 4-6-0	Denmead	1854		Captured 1861
206	Hayes 4-6-0	Mt. Clare	1854		
208	"Dutch Wagon" 4-4-0	Murry & Hazlehurst	1854	CSA Gen. Huger	Captured 1861
225	Tyson 4-6-0	A&W Denmead	1857	CSA Hercules	Captured 1861
226	Tyson 4-6-0	A&W Denmead	1857	CSA Gen. Lee	Captured 1861
231	4-4-0	Mason	1857	CSA Holden Rhodes	Captured 1861
232	4-4-0	Mason	1857		
235	4-4-0	Mason	1857	CSA Powhatan	Captured 1861
238	Perkins 4-4-0	Mt. Clare	1865	Lincoln's Funeral Train	
239	Perkins 4-4-0	Mt Clare	1865		

*For additional information see William D. Edson, *Steam Locomotives of the Baltimore & Ohio, An All-Time Roster*.

ENDNOTES

Chapter 1

1. Thirty-fourth Annual Report of the President and Directors to the Stockholders of the Baltimore and Ohio Railroad Company, (Baltimore: 1860), pp. 156, 236; Angus James Johnston II, *Virginia Railroads in the Civil War*, (University of North Carolina Press: 1961), p. 11; William G. Thomas, *The Iron Way: Railroads, the Civil War, and the Making of Modern America*, (Yale University Press: 2011), pp. 47-48, 217.
2. *Thirty-fourth Annual Report*, pp. 5, 78.
3. James D. Dilts, *The Great Road: The Building of the Baltimore & Ohio, The Nation's First Railroad, 1828-1855*, (Stanford University Press: 1993), pp. 2-3.
4. Patricia L. Faust, Editor, *Historical Times Illustrated Encyclopedia of the Civil War*, (Harper & Row: 1986), pp. 66-67, 408. Hereafter cited as Faust.
5. Oswald G. Villard, *John Brown A Biography Fifty Years After*, (Houghton Mifflin Co: 1910), pp. 402-403, 426, 429.
6. Edward Hungerford, *The Story of the Baltimore & Ohio Railroad 1827-1927*, (G. P. Putnam's Sons: 1928), Vol. I, pp 336-341, Matthew Page Andrews, "Heyward Shepherd, Victim of Violence," presented at the dedication of the Heyward Shepherd Memorial on October 10, 1931; Villard, pp. 443-444.
7. David M. Sullivan, *The United States Marine Corps in the Civil War – The First Year*, (White Mane Publishing Co.: 1997), pp. 4-7, 9.
8. Gregory A. Stiverson, "In Readiness To Do Our Duty," *The Frederick Militia and John Brown's Raid on Harpers Ferry, October 17-18, 1859*, (Maryland State Archives: 1991), pp. 3-4, Stiverson presents a complete transcription and analysis of the after action report submitted by Colonel Edward Shriver of the Maryland Militia covering the activities of the three militia companies sent by train From Frederick, Maryland, to Harpers Ferry on October 17, 1859.
9. Sullivan, pp. 12-15, 17, 20.
10. Sullivan, p. 23.
11. Sullivan, pp. 25, 26.

Chapter 2

12. Jean H. Baker, *The Politics of Continuity: Maryland Political Parties from 1858 to 1870*, (Johns Hopkins University Press: 1973, pp. 3-5; Lawrence M. Denton, *A Southern Star For Maryland: Maryland and the Secession Crisis*, (Publishing Concepts: 1995), pp. 23-24, 29-30.
13. Emerson D. Fite, *The Presidential Campaign of 1860*, (New York: 1911), p. 107; Scott Sumter Sheads & Daniel Carroll Toomey, *Baltimore During the Civil War*, (Toomey Press: 1997), pp. 9-10.

14. Victor Searcher, *Lincoln's Journey to Greatness: A Factual Account of the Twelve-day Inaugural Trip*, (John C. Winston Company: 1960), pp. 3-5 and inside cover.
15. Allan Pinkerton, *History and Evidence of the Passage of Abraham Lincoln from Harrisburg, Pa., to Washington, D.C., on the 22d and 23d of February, 1861*, (Pinkerton's National Detective Agency: 1868), pp. 15-16; Michael L. Kline, *The Baltimore Plot: The First Conspiracy to Assassinate Abraham Lincoln*, (Westholme Publishing, LLC: 2008), pp. 313-314; Searcher, p. 259.
16. Edward Stanley Lanis, "Allan Pinkerton and the Baltimore Assassination Plot Against Lincoln," *Maryland Historical Magazine*, Volume XLV, March, 1950, Number 1, pp. 8-9; Jay Bonansinga, *Pinkerton's War: The Civil War's Greatest Spy and the Birth of the U.S. Secret Service*, (Lyons Press: 2012), pp. 121-122; Kline, pp. 309, 310.
17. Carl Sandburg, *Abraham Lincoln: The War Years*, (Harcourt, Brace & Company: 1939), Vol. I, p. 135; E. B. Long, *The Civil War Day By Day*, (Doubleday & Company, Inc,: 1971), p. 56.
18. Ezra J. Warner, *Generals in Gray: Lives of the Confederate Commanders*, (Louisiana State University Press: 1959), pp. 232-233, John Lockwood and Charles Lockwood, *The Siege of Washington: The Untold Story of the Twelve Days that Shocked the Union*, (Oxford University Press: 2011), p. 66; Sheads and Toomey, pp. 13-14.
19. John W. Hanson, *Historical Sketch of the Old Sixth Regiment*, (Lee and Shepard: 1866), pp. 22-23; Charles P. Dare, *Philadelphia, Wilmington and Baltimore Railroad Guide*, (Fitzgibbon & Van Ness: 1856), pp. 57-59; Samuel P. Bates, *History of Pennsylvania Volunteers, 1861-5*, (B. Singerly: 1869) Vol. I; *Laws and Ordinances Related to the Baltimore and Ohio Railroad Company*, (John Murphy & Co.: 1850), pp. 134.
20. George W. Nason, *Minute Men of 61*, (Smith & McChance: 1910) pp. 194-196; George W. Brown, *Baltimore on the 19th of April*, (Johns Hopkins University: 1887), pp. 49-51; Report of Colonel Edward F. Jones, Sixth Massachusetts Militia, *Official Records of the War of the Rebellion*, (G. P. O.: 1887), Series I, Vol. 2, pp. 7-9. (Hereafter cited as *OR's* and refer to Series I unless otherwise stated).
21. George L. Radcliff, *Governor Thomas H. Hicks of Maryland and the Civil War*, (The Johns Hopkins Press: 1901), pp. 55-56; Brown, pp. 64-65, 77; J. M. Harris, *A Reminiscence of the Troublous Times of April, 1861*(Baltimore: 1891), Maryland Historical Society Fund Publication No. 21, pp. 10-11, 18, 22.; Leslie R. Tucker, *Major General Isaac Ridgeway Trimble*, (McFarland & Co., Inc.: 2005), pp. 47, 67, 86.
22. Warner, *Generals in Blue*, pp. 60-62; Benjamin F. Butler, *Butlers Book*, (A. M. Thayer & CO.: 1892), pp. 190-191; Ezra J. Warner, *Generals in Gray*, (Louisiana State Press: 1959), p. 10.
23. William J. Roehrenbeck, *The Regiment that Saved the Capital*, (Thomas Yoseloff: 1961), pp. 91-93; John E. Merriken, *Annapolis and Elk Ridge*, "The Bulletin" published by the National Railroad Historical Society, Vol. 38, Number 6, 1973, pp. 16-18.

24. Butler, pp. 200-203; William Swinton, *History of the Seventh Regiment, National Guard, State of New York, During the Civil War*, (Fields, Osgood, & Co.: 1870), 95-96; Roehrenbeck, pp. 107-108.

25. Swinton, pp. 97, 100-109; Roehrenbeck, pp. 109, 112-115, 121-122.

26. *OR's*, Vol. 2, pp. 607, 623-624.

27. Ibid, pp. 29, 634, 639; Sandburg, Vol. 1, pp. 275-276; "The Philadelphia Inquirer," May 20, 1861; Edward Hungerford, *The Story of the Baltimore & Ohio Railroad 1827-1927*, (G. P. Putnam's Sons: 1928), Vol. 1, pp. 78-79, 231.

28. McHenry Howard, *Recollection of a Maryland Confederate Soldier and Staff Officer Under Johnston, Jackson and Lee*, (William and Wilkins Co.: 1914); Butler, pp. 288-289, 231-232; Sheads and Toomey, pp. 30-31.

29. Stephen E. Ambrose, *Undaunted Courage*, (Simon & Schuster: 1996), p. 85; James D. Dilts, *The Great Road*, (Stanford University Press: 1993), pp. 185-186.

30. John D. Imboden, "Jackson at Harpers Ferry," *Battles and Leaders of the Civil War*, (Castle: 1884), Vol. I, pp. 111, 114, 125; *OR's*, Vol. II, pp. 3-6.

31. Ben Ritter, "A Short History of the Winchester & Potomac Railroad 1831-1866," Privately printed monograph, no date, pp. 1, 4; Imboden, pp. 117-118;

32. *OR's*, Vol. 2, p. 784-785, 822; Timothy R. Snyder, "Border Strife on the Upper Potomac: Confederate Incursions from Harpers Ferry, April-June 1861," *Maryland Historical* Magazine, Vol. 97, 1 (Spring 2002), p. 79, 82, 88-89; Letter from President J. W. Garrett to "Col. Jackson, Commanding at Harpers Ferry" dated May 10, 1861, B&O Railroad Museum archives; Warner, *Generals in Blue*, p. 209; *Southern Historical Society Papers*, (Kraus Reprint Co.: 1977), p. 96 (Hereafter referred to as *SHSP*).

33. Festus P. Summers, *The Baltimore and Ohio in the Civil War*, (Stan Clark Military Books: 1992 reprint), pp. 66-67; Imboden, pp. 122-123; Snyder, p. 91.

34. Ritter, p. 2; Arthur Candenquist, "The Great Train Robbery," *Civil War*, Vol. IX, No. 6, November-December 1991, pp. 42-43; William G. Thomas, *The Iron Way, Railroads , the Civil War and the Making of Modern America*, (Yale University Press: 2011), p. 135; *National Intelligencer*, (Washington, DC), July 12, 1861.

35. *OR's*, Vol. 2, p. 881, 889-890, 908, 911-912; Warner, *Generals in Gray*, pp. 161-162.

36. Faust, pp. 561-562; *OR's*, Vol. II, 579.

37. Ibid, pp. 660-661, 689.

38. Ibid, pp. 670-671, 672.

39. Ibid, pp. 675, 679, 897, 924; Snyder, pp. 102-103; James I. Robertson, Jr., *Stonewall Jackson: The Man, The Soldier, The Legend*, (Macmillan Publishing USA: 1997), p. 243; *Thirty-fifth Annual Report of the Baltimore and Ohio Railroad Company*, (Baltimore: 1863), p. 47; George Edgar Turner, *Victory Rode the Rails, The Strategic Place of Railroads in the Civil War*, (Bobbs-Merrell Co.: 1953), pp. 75-76.

40. Robertson, p. 244; Fritz and Mark Haselberger, "The Burning of the 21st Bridge At New Creek," *West Virginia History*, Vol. XXVII, No. 1, October, 1965, pp. 57, 59-61; William H. Lowdermilk, *History of Cumberland*, (James Akglin: 1878), pp. 400-401; *OR's*, Vol. 2, pp. 131-132, 945.

41. Gary Gimbel, "The End of Innocence, The Battle of Falling Waters," *Blue & Gray Magazine,* Vol. XXII, Issue 4, Fall, 2005; pp. 8, 12; *OR's,* Vol. 1, p. 472; *Thirty-Fifth Annual Report B&ORR,* p. 7.

42. C. G. Hearn, "The Great Locomotive March," *Civil War Times Illustrated,* Vol. XXV, No. 8, December 1986, p. 29; Candenquist, p. 43; Turner, pp. 88-89; *OR's,* Vol. 2, p. 949; Obituary of Charles Briscoe Keeler, *Winchester Star,* September 15, 1922.

43. *OR's,* Vol. 1, pp. 185-186, 160-161.

44. Ibid, pp. 157, 164-165, 166-167; Johnston II, pp. 31-32.

45. *War Time Diary of Miss Julia Chase,* Winchester, Virginia, 1861-1865, (The Hadley Library: 191) pp. 10, 11, 13; *The Diary of Sarah Morgan McKown 1860-1899,* compiled by James V. Hutton, Jr., The Handley Library, Winchester, Virginia, no date, p. 23.

46. Laura Virginia Hale, *Four Valiant Years In The Lower Shenandoah Valley 1861-1865,* (Hathaway Publishing: 1986), pp. 38-41; Candenquist, pp. 43, 47; Hungerford, Vol. 2, pp. 11-14, Report of Thatcher Perkins, Master of Machinery Baltimore & Ohio Railroad, to President John W. Garrett dated February 14, 1862, listing locomotives damaged or removed by Confederate Forces, B&O Archives.

47. *OR's,* Vol. 2, pp. 789, 790-791.

48. George A. Porterfield, "A Narrative of the Service of Colonel Geo. A. Porterfield in North-western Virginia in 1861-62," *SHSP,* Vol. XVI, pp. 83-85; Steve French, "Porterfield never recovers after Philippi," *The Washington Times,* June 14, 2003; *OR's,* Vol. 2, pp. 802-803, 827-828, 840; W. Hunter Lesser, *Rebels at the Gates, Lee and McClellan on the Front Line of a Nation Divided,* (Sourcebooks, Inc: 2004), 52-53.

49. Warner, *Generals in Blue,* 290-292; Clayton R. Newell, *Lee vs. McClellan, The First Campaign,* Regnery Publishing, Inc.: 1996), pp. 19, 54-55; Stephen W. Sears, editor, *The Civil War Papers of George B. McClellan,* (Ticknor & Fields: 1989), p. 1. *OR's,* Vol. 2, p. 843.

50. David L. McKain, *The Civil War and Northwestern Virginia,* (David L. McKain: 2004), pp. 16-17.

51. Lesser, pp. 25-29, 51-52; Theodore F. Lang, *Loyal West Virginia From 1861 to 1865,* (Deutsch Publishing Co.: 1895), p. 241; Warner, *Generals in Blue,* pp. 260-261; C. J. Rawling, *History of the First Regiment Virginia Infantry,* (J. B. Lippincott Co.: 1887), p. 17.

52. Col. Robert White, *Confederate Military History,* (Confederate Publishing Co.: 1899), Vol. 2, West Virginia, p. 14; Newell, p. 80.

53. Summers, pp. 72-73; Turner, p. 81; *OR's,* Vol. 2, pp. 45-46, 48-49.

54. Lesser, p. 58; Rawling, pp. 23-24; Summers, p. 76; *OR's,* pp. 49-50.

55. Newell, p. 117; Summers, pp. 83-84.

56. *OR's,* Vol. 2, pp. 66-67; White, pp. 15-16

57. Martin K. Fleming, "The Northwestern Virginia Campaign of 1861," *Blue & Gray Magazine,* Vol. X, Issue 6, August 1993, pp. 14-16; *SHSP,* Vol. XXXIV, pp. 289, 290-291; Lesser, pp. 61, 66-68; Newell, pp. 95-97; *OR's,* Vol. 2, pp. 68, 72-74.

58. Warner, *Generals in Gray*, p. 100; *OR's*, Vol. 1, pp. 239, 915.
59. William R. Plum, *The Military Telegraph During the Civil War in the United States*, (Jansen, McClurg & Co.: 1882), Vol. 1, pp. 94, 97-98; *OR's*, pp. 198-199, 236-238;
60. Faust, p. 633; Plum, p. 98; Fleming, pp. 17, 48-49, 53.
61. Faust, pp. 185, 426; Turner, pp. 83-85; *OR's*, Vol. 2, pp. 224-235.
62. Lesser, pp. 159-160, 215-217.
63. *OR's* Vol. 2, p. 753; Sears, pp. 55, 67.

Chapter 3

64. Harold A. Williams, *Robert Garrett & Sons, Incorporated, Origin and Development 1840-1965*, (Baltimore: 1965), pp. 2-3, 8.
65. Ibid, p. 12.
66. Ibid, p. 24; Robert Browning Garrett, "John Work Garrett, Mr. Baltimore And Ohio Railroad," *The Glades Star*, Vol. 4, No. 6, September, 1970, pp. 88-90.
67. Summers, p. 46.
68. Ibid, p. 48
69. Ibid, p. 49.
70. *OR's*, Vol. 2, p. 578.
71. Hungerford, Vol. 1, p. 359; Summers, p. 53; *The Papers of William Prescott Smith*, Letters and telegrams, 1861-1864, University of Louisville Ekstrom Library, Special Collections call number E 941.S61874Z; B&O Railroad Museum , Garrett Collection in document file marked 1859-72 Miscellaneous Memos in the President's Handwriting," hereafter referred to as "Garrett File."
72. Hungerford, Vol. 1, p. 369; Summers, p. 55; *OR's*, Vol. 51, pt. 2, p. 21.
73. *OR's*, Vol. 2, pp. 596-597, 603-604.
74. *OR's*, Vol. 2, pp. 615, 617
75. Turner, p. 47, 60; Summers, pp. 102-104.

Chapter 4

76. Charles P. Dare, *Philadelphia, Wilmington and Baltimore Railroad Guide*, (Fitzgibbon & Van Ness: 1856), pp. 11, 17, 19-21.
77. Norman B. Wilkinson, *The Brandywine Home Front During the Civil War 1861-1865*, (Kaumagraph Co.: 1966), p. 133; Dare, p. 25; Thomas Weber, *The Northern Railroads in the Civil War*, Indiana University Press: 1952, p. 54.
78. Jeffery K. Smart, "Burning Bridges: The Events Leading up to the Military Occupation of Harford County in 1861," *Harford Historical Bulletin*, Number 72, Spring 1997, p. 27; Smart, pp. 41, 44.
79. *OR's*, Vol. 2, pp. 583-585; Smart, p. 38.
80. Smart, pp. 49-51; *OR's*, pp. 631-632.
81. Alan P. Koenig, *Ironclads on Rails; Armor Returns to the Battlefield, 1861-65*, Doctorial dissertation University of Nebraska – Lincoln, 1995, pp. 58-60; Edwin P.

Alexandria, *Civil War Railroads & Models*, (Clarkson N. Potter, Inc.: 1977), pp. 214-217.

82. Sheads and Toomey, pp. 35-36; Samuel Tyler, *Memoir of Roger Brook Taney, LL.D.*, (John Murphy & Co. : 1872), pp. 640-641.

83. Charles J. Stille, *History of the United States Sanitary Commission*, reprint of the 1866 edition, (Corner House Historical Publications: 1997), pp. 161-162; Faust, p. 656.

84. George A. Otis, *A Report on a Plan for Transporting Wounded Soldiers by Railway in Time of War*, (War Department: 1875), pp. 9-10, 21; Alan Hawk, "An Ambulating Hospital: or How the Hospital Train Transformed Army Medicine," *Civil War History*, Vol. XLVIII, No. 3, September 2002, p. 209.

85. Francis A. Lord, PH. D., *They Fought for the Union*, (Bonanza Books: 1960), p. 95; Hawk, pp. 212-213; Otis, p. 17.

Chapter 5

86. Hungerford, Vol. 1, pp. 282-284;
87. David E. Markle, Editor, *The Telegraph Goes to War, The Personal Diary of David Homer Bates, Lincoln's Telegraph Operator*, Edmonston Publishing, Inc.: 2003), p. 3.
88. Tom Wheeler, *Mr. Lincoln's T-Mails, How Abraham Lincoln Used the Telegraph to Win the Civil War*, (Collins: 2006), p. 24; William R. Plum, LL. B., *The Military Telegraph During the Civil War in the United States* (Jansen, McClung & Co.: 1882), p. 63; Markle, p. 4; Bates, pp. 35-36.
89. Markle, p. 8.
90. David Homer Bates, *Lincoln In The Telegraph Office*, (The Century Co.: 1907), pp. 14-16, 27.
91. Plum, p. 70.
92. Ibid, pp. 92-93.
93. Ibid, pp. 94, 97-98, 101.
94. Ibid, p. 130; Bates, pp. 27, 30-32; Roger D. Hunt & Jack R. Brown, *Brevet Brigadier Generals In Blue*, Olde Soldier Books: 1990), p. 580; Plum, p. 130.
95. Markle, pp. 10, 14; Bates, p. 27
96. Markle, pp. 20-21; Bates, pp. 36-37.

Chapter 6

97. *Thirty-fifth Annual Report of the President and Directors to the Stockholders of the Baltimore and Ohio Railroad Company For the Year Ending September 30, 1861*, Baltimore: 1863), pp. 6-7; *Thirty-fifth Annual Report B&ORR*, p. 50.
98. Frederick H. Dyer, *A Compendium of the War of the Rebellion*, (Thomas Yoseloff: 1959), Vol. 1, pp. 270, 335; Warner, *Generals in Blue*, pp. 125-126; *OR's*, Vol. 5, pp. 562-563.
99. Lang, pp. 321-323; *OR's*, Vol. 5, pp. 552, 604, 647, 691.

100. Warner, *Generals in Blue*, pp. 247-248; Summers, pp. 104-105; *OR's*, Vol. 5, p. 625.
101. *OR's*, Vol. 5, pp. 378-380; Summers, p. 105.
102. James W. Thomas, LL.D. and Judge T. J. C. Williams, *History of Allegany County Maryland*, (L. R. Titsworth & Co.: 1923), pp. 400-401; *OR's*, Vol. 5, pp. 381-382.
103. *OR's*, Vol. 5, pp. 925, 936-937; Robertson, p. 283.
104. *Thirty-sixth Annual Report of the Presidents and Directors to the Stockholders of the Baltimore & Ohio Railroad Company, For the Year ending September 30, 1862.* (J. B. Rose & Co.: 1864), pp. 47-48.
105. *OR's*, Vol. 5, p. 976.
106. Arthur Candenquist, "The World's First Military Railroad," *Civil War Times*, Vol. XLIX, No. 3, June 2010, pp. 38-40, 43.
107. Candenquist, p. 42, Tucker, p. 86.
108. Snyder, p. 68, *Thirty-fifth Annual Report B&ORR*, p. 49.
109. George B. Abdill, *Civil War Railroads, Pictorial History of the Iron Horse – 1861 thru 1865*, (Bonanza Books: 1961), pp. 70-71.
110. Summers, pp. 105-106.

Chapter 7

111. Warner, *Generals in Blue*, pp. 407-409; *OR's*, Vol. 1, pp. 639, 648, 760; *OR's*, Vol. 2, p. 171; Frank J. Welcher, *The Union Army, 1861-1865, Organizations and Operations*, (Indiana University Press: 1989), Vol. I, pp. 20-21.
112. William B. Jordan, editor, *The Civil War Journals of John Meade Gould 1861-1865*, (Butternut & Blue: 1997), pp. 68, 74.
113. Ibid, p. 75.
114. Ibid, p. 77.
115. Richard Eddy, *History of the Sixth Regiment New York State Volunteers*, (Richard Eddy: 1864), pp. 74-75.
116. Ibid, p. 55.
117. Ibid, pp. 63-64.
118. Jordan, pp. 83, 99.
119. Francis B. Heitman, *Historical Registration and Dictionary of the United States Army*, (G.P.O: 1903), Vol. 1, 708; Dyer, p. 339; Eddy, p. 85;
120. Original broadside of General Order No. 18 issued at Relay on March 17, 1862, Harpers Ferry National Park Catalog No. 168625.
121. Gould, pp. 109, 114, 122.
122. *OR's*, Vo. 12, Part III, p. 211.
123. Eddy, pp. 100, 102-103.
124. Warner, *Generals in Blue*, pp. 420-420; Heitman, Vol. I, p. 892.
125. *OR's*, Vol. 12, Part III, pp. 342, 663; Warner, *Generals in Blue*, pp. 573-574.
126. Steve French, "Daring Raid of Winchester Mail Train," *The Washington Times*, Saturday, June 24, 2006, p. D5; Paul R. Teetor, *A Matter of Hours, Treason at Harpers Ferry*, (Fairleigh Dickinson University Press: pp. 43-44.
127. Faust, pp. 340-341; *OR's*, Vol. 19, Part I, pp. 799-780.; Daniel Carroll Toomey,

The Civil War in Maryland, (Toomey Press: 1983), pp. 52-54; Welcher, Vol. I, pp. 22-23.
128. OR's, Vol. 19, Part II, pp. 506-507.

Chapter 8

129. Peter A. Hansen, "The Rail Splitter and the Railroads, *Trains*, February 2009, pp. 32-35; Stephen E. Ambrose, *Nothing Like It in the World, The Men Who Built the Transcontinental Railroad 1863-1869*, (Simon & Schuster: 2000), p. 80.
130. Francis A. Lord, *Lincoln's Railroad Man: Herman Haupt*, (Fairleigh Dickinson University Press: 1969), p. 41; Bates, p. 22.
131. Weber, pp. 135-136; Hunt & Brown, p. 390; Lord, pp. 42-43.
132. Lord, pp. 21-24, 26-27, 54, 60.
133. William A. Danaway, *The African American Family in Slavery and Emancipation*, (Cambridge University Press: 2003), pp. 189, 205; Thomas, pp. 124-125; Lord, pp. 96-97, 100.
134. Turner, p. 312; Lord, pp. 140-141, 317; OR's, Series III, VOL. 5, pp. 78-80.

Chapter 9

135. OR's, Vol. 5, pp. 965-966; *Allan, SHSP,* pp. 118-119.
136. Robertson, pp. 304, 308-309; *Thirty-six Annual Report B&ORR*, p. 49; OR's, Vol. 5, pp. 396-398. Summers, p. 31-32
137. Dr. Richard A. Sauers, "Stonewall Jackson's Romney Campaign January 1-10, 1862," *Blue & Gray Magazine*, Vol. XXII, Winter 2006, Issue 6, pp. 64-65; OR's, Vol. 5, pp. 1036, 1039.
138. OR's, Vol. 5, pp. 1046-1047, 1053-1055;
139. William E. Bain, editor, *B&O in the Civil War from the papers of Wm. Prescott Smith*, (Sage Books, :1966), p. 37-38.
140. OR's, Vol. 5, p. 639.
141. Warner, *Generals in Blue*, pp. 17-18; Toomey, *The Civil War in Maryland*, p. 29.
142. OR's, Vo. 5, p. 703-704; Dyer, p. 255.
143. OR's, Vol. 5. pp. 677-678, 692-693.
144. OR's, Vol. 5, pp. 727-728.
145. Robertson, p. 333.
146. Dyer, p. 300; OR's, Vol. 5, p. 746; Summers, pp. 114-115.
147. *Thirty-sixth Annual Report B&ORR*, p. 7.
148. OR's, Vol. 51, Part I, p. 548; Vol. 12, Part III, p. 6.
149. *Thirty-sixth Annual Report B&ORR*, pp. 6-7, 41, 50-51, 53.
150. *Thirty-fifth Annual Report B&ORR*, p. 7; *Thirty-sixth Annual Report B&ORR*, pp. 4, 49-50.
151. Letter from Thatcher Perkins to John W. Garrett dated March 12, 1862, B&O Railroad Museum archives; *Thirty-sixth Annual Report B&ORR*, p. 53.
152. OR's, Vol. 12, Part III, p. 6, 22.

153. Faust, p. 415.
154. Daniel Carroll Toomey, *Hero at Front Royal, The Life of General John R. Kenly,* (Toomey Press: 2009), pp. 44-45, 55, *Thirty-sixth Annual Report B&ORR,* pp. 54-55.
155. Summers, p. 22; *Thirty-sixth Annual Report B&ORR,* pp. 53-55.

Chapter 10

156. *Thirty-sixth Annual Report of the B&ORR,* pp. 54-55.
157. Summers, pp. 163-165; *OR's,* Vol. 12 Part III, pp. 560-561.
158. Clifford Dowdey and Louis H. Manarin, editors, *The Wartime Papers of R. E. Lee,* pp. 292-293.
159. *OR's,* Vol. 19, Part I, pp. 757-758.
160. Tracy Evans, "Invitation to Battle, Special Order 191 and the 1862 Maryland Campaign," *The Sentinel,* Vol. II, No. 2, Summer 2012, pp. 14-17; *OR's,* Vol. 19, Part I, pp. 24-26.
161. Plum, Vol. I, pp. 236-237.
162. *Thirty-sixth Annual Report of the B&ORR,* pp. 55-57.
163. John H. White, Jr., *American Single Locomotives and the "Pioneer,"* (Smithsonian Institution Press: 1973), pp. 23-24.
164. "Swiftest on the C.V., The Power Train that Came here in the Year 1862," *Hagerstown Daily Mail,* January 9, 1897, *OR's,* Vol. 19, Part II, p. 323, Harsh, p. 439.
165. Turner, pp. 215-217.
166. William J. Miller, *The Training of an Army,* (White Mane Publishing Co.: 1990), p. 129.
167. Edward G. Longrace, *To Gettysburg and Beyond,* (Longstreet House: 1988), pp. 42-43.; Jonathan Letterman, M.D., *Medical Recollections of the Army of the Potomac,* (D. Appleton and Co.: 1866), 44-45; Sheads and Toomey, pp. 176-177.

Chapter 11

168. James V. Murfin, *The Gleam of Bayonets,* (Thomas Yoseloff: 1965), pp. 304- 306.
169. Hungerford, Vol. 2, pp. 24-25; *Thirty-Sixth Annual Report of the B&ORR,* p. 56.
170. Henry Kyd Douglas, *I Rode With Stonewall,* (University of North Carolina Press: 1940), p. 187.
171. John W. Schildt, *Four Days in October,* pp. 9, 11, 12, 17, 28, 36, 38.
172. Ibid, 49, 54-55, John W. Schildt, *Lincoln's Wartime Travels,* (John Schildt, 2010), pp. 47, 49.
173. Warner, *Generals in Gray,* p. 147, Faust, p. 561.
174. Steve French, *Rebel Chronicles, Raiders, Scouts, and Train Robbers of the Upper-Potomac,* (New Horizons Publishing Co.: 2012), pp. 153-154; *OR's,* Vol. 19, Part II, pp. 19-25.
175. *Southern Revenge, Civil War History of Chambersburg, Pennsylvania,* (Greater Chambersburg Chamber of Commerce: 1989), pp. 49-50, 53; Toomey, *Civil War in Maryland,* p. 65.

176. *Southern Revenge*, pp. 57, 60, 61.
177. Southern Revenge, p. 62; Toomey, *Civil War in Maryland*, pp. 66-67.
178. Johnston, pp. 102, 105; *Thirty-seventh Annual Report...For the Year ending September 30, 1863*, p. 42; General J. H. Lane, "Twenty-eighth North Carolina Infantry," *SHSP*, Vol. XXIV, p. 335.
179. *Thirty-seventh Annual Report B&ORR*, p. 42.
180. Ibid, p. 43.
181. Charles B. Clark, "Suppression and Control of Maryland, 1861-1865," *Maryland Historical Magazine*, Vol. 54, No. 3, September 1959, pp. 268-269; Warner, *Generals in Blue*, pp. 422-423; *OR's*, Vol. 21, pp. 865, 874.

Chapter 12

182. Michael E. Workman, Ph.D., "Worth To Us An Army," Rowlesburg In The Civil War, (Rowlesburg Printing: 2008), p. 8: Edward Steers, Jr., *"Montani Semper Liberi*, The Making of West Virginia," *North & South*, Vol. 3, Number 2, January 2000, p. 19.
183. Lang, p. 124.
184. *OR's*, Vol. 2, p. 713: Lang, p. 126; Steers, pp. 21-22.
185. James M. McPherson, *Battle Cry of Freedom, The Civil War Era*, (Ballantine Books: 1988). pp. 298-299, 303; Lesser, pp. 237, 262-263; Steers, pp. 23, 28.
186. Summers, pp. 118, 191, 193; Workman, pp. 10-11; Lesser, pp. 78-79.
187. Steers, p. 28; Lesser, p. 263.
188. Steers, pp. 28-30.
189. Ibid, p. 33.

Chapter 13

190. *OR's*, Vol. 21, p. 947.
191. Ibid, pp. 963-964.
192. Summers, p. 84; *OR's*, Vol. 2, p. 239.
193. Workman, pp. 5-6.
194. Darrell L. Collins, *The Jones-Imboden Raid*, (McFarland & Company, Inc.: 2007), p. 6; *OR's*, Vol. 25, Part II, pp. 656, 658.
195. *OR's*, Vol. 25, Part II, p. 659.
196. Warner, Generals in Gray, pp. 106-107.
197. *OR's* Vol. 25, Part II, pp. 652-653.
198. Ibid, pp. 710-711.
199. Ibid, pp. 158-159;
200. White, p. 74: Collins, pp. 25, 27.
201. *OR's*, pp. 93-94; Collins, pp. 33-36.
202. Collins, pp. 44-45; *OR's, Vol.* 25, Part II, pp. 247-248.
203. *OR's*, Vol. 25, Part I, pp. 100-101.
204. Collins, pp. 56-58.

205. Robert J. Driver, Jr., *First and Second Maryland Cavalry, C.S.A.*, (Rockbridge Publishing: 1999), p. 35; *OR's*, Vol. 25, Part I, p. 116; Collins, pp. 63-65.
206. White, p. 75; Collins, pp. 67-68, 70; Driver, p. 37-38; *OR's*, Vol. 25, Part II, p. 252.
207. Lang, pp. 258-260; Workman, p. 21.
208. Steve French, *The Jones-Imboden Raid Against the B&O Railroad at Rowlesburg, Virginia, April 1863*, (The Blue & Gray Education Society: 2001), p. 33; Delauter, p. 39;
209. Collins, p. 82.
210. French, "The 1863 Battle of Rowlesburg, West Virginia," *The Morgan Messenger*, October 20, 1999, p. 11; Collins, pp. 82-84, 87; *OR's*, Vol. 25, Part 1, p. 117.
211. *OR's*, Vol. 25, Part II, pp. 286-287, 296.
212. French, *The Jones-Imboden Raid...*, pp. 33; *Thirty-seventh Annual Report B&ORR*, pp. 45-46; Collins, pp. 98-99.
213. Ruth Ashby and Iret Ashby, "Company O's Picket," *The Glades Star*, Vol. 2, No. 36, March 1960, pp. 566-568; Collins, pp. 89-92; *OR's*, Vol. 25, Part I, p. 134; *Thirty-seventh Annual Report B&ORR*, p. 45-46; Roger U. Delauter, Jr., *McNeill's Rangers*, (H. E. Howard, Inc: 1986), pp. 39-40.
214. *OR's*, Vol. 25, p. 134; French, *The Jones Imboden Raid*, p. 37; Collins, p. 95.
215. Driver, *First and Second Maryland Cavalry, C. S. A.*, p. 41; Collins, 101-104.
216. *OR's, Vol.* 25, Part II, p. 318.
217. Collins, pp. 104-106; *OR's*, Vol. 25, Part II, pp. 373, 375-376
218. French, *The Jones-Imboden Raid*, p. 50; *OR's*, Vol. 25, Part II, p. 283.
219. Charles Camper and J. W. Kirkley, *Historical Record of the First Regiment Maryland Infantry*, (Gibson Brothers Printers: 1871), pp. 99-100; *OR's*, Vol. 25, Part II, p. 317.
220. Collins, pp. 113-114; *OR's*, Vol. 25, Part I, pp. 130, 134.
221. Collins, pp. 118-119, 124.
222. *OR's*, Vol. 25, Part I, p. 128.
223. *Thirty-seventh Annual Report of the B&ORR*, p. 46; Collins, pp. 125-126; *OR's*, Vol. 25, Part I, pp. 118, 120, 122-123.
224. Collins, p. 140.
225. *OR's*, Vol. 25, Part I, pp. 126, 128.
226. Collins, pp. 146-147; *OR's*, Vol. 25, Part I, p. 115.
227. Collins, p. 152; *OR's*, Vol. 25, Part I, pp. 119-120.
228. Collins, pp. 156, 158; *OR's* Vol. 25, Part I, pp. 119-120, 111, 134.
229. Collins, p. 159, *OR's*, Vol. 25, Part I, pp. 120, 126-127, 136-137.
230. Frank M. Myers, *The Comanches*, (Continental Book Co.: 1956), pp. 172-173; Steve French, "Rebels made Burning Springs live up to its name," *The Washington Times*, December 14, 1996, p. B3; Collins, pp. 161, 164-165; *OR's*, Vol. 25, Part I, p. 120; Part II, pp. 262, 462; McKain, pp. 95-96.
231. *OR's*, Vol. 25, Part I, p. 103; Part II, pp 199-800; Collins, pp. 179, 181, 183-184.
232. Collins, pp. 185-187.

Chapter 14

233. Heitman, Vol. I, pp. 818, 952; *OR's*, Vol. 25, Part II, p. 148.
234. H. E. Matheny, *Wood County, West Virginia in Civil War Times*, (Trans-Allegheny Books, Inc.: 1987), pp. 352-360.
235. "Plan for Military Blockhouses" consists of a series of drawings and specifications for blockhouses built for "The Baltimore and Ohio System," B&O Railroad Museum Archives.
236. Sidney F. Shaw, "The B. & O. R. R. The Base of Operations for the Federal Army in 1863-65: Reminiscences of Maj. S. F. Shaw," *Book of the Royal Blue*, Vol. II, October 1898, p. 11; Lang, p. 297.
237. William G. Craighill, Captain Engineers, report on existing blockhouses on the main line of the B&ORR and the Northwestern Virginia Railroad dated April 2, 1866, B&O Railroad Museum Archives; Workman, p. 39.

Chapter 15

238. Warner, *Generals in Blue*, pp. 233-234.
239. *OR's*, Vol. 27, Part III, p. 865, Johnston, p. 291.
240. Thirty-seventh Annual Report B&ORR, p. 48; Myers, pp. 188-191.
241. William H. Loudermilk, *History of Cumberland*, (James Anglin: 1878), pp. 409-412; Faust, pp. 834-835.
242. Warner, Generals in Blue, pp. 161, 162; Camper & Kirkley, pp. 101-102.
243. *OR's*, Vol. 27, Part III, p. 369.
244. Steve French, *Imboden's Brigade in the Gettysburg Campaign*, (Steve French: 2008), pp. 20-21; *OR's*, Vol. 27, Part II, pp. 296-297; Part III, pp. 905-906.
245. R. L. T. Beal, *History of the Ninth Virginia Cavalry*, (Richmond: 1899), p. 79-80; *OR's*, Vol. 27, Part II, pp. 694-695.
246. George C. Keidel, "Jeb Stuart in Maryland, June, 1863," *The Maryland Historical Magazine*, Vol. 34, Number 2, June 1936, pp. 161-164; *Just South of Gettysburg, Carroll County, Maryland in the Civil War*, edited by Frederick Shriver Klein, (Historical Society of Carroll County, MD: 1963), p. 79; *OR's*, Vol. 27, Part II, pp. 201-203.
247. Warner, *Generals in Blue*, pp. 315-316.
248. *OR's* Vol. 27, Part III, pp. 369-370.
249. Lord, pp. 216-217.
250. *OR's*, Vol. 27, Part II, pp. 316, 995-999; Part III, pp. 360, 377, 914; Myers, p. 194; Scott L. Mingus, Sr., *Flames Beyond Gettysburg: The Gordon Expedition, June 1863*, Ironclad Publishing, pp. 40, 237, 246-247.
251. Harold A. Williams, *The Western Maryland Railroad Story, A Chronicle of the First Century, 1852-1952*, (Western Maryland Railroad: 1952), pp. 12, 14, 25, 34-35.
252. Lord, pp. 218-220, 224; *OR's*, Vo. 27, Part III, p. 494.
253. Otis, p. 8, Heitman, pp. 998-999; Lord, p. 220.
254. Plum, Vol. 2, p. 21.

255. *OR's,* Vol. 25, Part III, pp. 575, 592-593, 609-610; Lord, p. 235; Garrett to Halleck, B&O Archives.
256. Heitman, p. 702; Koenig, pp. 94-96, 105, *OR's, Vol.* 27, Part III. pp. 589, 607-608.
257. Thirty-seventh Annual Report B&ORR, pp. 49-50, 52.

Chapter 16

258. Roger Pickenpaugh, *Rescue by Rail, Troop Transfer and the Civil War in the West, 1863,* (University of Nebraska Press: 1998), pp. 27-28.
259. Pickenpaugh, pp. 25-29
260. Edward B. Williams, "Reinforcements of Rail at Chickamauga," *America's Civil War,* January, 1996, pp. 47-49, 51; Turner, pp. 284-286.
261. Turner, pp. 289.
262. Bates, pp. 174-175.
263. Summers, p. 51; *OR's,* Vol. 29, Part I, p. 146.
264. *OR's,* Vol. 29, Part I, p. 152.
265. Summers, pp. 168-169.
266. *OR's,* Vol. 29, Part I, pp. 147-151, 153; Summers, p. 169.
267. Garrett File, Summers, p. 170; Pickenpaugh, pp. 54-56; *OR's,* Vol. 29, pp. 155, 157.
268. Pickenpaugh, pp. 73, 75, 77; *OR's,* Vol. 29, Part I, p. 158.
269. *OR's,* Vol. 29, Part I, pp. 158, 167-169.
270. Pickenpaugh, pp. 89-90.
271. Ibid, p. 94.
272. Ibid, pp. 95, 97, 130.
273. *OR's,* Vol. 29, Part I, pp. 183-184.
274. Pickenpaugh, pp. 131-132.
275. Ibid, p. 133, 135-136, 139.
276. Garrett File; *Thirty-eighth Annual Report of the President and Directors to the Stockholders of the Baltimore and Ohio Railroad Co. For the Year Ending September 30th, 1864,* p. 45.

Chapter 17

277. *OR's,* Vol. 25, Part II, p. 133; Vol. 27, Part III, pp. 696.
278. Schildt, *Lincoln's Wartime Travels,* p. 12, 78, Baine, pp. 80-81.
279. Summers, p. 36-37; Schildt, *Lincoln's Wartime Travels,* pp. 80-81, 85-86; Baine, p. 86.
280. Baine, pp. 84-87.
281. Summers, pp. 30-31.
282. *Thirty-Eighth Annual Report of the B&ORR,* pp. 9-10.
283. Plum, Vol. II, pp. 145-149.
284. J. Willard Brown, A.M., *The Signal Corps, U.S.A. in the Rebellion,* (U.S. Veteran Signal Corps Association: 1896) pp. 622-623; Heitman, Vol. I, p. 967.

285. *SHSP,* Vol. 9, pp. 268, 270; *Thirty-eighth Annual Report B&ORR,* p. 53.
286. Harry Gilmor, *Four Years in the Saddle,* (Harper & Brothers, Publishers: 1866), pp. 143-146; Steve French, "Train robber almost derails a career," *The Washington Times,* February 19, 2005, p. D5; Summers pp. 32-34;
287. Warner, *Generals in Blue,* pp. 535-536; Welcher, Vol. I, pp. pp. 18-19.
288. *Thirty-eighth Annual Report B&ORR,* pp. 53-54.
289. Robert W. Schoeberlein, "A Fair to Remember: Maryland Women in Aid of the Union," *Maryland Historical Magazine,* Vol. 90, No. 4, Winter 1995, pp. 471, 479-481; Schildt, *Lincoln's Wartime Travels,* pp. 89-90.
290. Jim Leeke, *A Hundred Days to Richmond, Ohio's "Hundred Days" Men in the Civil War,* (Indiana University Press: 1999), pp. XI-XIII.
291. Delauter, pp. 66-67; *Thirty-eighth Annual Report B&ORR,* pp. 54-55.
292. Warner, *Generals in Blue,* pp. 447-448; *OR's,* Vol. 37, Part I, pp. 395-396; Summers, p. 153. Welcher, pp. 23, 30.
293. Leek, pp. 39-40.

Chapter 18

294. *OR's,* Vol. 37, Part I, pp. 492-493; Dyer, Vol. I, pp. 257, 383.
295. Warner, Generals in Gray, pp. 79-80.
296. *OR's,* Vol. 37, Part I, pp. 160, 769; Part II, p. 4; Correspondence between Jubal Early and Robert E. Lee concerning advance into Maryland and destruction of B&O Railroad. Also mentions Point Lookout expedition. Huntington Library, San Marino, CA, Civil War Collection, numbers CW100 and CW101.
297. *OR's,* Vol. 27, Part I, pp. 175-176.
298. Steve French, "Sickness, death at Andersonville await Ohioans taken after skirmish." *The Washington Times,* October 20, 2001, p. B3.
299. Edward B. Stevens, M.D. and John A. Murphy, M.D., *The Cincinnati Lancet & Observer,* (E. B. Stevens, M.D.: 1865), Vol. 8, pp. 227-228; Koenig, pp. 95-96; H. Maxwell & Howard L. Swisher, *History of Hampshire County, West Virginia,* (A, B. Boughner: 1897), pp. 648, 650; *OR's,* Vol. 37, Part I, pp. 186-187.
300. Williams, pp. 184-186; Hungerford, Vol. II, pp. 17-19; *Thirty-Eighth Annual Report of the B&ORR,* pp. 56-57.
301. Bain, p. 102.
302. Ibid, pp. 114-115, 119
303. *OR's,* Vol. 37, Part II, p. 592.
304. Ibid, pp. 17-18, 37, 58-59, Part I, pp. 694-695.
305. Gail Stephens, *Shadow of Shiloh, Major General Lew Wallace in the Civil War,* (Indiana Historical Society Press: 2010), pp. 185-186; William Prescott Smith File; Jim Leeke, Editor, *Smoke Sound & Fury, The Civil War Memoirs of Major-General Lew Wallace, U.S. Volunteers,* (Strawberry Hill Press: 1998), pp. 218, 221.
306. Bain, p. 103; Leeke, *Sound, Smoke & Fury,* p. 229.
307. Frederick W. Wild, *Memoirs and History of Capt. F. W. Alexander's Baltimore Battery of Light Artillery U.S.V.,* (Baltimore: 1912), pp. 119-121; *OR's,* Vol. 37, Part II, pp. 62-64, 100, 110.

308. William Prescott Smith File; *OR's*, Vol. 37, Part II, pp. 101, 111-112.

309. Bain, p. 119; Stephens, p. 189.

310. William H. Wiegel, "History of Colonel William H. Weigel," One page synopsis of Weigel's life accompanied with a three page letter written to Secretary of War Edwin Stanton on December 26, 1864, requesting a promotion; Charles Albert Earp, "Profile of a Union Staff Officer," Unpublished manuscript covering the military career of Captain William H. Wiegel; Lew Wallace, *An Autobiography*, (Garrett Press: 1969), Vol. II, pp. 758-759, 764, 776; *SHSP*, Vol. 25, p. 174; Wild, pp. 131-132.

311. Leeke, *Sound & Fury*, p. 269.

312. Bain, p. 130.

313. *Thirty-eighth Annual Report of the B&ORR*, p. 58; *OR's*, Vol. 37, Part I, p. 349.

314. Edwin W. Beitzell, *Point Lookout Prison Camp for Confederates*, (E. W. Beitzell: 1972), pp. 2, 19, 20; Faust, p. 588; Royce G. Shingleton, *John Taylor Wood, Sea Ghost of the Confederacy*, (Athens: 1979), pp. 116-118.

315. Bradley T. Johnson, "My Ride Around Baltimore in Eighteen Hundred and Sixty-Four, *SHSP*, Vol. 30, p. 216-218; Daniel Carroll Toomey, *The Johnson-Gilmor Raid July 9-13, 1864*, (Toomey Press: 2005), pp. 14-15, 19; *Thirty-eighth Annual Report of the B&ORR*, p. 62.; *OR's*, Vol. 37, Part II, p. 103.

316. *OR's*, Vol. 37, Part II, pp. 155-156.

317. Gilmor, pp. 190-191, 194-196; Toomey, *Johnson-Gilmor Raid*, pp. 20, 24, 26.

318. Jerry L. Harlowe, *Mile Markers of the Baltimore & Frederick-Town Turnpike, 1805-2005*, (Patapsco Falls Press: 2005), pp. 71-75; Library of Congress, Robert Garrett family papers, Box 124, Folder July-September 1864.

Chapter 19

319. *Thirty-eighth Annual Report B&O*, pp. 58-59; William Prescott Smith File.

320. Fritz Haselberger, *Confederate Retaliation, McCausland's 1864 Raid*, (Burd Street Press: 2000), pp. 66, 69, 75-77.

321. *OR's*, Vol. 37, Part I, p. 355; *Southern Revenge*, pp. 114-116, 118, 127; Gilmor, pp. 14, 36; Haselberger, p. 85.

322. *Southern Revenge*, pp. 128-129.

323. *OR's*, Vol. 37, Part I, p. 356; Fielder C. Slingluff, "The Burning of Chambersburg," *SHSP*, Vol. 37, pp. 353-354;

324. *OR's*, Vol. 37, Part I, pp. 188-189; Toomey, *Civil War in Maryland*, pp. 135-136.

325. Gilmor, pp. 215-216; Leeke, p. 142.

326. W. W. Goldsborough, *The Maryland Line in the Confederate Army 1861-1865*, (Association of the Maryland Line: 1900), p. 210; Gilmor, pp. 217-221; Leeke, pp. 143-146; Koenig, pp. 107-109.

327. Haselberger, pp. 137-140; *OR's*, Vol. 43, Part I, p. 4; Leeke, pp. 146-149.

328. George W. Booth, *A Maryland Boy in Lee's Army*, (University of Nebraska Press: 200), Reprint of 1898 edition, pp. 133-134; *OR's*, Vol. 43, Part I, pp. 5-6; pp. 493-495; Haselberger, pp. 144-145, 151, 175.

329. B. F. Cooling, *Jubal Early's Raid on Washington 1864*, (Nautical & Aviation Publishing Co. of America: 1989), pp. 223-224; *OR's*, Vol. 43, Part I, pp. 695, 719.

330. *OR's*, Vol. 43, Part I, pp. 709, 721, 731, 719; Lang, pp. 322-322.

331. *OR's*, Vol. 43, Part I, pp. 730, 780-781.

332. Faust, p. 835; *OR's*, Vol. 43, Part I, pp. 708, 710-711.

333. Sallie Schulenberger, "Drums for Little Rebels and a Beaver Hat for Sallie," *Baltimore and Ohio Magazine*, May 1936, pp. 8-10; Williamson, pp. 260-267; *Thirty-ninth Annual Report of the President and Directors to the Stockholders of the Baltimore and Ohio Railroad Company for the Year Ending September 30th, 1865*, pp. 4, 39.

334. Jeffry Wert, "Attacking the Invincible, Rosser's Rebel Cavalry Takes New Creek, West Virginia," *The Civil War Times Illustrated*, Vol. 20, No. 10, February 1982, pp. 10-12, 14-15; Scott, pp. 181-185, 187-191; *Thirty-Ninth Annual Report of the B&ORR*, p. 40; *OR's*, Vol. 43, Part I, pp. 692-694, 696, 705-707.

335. *OR's*, Vol. 43, Part I, pp. 692, 695-696, 717, 742.

336. Ibid, pp. 683, 697, 709.

337. Ibid, pp. 682, 710, 717.

338. *Thirty-ninth Annual Report B&ORR*, pp. 40-41.

339. Ibid, p. 3; *Thirty-eighth Annual Report B&ORR*, p. 49.

Chapter 20

340. Hungerford, Vol. II, p. 58.

341. *OR's*, Vol. 47, Part II. See final report by Colonel Parson, Chief of Rail and River Transportation to Edwin M. Stanton, Secretary of War, dated February 2, 1865, pp. 214-219. For a real time account of this remarkable and for the most part unappreciated logistical accomplishment, see the 205 attachments on pages 219-284.

342. Steve French, *Rebel Chronicles*, p. 233; *Thirty-ninth Annual Report B&ORR*, p. 41; Snyder, p. 228.

343. *OR's*, Vol. 46, Part II, pp. 182-183, 188-189.

344. Rockford E. Toews, *Lincoln in Annapolis, February 1865*, (Maryland State Archives: 2009), pp. 9-11, 14-15, 21-23; Faust, pp. 335-336.

345. *Thirty-ninth Annual Report B&ORR*, pp. 41-42.

346. Warner, *Generals in Blue*, pp. 102-103; John W. Bailey, Jr., "The McNeill Rangers and the Capture of Generals Crook and Kelley," *Maryland Historical Magazine*, Vol. 62, No. 1, March 1967, p. 55.

347. J. W. Duffey, *Two Generals Kidnapped*, (Moorefield Examiner: 1944), pp. 1, 3, 7-8; Bailey, p. 54, 58.

348. Bailey, pp. 59; Duffey, pp. 11-13.

349. Bailey, pp. 62-63; Duffey, pp. 14, 18.

350. *Thirty-ninth Annual Report B&ORR*, pp. 42-43.

351. Long, p. 647.

352. Scott D. Trostel, p. 16, 19.

353. Dorothy M. Kunhardt and Phillip B. Kunhardt, Jr., *Twenty Days*, (Castle Books, 1965), pp. 119, 130-133; Faust, p. 780.

354. D. M. and P .B. Kunhardt, p. 140; Trostel, pp. 20-21, 28-29, 33; Abdill, p. 186.

355. Trostel, pp. 48-49, 51.

356. Sheads and Toomey, pp. 80-81.

357. Daniel Carroll Toomey, *Hero at Front Royal, The Life of General John R. Kenly*, (Toomey Press: 2009), p. 84.

358. Trostel, pp. 52-55, 206.

359. Ambrose, *Nothing like it in the World*, pp. 185-186.

360. Francis A. Lord, *They Fought for the Union*, (Bonanza Books: 1960), p. 7, *OR's*, Series III, Vol. 1, p. 22; Faust, pp. 736-737.

361. William B. Holberton, *Homeward Bound, The Demobilization of the Union and Confederate Armies, 1861-1865*, (Stackpole Books: 2001), pp. 7-8, 153; *OR's*, Series III, Vol. 5, pp. 1-3; Ida M. Tarbell, "How the Union Army was Disbanded," *Civil War Times Illustrated,*Vol. 6, No. 8, December 1967, pp. 4-6

362. Holberton, pp. 9-10, 154; Tarbell, p. 7.

363. Holberton, pp. 26-27, 51; Tarbell, p. 8.

364. Hungerford, Vol. II, pp. 61-62; McKain, pp. 109, 130; Holberton, p. 51, Tarbell, pp. 8-9.

Chapter 21

365. Lawrence W. Sagle, "Salvage Hunt Through Dixie," Unpublished manuscript written about 1958 when he was the Public Relations Representative for the B&O Railroad. This information was taken from a copy in the archives of the B&O Railroad Museum. The information contained in Chapter 21 is almost wholly derived from this report, p. 1.

366. Ibid, pp. 3-5.

367. Ibid, p. 14.

368. Ibid, pp. 15-18.

369. Ibid, pp. 19-22.

370. Ibid, p. 24.

371. Thomas T. Moebs, *Confederate States Navy Research Guide*, (Moebs Publishing Co.: 1991), p. 347; Donald G. Shomette, *Shipwrecks of the Civil War*, (Donic Ltd.: 1973), pp. 330-331; Paul H. Silverstone, *War Ships of the Civil War Navies*, (Naval Institute Press: 1989), p. 205.

372. Sagle, p. 26.

373. Ibid, p. 27-28.

374. Ibid, pp. 30, 32.

375. Ibid, p. 33.

376. Ibid, p. 35.

377. Ibid, pp. 40-41.

378. Ibid, p. 43.

379. Ibid, pp. 44-47.

380. Ibid, p. 48.
381. Ibid, p. 50.
382. Ibid, pp. 9, 50-52.
383. Hungerford, Vol. II, p. 135.

Chapter 22

384. Herbert Harwood, Jr., *Impossible Challenge II*, (Barnard Roberts & Co.: 1979), pp. 113-114.
385. "Death Claims Engineer," obituary for Joseph H. Toomey, Sr., *Winchester Star*, January 13, 1912, p. 5; Ritter, p. 5, *OR's*, Series III, Vol. 5, p. 466.
386. Harwood, pp. 118-119.
387. John F. Stover, *History of the Baltimore and Ohio Railroad*, (Purdue University Press: 1987), p. 118, 127; Hungerford, Vol. II, pp. 69, 107; *Thirty-ninth Annual Report of the B&ORR*, p. 10.
388. William D. Edson, Steam Locomotives of the Baltimore & Ohio, An All-Time Roster, (William D. Edson: 1992), p. 16; Thirty-ninth Annual Report of the B&ORR, pp. 52-54; Warner, Generals on Blue, p. 407-409; Abdill, p. 45; Stover, p. 119.
389. Daniel Carroll Toomey, *Union Civil War Veterans' Organizations in Maryland*, (Toomey Press: 2004), pp. 1-3.
390. "Baltimore & Ohio to Washington," Route guide published by the B&O Railroad in 1902 for the 36th Annual Encampment of the Grand Army of the Republic.
391. "Gen. Kelley's Funeral," *The Evening Star*, Saturday, July 18, 1891, p. 4.
392. "COMMANDER IN CHIEF AND DEPARTMENT OF MARYLAND, G.A.R., SPECIAL TRAIN TO DENVER, COL.," Route guide published by the B&O Railroad in 1905 for the 39th annual encampment of the Grand Army of the Republic.
393. "Maryland Pays Tribute to Her Gallant Sons," *The News*, Chattanooga, Tenn, Thursday, October 8, 1903.
394. *Fiftieth Anniversary of the Battle of Gettysburg, Report of the Pennsylvania Commission*, (Wm. Stanley, State Printer: 1915), pp. ix, 19-20, 30-31, 34-35, 113.
395. 'Exhibit of the Baltimore and Ohio Railroad at the NATIONAL ANTIETAM COMMEMORATION September 4-17, 1937," Exhibit brochure published by the B&O Railroad for the 75th anniversary of the battle of Antietam, 1937.
396. Paul L. Roy, *The Last Reunion of the Blue and Gray*, (The Bookmart: 1950), pp. 17, 31, 33, 111, 137; Charles Albert Earp, *The 75th Reunion at Gettysburg, My Interviews with the Veterans*, (Toomey Press: 2003), pp. 8-9, 29.

BIBLIOGRAPHY

Books & Pamphlets

Abdill, George B. *Civil War Railroads, Pictorial Story of the Iron Horse – 1861 thru 1865*. New York: Bonanza Books, 1961.

Alexander, Edwin P. *Civil War Railroads & Models*. New York: Clarkson N. Potter, Inc., 1977.

Alexander, Ted, et al. *Civil War History of Chambersburg, Pennsylvania*. Chambersburg: Greater Chambersburg Chamber of Commerce, 1989.

Ambrose, Stephen E. *Undaunted Courage*. New York: Simon & Schuster, 1996. *Nothing Like it in the World; The Men Who Built the Transcontinental Railroad 1863-1869*. New York: Simon & Schuster, 2000.

Andrews, Matthew Page. "Heyward Shepherd, Victim of Violence," Program for the dedication of the Heyward Shepherd Monument, Harpers Ferry: 1931.

Bain, William E. editor. *B&O in the Civil War from the papers of Wm. Prescott Smith*. Denver: Sage Books, 1966.

Baker, Jean H. *The Politics of Continuity: Maryland Political Parties from 1858 to 1870*, Baltimore: Johns Hopkins University Press, 1973.

Bates, David Homer. *Lincoln in the Telegraph Office*. New York: The Century Co., 1907.

Bates, Samuel P. *History of the Pennsylvania Volunteers, 1861-5*, Harrisburg, State Printer, 1869.

Beale, Richard L. T. *History of the Ninth Virginia Cavalry*, Richmond: B. F. Johnson Publishing Co., 1899.

Beitzell, Edwin W. *Point Lookout Prison Camp for Confederates*. Abell, MD: E. W. Beitzell, 1972.

Bonansiga, Jay. *Pinkerton's War: The Civil War's Greatest Spy and the Birth of the U.S. Secret Service*, Gilford, CT: Lyons Press, 2012.

Booth, George W. *A Maryland Boy in Lee's Army*. Lincoln: University of Nebraska Press, 2000. Reprint of 1898 edition.

Brown, J. Willard. *The Signal Corps, U.S.A. in the Rebellion*. Boston: U.S. Veteran Signal Corps Association, 1896.

Butler, Benjamin F. *Butler's Book*, Boston: A. M. Thayer & Co., 1892.

Camper, Charles and Kirkley, J. W. *Historical Record of the First Regiment Infantry*, Washington: Gibson Brothers, 1871.

Collins, Darrell. *The Jones-Imboden Raid*. Jefferson, NC: McFarland & Company, 2007.

Colling, B. F. *Jubal Early's Raid on Washington 1864*. Baltimore: Nautical & Aviation Publishing Co., 1989.

Danaway, William A. *The African American Family in Slavery and Emancipation*. Boston: Cambridge University Press, 2003.

Dare, Charles P. *Philadelphia, Wilmington and Baltimore Guide*, Philadelphia: Fitzgibbon & Van Ness, 1856.

Denton, Lawrence M. *A Southern Star For Maryland: Maryland and the Secession Crises*, Baltimore: Publishing Concepts, 1995.

Dilts, James D. *The Great Road: The Building of the Baltimore & Ohio, The Nation's First Railroad, 1828-1855*, Stanford: Stanford University Press, 1993.

Douglas, Henry Kyd. *I Rode with Stonewall*. Chapel Hill: University of North Carolina Press, 1940.

Dowdey, Clifford and Manarin, Louis H. editors. *The War Time Papers of Robert E. Lee*. Boston: Little Brown & Company, 1961.

Driver, Robert J. Jr. *First and Second Maryland Cavalry, C. S. A.* Charlottesville: Rockbridge Publishing, 1999.

Duffey, J. W. *Two Generals Kidnapped*. Moorefield: Moorefield Examiner, 1971 reprint of 1944 edition.

Dyer, Frederick H. *A Compendium of the War of the Rebellion*. New York: Thomas Yoseloff, 1959.

Earp, Charles A. *The 75th Reunion at Gettysburg, My Interviews with the Veterans*. Baltimore: Toomey Press, 2003.

Eddy, Richard. *History of the Sixth Regiment New York Volunteers*. Boston: Richard Eddy, 1864.

Edson, William D. *Steam Locomotives of the Baltimore & Ohio, An All Time Roster*. Potomac, MD: W. D. Edson, 1992.

Faust, Patricia L. Editor. *Historical Times Illustrated Encyclopedia of the Civil War*, New York: Harper & Row, 1986.

Fite, Emerson. *The Presidential Campaign of 1860*, New York: P. Smith, 1911.

French, Steve. *Rebel Chronicles, Raiders, Scouts, and Train Robbers of the Upper-Potomac*. Hammond, IN: New Horizons Publishing Co., 2012. *The Jones-Imboden Raid Against the B&O Railroad at Rowlesburg, Virginia, April 1863*, Danville, VA: The Blue & Gray Education Society, 2001. *Imboden's Brigade in the Gettysburg Campaign*, Hedgesville, WV: Steve French, 2008.

Gilmor, Harry. *Four Years in the Saddle*. New York: Harper & Brothers, 1866.

Goldsborough, W. W. *The Maryland Line in the Confederate Army 1861-1865*. Baltimore: Association of the Maryland Line, 1900.

Hale, Laura Virginia. *Four Valiant Years in the Lower Shenandoah Valley*. Front Royal, VA: Hathaway Publishing, 1986.

Hanson, John W. *Historical Sketch of the Old Sixth Regiment*, Boston: Lee and Shepard, 1866.

Harlowe, Jerry L. *Mile Markers of the Baltimore & Frederick-Town Turnpike, 1805-2005*. Baltimore: Patapsco Falls Press: 2005.

Haselberger, Fritz. *Confederate Retaliation, McCausland's 1864 Raid*. Shippensburg, PA: 2000.

Heitman, Francis B. *Historical Registration and Dictionary of the United States Army*. Urbana, IL: 1965 reprint of the 1903 edition.

Holberton, William B. *Homeward Bound, The Demobilization of the Union and Confederate Armies, 1861-1865*. Mechanicsburg: Stockpole Books, 2001.

Howard, McHenry. *Recollections of a Maryland Confederate Soldiers and Staff Officer Under Johnson, Jackson and Lee.* Baltimore: William and Wilkins Co., 1914.

Hungerford, Edward. *The Story of the Baltimore & Ohio Railroad 1827-1927,* New York: G. P. Putnam's Sons, 1928.

Hunt, Roger D. & Brown, Jack R. *Brevet Brigadier Generals in Blue.* Gaithersburg, MD: Olde Soldiers Books, 1990.

Imboden, John D. "Jackson at Harpers Ferry." *Battles and Leaders of the Civil War.* New York: Castle, 1884.

Johnston II, Angus James. *Virginia Railroads in the Civil War,* Chapel Hill: University of North Carolina Press. 1961.

Jordon, William B. Editor. *The Civil War Journals of John Gould 1861-1865.* Baltimore: Butternut & Blue, 1997.

Kline, Frederick Shriver, Editor. *Just South of Gettysburg, Carroll County, Maryland in the Civil War.* Westminster: Historical Society of Carroll County, 1963.

Kunhardt, Dorothy M. and Phillip B. *Twenty Days,* New York: Castle Books, 1965.

Lang, Theodore F. *Loyal West Virginia From 1861 to 1865.* Baltimore: Deutsch Publishing Co. 1895.

Leeke, Jim. *A Hundred Days to Richmond, Ohio's "Hundred Days" Men in the Civil War.* Indianapolis: Indiana University Press, 1999. Editor, *Smoke, Sound & Fury, The Civil War Memoirs of Major-General Lew Wallace, U.S. Volunteers.* Portland, OR: Strawberry Hill Press, 1998.

Lesser, W. Hunter. *Rebels at the Gates, Lee and McClellan on the Front Line of a Nation Divided.* Naperville, IL: Sourcebooks, Inc. 2004.

Letterman, Jonathan. *Medical Recollections of the Army of the Potomac.* New York: D. Appelton and Co., 1866.

Lockwood, John and Lockwood, Charles. *The Siege of Washington: The Untold Story of the Twelve Days that Shocked the Union,* New York: Oxford University Press, 2011.

Long, E. B. *The Civil War Day By Day,* Garden City, NY: Doubleday & Company, 1971.

Longrace, Edward G. *To Gettysburg and Beyond.* Hightstown, NJ: Longstreet House, 1988.

Lord, Francis A. *They Fought For the Union.* New York: Bonanza Books, 1960. *Lincoln's Railroad Man: Herman Haupt.* Rutherford, NJ: Fairleigh Dickinson University Press, 1969.

Lowdermilk, William H. *History of Cumberland.* Washington: James Akglin, 1878.

McKain, David L. *The Civil War and Northwestern Virginia.* Parkersburg, WV: David L. McKain 2004.

McPherson, James M. *Battle Cry of Freedom, The Civil War Era.* New York: Ballantine Books, 1988.

Markel, David E. Editor. *The Telegraph Goes to War, The Personal Diaries of David Homer Bates,* Lincoln's Telegraph *Operator.* Hamilton, NY: Edmonston Publishing, Inc., 2008.

Matheny, H.E. *Wood County, West Virginia in Civil War Times.* Parkersburg: Trans-Allegheny Books, 1987.

Maxwell, Hu. and Swisher, Howard L. *History of Hampshire County, West Virginia.* Kingwood, WV: A. B. Boughner, 1897.

Miller, William J. *The Training of an Army.* Shippensburg, PA: White Mane Publishing Co., 1990.

Mingus, Scott L. Sr. *Flames Beyond Gettysburg; The Gordon Expedition, June 1863. Columbus*: Iron Clad Publishing, 2009.

Moebs, Thomas T. *Confederate States Navy Research Guide,* Williamsburg, VA: Moebes Publishing Co., 1991.

Murfin, James V. *The Gleam of Bayonets.* New York: Thomas Yoseloff, 1965.

Myers, Frank M. *The Comanches,* Marietta, GA: 1956 of the 1871 edition.

Nason, George W. *Minute Men of 61,* Boston: Smith & McChance, 1910.

Newell, Clayton R. *Lee vs. McClellan, The Campaign.* Washington, DC: Regnery Publishing, Inc., 1996.

Otis, George A. *A Report on a Plan for Transporting Wounded Soldiers by Rail in Time of War.* Washington, DC: War Department, 1875.

Pennsylvania, State of. *Fiftieth Anniversary of the Battle of Gettysburg, Report of the Pennsylvania Commission.* Harrisburg: State Printer, 1915.

Pickenpaugh, Roger. *Rescue by Rail, Troop Transfer and the Civil War in the West, 1863.* Lincoln: University of Nebraska Press, 1998.

Pinkerton, Allan and William A. *History of the Passage of Abraham Lincoln from Harrisburg, Pa, to Washington, D.C on the 22D and 23D of February, 1861,* New York, Pinkerton's National Detective Agency, 1942.

Plum, William R. *The Military Telegraph During the Civil War in the United States.* Chicago: Jansen, McClung & Co., 1882.

Rawling, C. J. *History of the First Regiment Virginia Infantry.* Philadelphia: J. B. Lippincott Co. 1887.

Robertson, Jr., James I. *Stonewall Jackson: The Man, The Soldier, The Legend.* New York: Macmillan Publishing USA, 1997.

Roehrenbeck, William J. *The Regiment That Saved the Capital,* New York: Thomas Yoseloff, 1961.

Roy, Paul L. *The Last Reunion of the Blue and Gray.* Gettysburg: P. L. Roy, 1950.

Sandburg, Carl. *Abraham Lincoln: The War Years,* New York: Harcourt, Brace & Company, 1939.

Schildt, John W. *Lincoln's Wartime Travels.* Sharpsburg: John Schildt, 2010.

Searcher, Victor. *Lincoln's Journey to Greatness: A Factual Account of the Twelve-day Inaugural Trip,* Philadelphia: John C. Weston Co., 1960.

Sheads, Scott Sumter and Toomey, Daniel Carroll. *Baltimore During the Civil War.* Baltimore: Toomey Press, 2003.

Shingleton, Royce G. *John Taylor Wood, Sea Ghost of the Confederacy.* Athens: University of Georgia Press, 1979.

Shomette, Donald G. *Shipwrecks of the Civil War.* Washington, DC: Donic Ltd, 1973.

Silverstone, Paul H. *War Ships of the Civil War Navies.* Annapolis: Naval Institute Press, 1989.

Stephens, Gail. *Shadow of Shiloh, Major General Lew Wallace in the Civil War*. Indianapolis: Indiana Historical Society Press, 2010.

Stille, Charles J. *History of the United States Sanitary Commission*. New York: Corner House Historical Publication, 1997 reprint of 1866 edition.

Stiverson, Gregory A. *"In Readiness To Do Our Duty," The Frederick Militia and John Brown's Raid on Harpers Ferry*, October 17-18, 1859, Annapolis: Maryland State Archives, 1991.

Stover, John F. *History of the Baltimore and Ohio Railroad*. Lafayette, IN: Purdue University Press, 1987.

Summers, Festus. *The Baltimore and Ohio in the Civil War*. Gettysburg: Stan Clark Military Books, 1992 reprint of 1939 edition.

Swinton, William. *History of the Seventh Regiment, National Guard, State of New York, During the Civil War*, New York: Fields, Osgood, & Co., 1870.

Sullivan, David M. *The United States Marine Corps in the Civil War – The First Year*, Shippensburg, PA: White Mane Publishing Co., 1997.

Teeter, Paul R. *A Matter of Hours, Treason at Harper's Ferry*. London and Toronto: Fairleigh Dickinson University Press, 1982.

Thomas, James W. and Williams, Judge T. J. C. *History of Allegany County Maryland*. Baltimore: L. R. Titsworth & Co., 1923.

Thomas, William G. *The Iron Way: Railroads, the Civil War, and the Making of Modern America*. New Haven & London: Yale University Press, 2011.

Toews, Rockford E. *Lincoln in Annapolis, February 1865*. Annapolis: Maryland State Archives, 2009.

Toomey, Daniel Carroll. *The Civil War in Maryland*. Baltimore: Toomey Press, 1983. *Hero at Front Royal, The Life of General John R. Kenly*. Baltimore: Toomey Press, 2009. *Union Civil War Veterans' Organizations in Maryland*. Baltimore: Toomey Press, 2004.

Turner, George Edgar. *Victory Rode the Rails, The Strategic Place of Railroads in the Civil War*. New York: Bobbs- Merrill Co., 1983.

Tyler, Samuel. *Memoir of Roger Brook Taney, LL.D.* Baltimore: John Murphy & Co., 1872.

U.S. War Department. *The War of the Rebellion A Compilation of the Official Records of the Union and Confederate Armies, 70 volumes*. Harrisburg: Historical Times, Inc., 1985.

Villard, Oswald G. *John Brown A Biography Fifth Years After*. Boston: Houghton Mifflin Co., 1910.

Wallace, Lew. *An Autobiography*. New York: Garrett Press: 1969.

Warner, Ezra J. *General in Gray: Lives of the Confederate Commanders*. Baton Rouge: Louisiana State University Press, 1959. *Generals in Blue: Lives of the Union Commanders*, Louisiana State University Press, 1964.

Weber, Thomas. *The Northern Railroad in the Civil War*. New York: Indiana University Press, 1952.

Wheeler, Tom. *Mr. Lincoln's T-Mails, How Abraham Lincoln Used the Telegraph to Win the Civil War*. New York: Collins, 2006.

White, John H. Jr. *American Single Locomotives and the "Pioneer."* Washington, DC: Smithsonian Institution Press, 1973.

White, Col. Robert. *Confederate Military History Vol. 2 West Virginia.* Atlanta: Confederate Publishing Co., 1899.

Wilkinson, Norman B. *The Brandywine Home Front During the Civil War 1861-1865.* Wilmington: Kaumagraph Co., 1966.

Wild, Frederick W. *Memoirs and History of Capt. F. W. Alexander's Baltimore Battery of Light Artillery U.S.V.* Baltimore: F. W. Wild, 1912.

William, Harold A. *Robert Garrett & Sons, Incorporated, Origin and Development 1840-1965.* Baltimore: Robert Garrett and Sons, Inc., 1965. *The Western Maryland Railroad Story, A Chronicle of the First Century, 1852-1952.* Baltimore: Western Maryland Railroad, 1952.

Workman, Michael E., Ph.D. *"Worth To Us An Army," Rowlesburg in the Civil War.* Rowlesburg, WV: Rowlesburg Printing, 2008.

Manuscripts

Baltimore & Ohio Railroad Museum, Hays T. Watkins Research Library, Baltimore, Maryland Baltimore & Ohio Railroad Company Records Collection, 1159-1870.

Handley Library, Winchester, Virginia Ben Ritter,"A Short History of the Winchester & Potomac Railroad 1831-1833." War Time Diary of Miss Julia Chase, Winchester, Virginia, 1861-1865. The War Time Diary of Sara Morgan McKown 1860-1899.

Huntington Library, San Marino, CA Civil War Collection Numbers CW 100 and CW 101.

Library of Congress

Robert Garrett Family Papers.

Maryland Historical Society B&O Papers, File MS 1135

Smithsonian Institution, Archives Center John W. Garrett Collection #171. "Salvage Hunt Through Dixie," Unpublished manuscript by Lawrence W. Sagle, 1958.

University of Louisville Ekstrom Library The Papers of William Prescott Smith; Letters and Telegrams.

University of Nebraska – Lincoln "Armor Returns to the Battlefield, 1861-1865," Doctorial Theses by Alan R. Koenig, 1995.

Newspapers

Hagerstown Daily Mail
National Intelligence.
Philadelphia Inquirer.
The News, Chattanooga, TN.
Winchester Star

Periodicals

Ashby, Ruth and Ashby, Iret. "Company O's Picket." *The Glades Star* Vol. 2, No. 36, (March 1960) pp. 566-568. Bailey, John W. Jr. "The McNeil Rangers and the Capture of Generals Crook and Kelly." *Maryland Historical Magazine* Vol. LXII, No. 1, (March 1967) p. 55.

Candenquist, Arthur. "The Great Train Robbery." *Civil War* Vol. IX, No. 6, (November-December 1991) pp. 42-43. "The World's First Military Railroad." *Civil War Times* Vol. XLIX, No. 3, (June 2010) pp. 38-40, 43.

Clark, Charles B. "Suppression and Control of Maryland, 1861-1865." *Maryland Historical Magazine* Vol. LIV, No. 3, (September 1959) pp. 268-269.

Evans, Tracy. "Invitation to Battle, Special Order 191 and the 1862 Maryland Campaign." *The Sentinel* Vol. II, No. 2, (Summer 2012) pp. 14-17.

Fleming, Martin K. "The Northwestern Virginia Campaign of 1861." *Blue and Gray Magazine.* Vol. X, No. 6, (August 1993) pp. 14-16.

French, Steve. "Porterfield never recovers after Philippi." *The Washington Times,* (June 14, 2003). "Daring Raid of Winchester Mail Train." *The Washington Times.* (June 24, 2006) p. D5. "The 1863 Battle at Rowlesburg, West Virginia." *The Morgan Messenger,* (October 20, 1999) p. 11. "Rebels made Burning Springs live up to its name." *The Washington Times,* (December 14, 1996) p. B3. "Train Robber almost derails a career." *The Washington Times,* (February 19, 2005) p. D5. "Sickness, death at Andersonville await Ohioans taken after skirmish." *The Washington Times,* (October 20, 2001) p. B3.

Gimbel, Gary. "The End of Innocence, The Battle of Falling Waters." *Blue & Gray Magazine* Vol. XXII, No. 4 (Fall 2005) pp. 8, 12.

Garrett, Robert Browning. "John Work Garrett." *The Glades Star* Vol. 4, No. 6 (September 1970) pp. 88-90.

Hansen, Peter A. "The Rail Splitter and the Railroads." *Trains,* (February 2009) pp. 32-35.

Harris, J. M. "A Reminiscence of the Troublous Times of April, 1861." *Maryland Historical Society Fund Publication* No. 31 (1891): pp. 10-11, 18, 22.

Hawk, Alan. "An Ambulating Hospital; or How the Hospital Train Transformed Army Medicine." *Civil War History* Vol. XLVIII, No. 3 (September 2002) p. 209.

Haselberger, Fritz and Mark. "The Burning of the 21st Bridges At New Creek." *West Virginia History* Vol. XXVII, No. 1 (October 1965) pp. 57, 59-61.

Hearn, C. G. "The Great Locomotive March." *Civil War Times Illustrated,* Vol. XXV, No. 8 (December 1986) p. 29.

Johnson, Bradley T. "My Ride Around Baltimore in Eighteen Hundred and Sixty-Four." *Southern Historical Society Papers.* Vol. XXX, (January-December, 1902) pp. 216-218.

Keidel, George C. "Jeb Stuart in Maryland, June 1863." *The Maryland Historical Magazine* Vol. XXXIV, No. 2 (June 1936) pp. 161-164.

Lane, Gen. J. H. *"Twenty-eighth North Carolina Infantry."* SHSP, Vol. XXIV (January-December, 1896) p. 335. Lanis, Edward Stanley. "Allan Pinkerton and the Baltimore Assassination Plot Against Lincoln." *Maryland Historical Magazine,* XLV, (March 1950): pp. 8-9.

Merriken, John E. "Annapolis and Elk Ridge." *The Bulletin* Vol. 38, (No. 6, 1973) pp. 16-18.

Sauers, Dr. Richard A. "Stonewall Jackson's Romney Campaign January 1-10, 1862." *Blue & Gray Magazine* Vol. XXII, (Winter 2006) pp. 64-65.

Schoeberlein, Robert W. "A Fair to Remember: Maryland Women in Aid of the Union." *Maryland Historical Magazine* Vol. XL, No. 4, (Winter 1995) pp. 471, 479-481.

Schulenberger, Sallie, "Drums for Little Rebels and a Beaver Hat for Sallie." *Baltimore and Ohio Magazine.*, (May 1936) pp. 8-10.

Shaw, Sidney F. "The B. & O. R. R. The Base of Operations for the Federal Army 1863-65: Reminiscences of Maj. S. F. Shaw." *Book of the Royal Blue* Vol. II, (October 1898) p. 11.

Slingluff, Filder C. "The Burning of Chambersburg." *Southern Historical Society Papers* Vol. XVII, (January- December 1909) pp. 353-354.

Smart, Jeffery K. "Burning Bridges: The Events Leading up to the Military Occupation of Harford County in 1861." Harford Historical Bulletin No. 72, (Spring 1997) P. 27.

Smith, James Power. "With Stonewall Jackson in the Army of Northern Virginia." *Southern Historical Society Papers* No. XLIII, (September 1920) pp. 96-97.

Snyder, Timothy R. "Border Strife on the Upper Potomac: Confederate Incursions from Harpers Ferry April-June 1861." *Maryland Historical Magazine* Vol. 97, (Spring 2002) pp. 79, 82, 88-89.

Steers, Ed Jr. *"Montani Semper Liberi.* The Making of West Virginia." *North & South*, Vol. 3, No. 2, (January 2000) p. 19.

Stevens, Dr. Edward B. and Murphy, Dr. John A. "Correspondence.*" The Cincinnati Lancet & Observer.* Vol. VIII, (August, 1865) pp. 227-228.

Tarbell, Ida M. "How the Union Army was Disbanded." *Civil War Times Illustrated* Vol. 6, No. 8, (December 1967) pp. 4- 6.

Wert, Jeffry. "Attacking the Invincible, Rosser's Rebel Cavalry Takes New Creek, West Virginia." *The Civil War Times Illustrated*, Vol. 20, No. 10 (February 1982) pp. 10-12, 14-15.

Williams, Edward B. "Reinforcements of Rail at Chickamauga." *America's Civil War,* (January, 1996) 47-49, 51.

Radcliffe, George L. "Governor Thomas H. Hicks of Maryland and the Civil War."*Johns Hopkins University Studies in Historical and Political Science* Series XIX, Nos. 11-12 (November-December 1901): 55-56.

Baltimore & Ohio Annual Reports and related documents

Laws and Ordinances Related to the Baltimore and Ohio Railroad Company. Baltimore: John Murphy & Co., 1850.

Thirty-Third Annual Report of the President and Directors to the Stockholders of the Baltimore & Ohio Railroad Company. Baltimore: 1859.

Thirty-Fourth Annual Report. Baltimore: 1860.

Thirty-Fifth Annual Report. Baltimore: 1863.

Thirty-Sixth Annual Report. Baltimore: 1864.

Thirty-Seventh Annual Report. Baltimore: 1865.

Thirty-Eighth Annual Report. Baltimore: 1866.

Thirty-Ninth Annual Report. Baltimore: 1867.

INDEX

Q

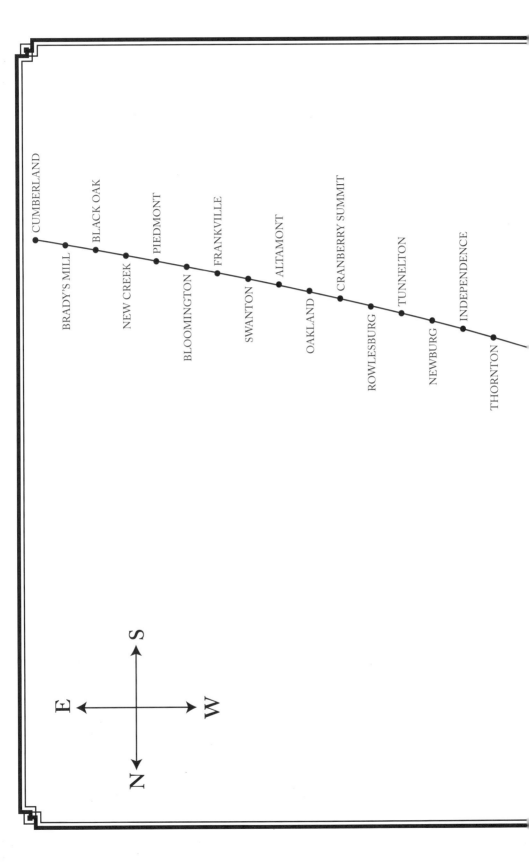